Mick Middles decided to become a professional writer in December 1977. In January 1978 he was appointed Manchester correspondent for *Sounds*, and his work has also appeared in *The Face*, *Smash Hits*, *Jamming*, *Zigzag*, *City Life*, the *Guardian* and *Cricket World*. In 1985 he wrote the successful pop biography *The Smiths: The Complete Story*, after which he edited the Manchester music monthly, *Muze Magazine*. In 1986 he began writing for the *Manchester Evening News* and instigated the influential pop column 'The Word' before progressing to general columnist and feature writer in 1987. He collaborated with legendary West Indies cricket captain Viv Richards to produce *Hitting Across the Line*, the cricketer's outspoken autobiography published by Headline on the eve of the England v West Indies Test at Lord's in 1991. He now writes regularly for the *Manchester Evening News* and the *Daily Telegraph*.

Mick Middles lives in Stockport with his wife, Karen, and two cats.

Also by Mick Middles

The Smiths: The Complete Story
Viv Richards: Hitting Across the Line*

* *Available from Headline*

Red Mick

The Biography of Mick Hucknall of Simply Red

Mick Middles

HEADLINE

First published in 1993
by HEADLINE BOOK PUBLISHING PLC

First published in this edition in 1993
by HEADLINE BOOK PUBLISHING

10 9 8 7 6 5 4 3 2 1

ISBN 0 7472 4420 0

Typeset by
Letterpart Limited, Reigate, Surrey

Printed and bound in Great Britain by
HarperCollins Manufacturing, Glasgow

HEADLINE BOOK PUBLISHING
A division of Hodder Headline PLC
Headline House
79 Great Titchfield Street
London W1P 7FN

For Karen

Contents

Acknowledgements

Special thanks are due to Mrs D. Middlehurst of Gwynedd and Brenda and Roy Shirley of Chelmsford, without whom this book would have perished when the old computer decided, wisely, to give up the ghost.

So many people gave up valuable time to answer my questions. A lot of them, for reasons which mostly escape me, wish to remain anonymous. However, hearty thanks must be extended to the following people: Roger Eagle, Sylvan Richardson, Aziz Ibrahim, Sandy Gort, Mike Rooke, Sue Swindells, Brian Turner, Tim Lee, Martin Ryan, John Nuttall, Derek Brandwood, Brian Beech, John Barratt, Rosemary Barratt, Bob Dickinson, Bob Kenyon, Mog, Tony (TJ) Davidson, Damian Brehony, Mike Hill, Yvette Livesey, Tony Michaelides, Steve Wright, Johnny Rogan, C.C., Mike Butler, Paul Morley, Michael Mackey, Lesley Lee, Tosh Ryan, John Wilde, Linda Ward, Hilary Jones, Eric Jackson, *City Life* magazine, *Manchester Evening News*, *NME*, *Melody Maker*, the *Guardian*, *The Times*, *Music Week*, *Q*, *Time Out* and the *Daily Mirror*.

Finally, thanks to Alan Brooke and Lorraine Jerram at Headline.

Introduction
Come On You Reds!

The boys would huddle aboard an old train, but not the romantic kind. Although pressed vertical by the sheer weight and volume of their fellow passengers, they would remain true to their rumbustious reputation.

The train, with gloomy, rickety carriages, would shuffle out of Oxford Road Station, reluctantly housing its volatile human cargo. Shouts would ring out, at irregular intervals – shouts and dirges, screams and chants – each and every one dedicated to a cause already made obvious by the proliferation of red, black and white woollen garments. Scarves tied aggressively around wrists that would often punch the air or, if space allowed, clap overhead.

It was early Saturday afternoon, the time most feared by locally based British Rail employees. It was also 1976 and the resurgent Manchester United of Coppell, Hill and Greenhoff, managed, most controversially by Tommy Docherty, were playing at home. To travel in such carriages while not blessed with an accent of the thickest Mancunian, and a heartily expressed fondness of Docherty and Co., was to risk an ambuscade of hateful stares, or far worse.

Alighting as ever at Warwick Road, the four teenage boys would be practically carried along with the flow, under the bridge and alongside the ghostly and, to these boys, mysterious Old Trafford Cricket Ground. Occasionally jumping in joyous anticipation, they would march on, pausing only to buy a glossily aromatic match programme. They were not a sartorially elegant bunch, though all four of them would surely debate that point. Their ungainly mix of tank-tops, petrol blue Oxford bags and spearpoint collared shirts would seem unsightly, even for the seventies.

One of them, a cheeky-faced handle-eared brat, named Hucknall, was even the proud owner of the start of a beer belly, an unusual attribute for a fifteen-year-old. Incredibly, the belly was already over a year old and had attained semi-legendary status in the playground of Audenshaw Grammar School, elevating Hucknall, or so he believed, above his comparatively infantile peers. (Oddly enough, the belly had even attracted the curiosity of no small number of local females, most of whom, to the astonishment and envy of Hucknall's friends, seemed quite fond of passing their biro-scribbled phone numbers to him usually on the ends of No. 6 cigarette packets.)

The foursome would squeeze excitedly through the turnstiles. Their comradely rhetoric was not overwhelmingly eloquent. 'Kill the foookin' Scouse bastaaards!' was a particularly common howl, and one which needs little explaining. It was mostly braggadocio. It was hip to act the part of the hooligan, if not follow through with the despicable consequences. It was standard machismo, not a particularly appealing trait, but one which was shared by just about every youngster in the ground unaccompanied by their parents. It was generated by too many hours spent reading Richard Allen books and chatting about the 'glorious' exploits of United's so-called 'Red Army'. It was something to believe in, a source of pride, a sense of comradeship. It was unfortunate that the afternoon would be heavily punctuated by too much spitting, swearing, punching and bragging. But that's how it was. If only they had known, particularly the one called Hucknall, what the future would hold.

JULY 1992

Alighting at Warwick Road Station, the crowd – bigger, it seemed than any football crowd, though significantly better behaved – surged from the platform and squeezed breathlessly through the bottleneck of the tunnel. Nobody seemed to mind. Nor had they allowed their recessional caution to curb their willingness to fork out £22 for a single ticket. It was, after all, a special occasion.

The crowd was – the guards, the touts, the officials all noted – quite staggeringly disparate. There were smartly dressed thirtysomething couples, carrying Evian water and chatting about the office. Bedenimed building society clerks cast irritated glances at all too giggly pubescent girls dressed in stripy cord trousers, endlessly running their fingers through long, crimped hair. Standard rock fans, parochially garbed in tight jeans and trainers, queued next to floppy young brats in square woollen skull caps. Tattooed biceps brushed against the cotton shirts of hi-fi shop salesmen. Fans of Beatles and Buzzcocks, Shakatak and the Shamen, Frank Sinatra and the Fall. Entire families marched briskly through the gates, sneaking in picnic hampers; teams of secretaries, doctors and dignitaries. Local radio outside broadcast units circulated, snatching 'vox pops' willy-nilly, pirate poster sellers cleverly sidestepped security and offloaded poorly printed T-shirts and four-page glossy 'programmes'. Forty-five thousand of them, all ignoring the natural lure of the football stadium, converging on Old Trafford Cricket Ground – much to the chagrin of the die-hard cricket fans who still held out some hope for Lancashire's already disastrous season – and filing, ever so politely, through the turnstiles. Police and security alike shrugged and joked, relaxing in the underwhelming ease of the operation.

Simply Red, the largest pop band ever to emerge from these parts, had come home – and how! What style! What panache! What arrogance, even. Slap bang in the middle of a murky Manchester summer, wholly dominated by open-air rock events which were mostly taking place at Maine Road Football Ground in Moss Side. It had been mooted that, like Bryan Adams and Prince, Simply Red might also like to make use of the facilities at the home of Manchester City Football Club. But somehow it just wouldn't have been right. The perfect venue, Hucknall's true place of worship as a grubby child and as a rock star, admittedly stood less than a quarter of a mile away. Nevertheless, for Simply Red singer Mick Hucknall, the streets of Old Trafford, from Warwick Road Station to the Stretford End were filled with ghostly evocations, with echoes of a Doc Martened past.

Not a hint, not a drop, not a flicker of antagonism darkened the proceedings as the awkward task of settling 45,000 people into position was carried out with consummate ease. Test matches held on that very ground had seen far more boisterous gatherings and even the *Manchester Evening News* was to note, with perhaps just a hint of irony that, 'It was more like a church fête than a pop concert.'

It was, too. There was hardly even a murmur of protest when health and safety chiefs, arguably paranoid beyond the call of duty in this company, ordered the shutters to come down on the bars three and a half hours before the end of the concert. An unthinkable action at a rock'n'roll event but, as the perpetrators of the recent 'Madchester' youth explosion would be all too willing to testify, this was nothing like a rock'n'roll event. This was an exercise in absolute professionalism, both musically and logistically.

The 45,000 strong crowd had gathered neatly, politely, but no less enthusiastic for all that, to sample an evening of quality and elegance, the two attributes so rare in the field of popular music which most readily spring to mind when the uncynical person thinks of Mick Hucknall and Simply Red. They are, it is true, detested almost without equal within the inkier pages of the British music press who, quite rightly, tend to promote music of a more esoteric nature. To them and the hipper sections of the music marketplace, Simply Red represent the ultimate 'bland out'. And Hucknall is a prime example of a man whose musical aspirations have softened beyond belief in order to capture the largest possible international audience.

But such thinking, although understandable, misses the point – and by a mile. As this book will testify, Hucknall spent many years clanging away on a beat-up guitar, screaming through bad PA systems in nicotine-filled hellholes. He had pursued the 'indie' dream to an alarming extent and had fun if not success. But in creating Simply Red he had mapped a way out of such bedlam. Simply Red would become an adventure into maturity, into adulthood. It would become an obsession too, a quest for musical perfection. The aim was to attain the highest possible levels, often regardless of personal consequences.

The cynics, of course, would point out that the music of Simply Red in no way matches the power and grace of Hucknall's true heroes: Miles Davis, Duke Ellington, James Brown, John Coltrane, John Lennon. But, once again, this is to miss the point. The majority of those artists couldn't possibly hope to straddle the scope of the music produced by Simply Red – and who can deny that Hucknall moves across the genres with immense style.

There isn't another voice in the higher echelons of popular music which emits such serenity and strength. When, at Old Trafford Cricket Ground or elsewhere, that voice fell so delicately into the Cole Porter classic *Every Time We Say Goodbye*, the watching eyes dampened and an awesome silence descended. Would even the great Ella Fitzgerald have produced such a poignant rendition? There were moments of inspiring delicacy. As the voice drifted, so cleverly, so tantalisingly through the famous line, 'There's no love song finer . . . but how strange, the change . . . from major to minor . . .' who could seriously deny that they were in the presence of one of the most extraordinary talents in popular music history?

There was, at Old Trafford, an arrogance that was not wholly palatable though. Unavoidably, as they were two thirds of the way through a massive eighteen-month world tour, the musicianship had been honed to blissful perfection – but too perfect, perhaps, for those who like a wobble in their ballads, a little uncertainty in their funk. At times it hardly even sounded live. And, of course, glowing with pride, Mick Hucknall flashed his ruby tooth, swirled the old dreadlocks, arched backwards to show off that unexpectedly thin waist and introduced the songs in an unbecoming strain of mid-Atlantic Mancunian. There was more than a hint of affectation, but who could blame him? He stood there, in total control of his craft, imposing a library-like silence on 45,000 gawping strangers. How did Mick Hucknall feel, standing on that stage, gazing towards Warwick Road Station? It was the very place where, sixteen years previously and nothing but a gawky guttersnipe, he had so often marched towards his beloved Stretford End.

Chapter 1
The Playground
Demagogue

Beneath an interior moon – a large, white, dominating sphere hanging thirty feet below the ceiling's apex – the children of Junior Four, St Laurence's Junior School, Denton, would go about their often terrible and disruptive business.

There would be hasty scribbling, fits of demented giggling, occasional punches thrown and a few tiny pockets of silent concentration. It was, in short, much like any other junior school on the fringes of Manchester.

Its rather severe Victorian appearance was softened considerably by peeling pastel-painted walls, more often than not decorated by the intriguingly inept artwork of the pupils. Even the rib-like radiators (many machismo points could be gained by holding your hand tightly against the intense heat of these metallic monsters for more than five seconds) failed to escape clumsy decoration. They were, according to season, adorned with tinsel, dried leaves or after an extreme downpour, damp, heavy duffelcoats.

It was a school with the usual problems. School dinners, for instance, would arrive daily at 10a.m. By the time the merciful dinner bell had rung, the meals would have sunk into unidentifiable, lukewarm mush tasting mostly of aluminium. Certain food would in time attain legendary status – the lumpy scoops of mashed potato, for example, or the pustulous rice pudding complete with dab of raspberry jam (to be whisked around, as frantically as possible, until a desirable

7

pink foam was formed). The Toad in the Hole was not unlike a wet sponge and the lemon meringue, definitely not for the faint of heart, was an indestructible white lump perched on yellow, rubbery base.

It was a poor school. A world apart from the affluence of nearby Stockport but not, perhaps, quite so impoverished as similar schools five miles down Hyde Road in Manchester's rapidly changing areas of inner-city desolation. Indeed, by comparison, Denton's hint of suburbia could be seen as positively rural. (It was an area desirable, perhaps, to those unhinged by the apocalyptic upheavals of slum clearance Manchester. It would have been seen as a move into cleaner air – even in the sixties. And, had they only known what an inhuman disaster was being planned by idiotic architects with notions of a concrete Utopia, Denton would have been teeming with ex-residents of Hulme and Moss Side, all relishing a life in the outer city. After all, Denton was *almost* in Cheshire.) Nevertheless, with the encroaching sprawl of the Haughton Green overspill estate just around the corner, Denton's tiny but teeming centre just a hundred yards in the opposite direction, and the omnipresent growl of nearby industry, St Laurence's junior school was positively brimming with northern imagery. The outside brick walls, still blackened from the receding terrors of smoky Cottonopolis, provided a somewhat satanic background for the children's playground activities. Ice slides in winter, hopscotch for the girls in summer while the ragamuffin boys would find inventive ways of torturing unlucky spiders – or weaker children.

St Laurence's was a school in some confusion in the mid-sixties. It was one of the very last schools to use the revolutionary and rather ridiculous ITA frenetic reading system. The consequences would have been catastrophic had not the headmaster ('An absolute genius' – Sandy Gort, former pupil) Mr Conki grasped the problem and swiftly backpedalled from this unfortunate method, brilliantly tackling the wave of semi-literacy in the classrooms. Mr Conki commanded respect and received it even from the wildest of pupils, much to the chagrin of less talented teachers.

Mick Hucknall was a cheerful, quite popular Junior Four

pupil. He was bright but not outstanding in any one subject. Former pupils all seem to remember him as, 'Always in the top few, especially at English.' Music tuition had a low profile in St Laurence's curriculum and for most kids, Hucknall included, it meant little more than the chance to slap a tambourine or ping a triangle.

He was also the class clown. His most forthright talent was his ability to lurch into a highly polished series of comic impressions, most of which could only be appreciated by those in the immediate vicinity. Barely a kid in the class or teacher in the school – except perhaps Conki – escaped a cheeky send up from the freckle-faced, red-headed little scally, Mick Hucknall.

'Sometimes his jokes could be quite cruel,' stated one fellow pupil before carefully adding, 'but I don't remember him being one of the really nasty lads.'

In the playground, on the greying, crumbly tarmac, Hucknall reigned supreme. Whenever a ring of pupils was formed, Hucknall could often be found lurking at the centre. His cheeky freckle-specked grinning face appealed to only the most gullible of teachers. Hucknall invented games, told stories, gleefully accepted any dares and challenges.

One pupil, Kevin Ogden (or 'Oggy' as he was commonly called) often found himself the butt of Hucknall's mockery. The jibing wasn't particularly offensive, but it was certainly repetitive. One morning, wandering down Two Trees Lane, Hucknall spotted an elderly woman calling to her dog. To Hucknall's utter delight he found out that the dog, a particularly scruffy looking mongrel, was called 'Oggy'. The woman, no doubt, must have wondered why the little red-haired schoolboy seemed to be bent double with mirth at the very name of her beloved pet.

Arriving at school, Hucknall gathered his schoolmates together to form a ring. The other kids were used to this, barely a morning went by without Hucknall spouting some, 'Guess what happened to me this morning' anecdote. Hucknall proceeded to tell the story of a dog named Oggy and then, just as the dog's hapless namesake sauntered through the school gates, his red-headed tormentor burst into song. This would appear to be the first song even written by Hucknall, and there would be no awards for its lyrical content.

'Oggy, Oggy, Oggy dog,' sang Hucknall. 'Oggy, Oggy, Oggy dog . . . Oggy's a dog, Oggy's a dog.'

It was a catchy little number though, and the entire playground would burst into song every time poor Kevin Ogden shuffled onto the tarmac. This went on for several weeks. From this tale, it can be seen that it was in the playground rather than the classroom where Hucknall most liked to shine. Tales of his bullying do still abound – and, no doubt, still fill many hours of gossip in Haughton Green tap rooms – but to linger too long on this subject would be to confuse the issue. This was, after all, a tough school. Most if not all of the snotty-nosed, snake-belted boys would find themselves embroiled in seemingly endless minor 'scraps'. Most boys had little choice but to adopt a rather comical attitude of infantile machismo, based on their ever-present desire to appear as grown up as possible.

Nevertheless, it has to be noted that Hucknall was generally regarded as an 'instigator' of playground trouble. The little gangs that formed would always be based around a leader and Hucknall would always be the leader. He would also be noted for his inventiveness in thinking up a suitable initiation ceremony whenever someone requested gang membership status. Running around the playground while flapping the arms was one of the more harmless tests. Inhaling a full drag of a Park Drive cigarette was not.

Cigarette smoking was, of course, seen as a symbol of maturity. At junior school, however, it was not that common. Quite often, after sneaking a cigarette from the packets of their parents or managing to get an older boy to purchase five Park Drive from the local corner shop, the pupils would 'pretend' to smoke. Anyone who had actually been seen smoking was afforded a quite fantastic degree of respect from the other boys. It was tasting adulthood in a way.

Many people, when recalling the playground antics of Hucknall, have tended to linger dramatically on his more bullish antics. In later years, nostalgic Dentonians would exchange endless tales of Hucknall's childhood obnoxiousness. But the truth is rather less dramatic. Hucknall did, at times, allow his naturally competitive edge to overflow into selfishness. But this was not untypical behaviour for a young boy trying to survive in a boisterous environment.

One aspect of Hucknall's playground life is often strangely forgotten. He would sing. Whenever he got hurt, be it physically or mentally, he would sneak into a corner and drift into song. This was the one truly unusual, if somewhat obviously relevant characteristic of the young Mick Hucknall. From an exceedingly early age, whenever things became too much to bear, he found himself drawn towards this unlikely form of escapism. Naturally, there were occasions when this tendency towards music did call into question the young lad's infantile machismo. Needless to say, whenever this happened, Hucknall would vigorously defend himself, fists flying.

Hucknall's brashness was, and still is, construed by many as an indication of childhood unhappiness. Although this might make a fine, heartfelt story – the stuff that tear-jerking TV movies are made of – nothing could be further from the truth. Mick Hucknall was a happy child and always had been.

He was born Michael James Hucknall, at St Mary's Hospital, Manchester, on 8 June 1961. (For what it's worth, he entered the world within twenty-four hours of Prince.) Within two years his parents separated. His father, Reg, moved to Haughton Green, Denton and continued to work as a barber in a seedy Stockport 'Brylcreem joint'. For a while, Mick's mother, Maureen, a hairdresser from Bredbury, Stockport, took the child into digs in Chorlton. During this time he would make regular and, by all accounts rumbustious, trips to see his grandmother, Florence Gibbons. It was Florence who, after looking after Mick for three weeks during Christmas, realised that her daughter just couldn't cope, both with the demands of the young child as well as having to hold down a full-time job. She took the painful decision to take the child to his father who was living with a friend, Nell.

As time progressed Mick settled contentedly into his new family. Nell rapidly became 'Auntie Nell' and each of her four daughters took it in turns to pamper the young boy, whose shock of brilliant red hair, and cheeks like two Cape Town apples helped him perfect a vision of angelic cuteness. This 'look', which he could seemingly turn on at will, helped him to win many chocolates from the ever adoring troupe of instant cousins, and from Nell and Reg.

Pop music entered his life rather strangely, via a collection of highly aromatic bubblegum cards featuring the rather vacuous antics of the Beatles. (The bubblegum cards were currency in St Laurence's playground where a child boasting a full set, as Hucknall did, would be generally regarded as 'the king'.) There was, of course, no escaping the Beatles at that time. Their influence was as profound to the little brats who scurried about in infant school playgrounds as it was to the teenage hordes. Mick adored them from an incredibly young age, and he was soon to be heard serenading Reg, Nell and the four daughters with curiously adept versions of Beatles classics. It was little more than a cute and entertaining turn which was wheeled out at Christmas or on Sundays when a vigorous rendition of *I Want To Hold Your Hand* might well be just the tonic to enliven a dull Denton evening.

Many people in the vicinity had begun to notice that the little cheeky scally, with rose red cheeks and 'sticky-out ears', would spend a wholly unreasonable amount of time each day exercising his lungs and testing his vocal chords. Some would ask, 'Is he all right? Is it normal?' Hucknall wasn't far from normal. He had something. A charisma? Possibly, but most people, given the benefit of hindsight would later state, 'I always knew he had something.' They didn't know anything of the sort. There were and still are far stranger, more charismatic, more eerie and more obviously talented children than Hucknall on every street, on every similar estate. It was curious to find a child, not well versed in middle-class practices like learning the piano or playing the violin horribly, or even blowing, to even more horrible effect, down a descant recorder.

Hucknall's Auntie Sheila took him to see the Beatles' film *A Hard Day's Night*. The madcap antics of the Fab Four obviously made a lasting impression on him although even then the fascination lay in the structure of the songs. Sheila – a heavy early influence – was earnestly 'into' the Beatles and studiously collected and coveted all their releases. Hucknall worshipped these slabs of plastic to what seemed like an unhealthy degree. From the age of five he would derive great satisfaction from gazing adoringly at the sleeves; feeling them, sniffing them, scrutinising them. He could, he would often boast, find the tracks he liked best simply by studying the width of the grooves.

It was an obsessive, train-spotter mentality. So strange, too, because Hucknall had little idea what the songs were about. He was drawn by the earthy beat, excited by the energy that filtered tinnily through the Dansette. It even upset him to discover that not every local child, however precocious, shared his natural obsession. But one boy did, at least to a point. His best friend since the heady days of three years of age was Neil Moss. Sitting upstairs in Hucknall's room, they would swap stories about John, Paul, George and Ringo. That was when they weren't running around the house, firing cap guns at each other, or playing at James Bond, or the Man From UNCLE, or playing 'three'n'in' with a plastic football out on the road (with the grids acting as goal posts).

But still Hucknall would sing – he would always sing. 'It was extraordinary,' Hucknall would say, twenty-five years later. 'I was obviously born to it. I was guided into singing. It *was* extraordinary, but there you go.'

His first concert, excluding his 'Oggy Dog' antics, took place at a wedding when he was six. Hucknall, resplendent in a pair of leather Austrian shorts – complete with bib and braces – gave a spirited rendition of *I Want To Hold Your Hand* in front of a band who were, to all intents and purposes, playing something completely different. Needless to say, his singing earned a rapturous, if somewhat biased response.

Hucknall's early culture, in line with the bubblegum cards, came from two sources: the television and the newsagents. He would regularly purchase *Beatles Monthly* magazines and songbooks, and before his eighth birthday he had memorised a huge portion of the massive Beatles' repertoire. His skill at dipping into this vast songbook to produce some unexpected and hastily adapted gem, be it *Norwegian Wood* or *Can't Buy Me Love*, certainly began to make those around him believe that this precocious child might have something musical to offer, something beyond looking cute and entertaining the family at Christmas.

Unbeknown to his teachers, Hucknall had already begun his parallel, unofficial education. He was indeed fortunate to have discovered the two finest teachers of the pop era – Mr Lennon and Mr McCartney. Their songwriting prowess, so prolific that it gushed through them in an almost spiritual manner, was changing the face of the music of the Western world. The young Hucknall, however, had no idea of the unparalleled breadth of their influence. The Beatles were simply the first pop stars he had experienced, and so young. No doubt he thought – if he thought about it at all – that all pop groups were exactly like the Beatles.

Television, of course, enriched his imagination considerably. He nurtured a healthy addiction, not only to the Beatles, but also to the images of the Rolling Stones, Granada film footage of John Lee Hooker and B.B. King – shown partly to appease the massive North-west club scene of the era – and the Supremes and Four Tops. 'I absolutely loved those shiny suits and all that twirling about,' he said later.

One more image, destined to remain forever implanted in Hucknall's mind, was a television shot of the side of Jimi Hendrix's head as cacophonous noise simply blasted out of the set, causing the ornaments to shiver and his dad to launch into a tirade of condemnation before storming out of the room. Hucknall looked once again at the set and wondered just what it was all about.

The evenings, as ever, were spent under the orange glow of the Denton street lamps. Within Hucknall's little gang a kind of too-young-to-be-a-soulboy chic became the norm. Basically, most of his contemporaries were happy to be decked out in the hand-me-downs of their older brothers. Therefore they would be a fairly accurate representation of the previous year's fashion with, of course, the added attractions of scuffed holes at the knees and elbows. Huge, deep, dark splodges of mud decorated Levi jackets and there were great, uncomfortable tears in the soles of ancient Doc Martens, too big really, but worn by the gleeful youngsters with equal pride.

Causing trouble was, as is the case with most healthy pre-teens, the main preoccupation and Hucknall was certainly no exception to this rule. One favourite pastime was to hang around the local phone box and bench staging mock fights, which neatly transformed into a chase whenever a hapless police car happened by (which was often in Denton). Sapping (nicking apples, even harshly acidic crab apples) from the trees of curmudgeonly local pensioners was also popular. Hucknall, playing the unlikely role of 'master of fair do's', once turned violently on a friend who had responded with the words, 'Aaah, sod off yer old git!' when challenged by a pensioner. This, in Hucknall's view apparently, was taking things a little too far.

Hucknall made himself 'violently sick' one day when, on the way home from school, he led a lightning gang raid on a garden-based crab apple tree on Mill Lane. After a series of dares, 'I bet you can't eat all of those apples . . .', Hucknall promptly sat down on the two-foot garden wall and ate his way through the entire haul – only to relieve himself over the gate of the garden next door. The following ten minutes was a mixture of giggling fits and ferocious vomiting.

The whole gang, especially Hucknall, seemed to be obsessed with their pushbikes. Much to the consternation of their parents their bikes were the uncomfortable-looking 'trackers'. It took a particularly adept hand, which Hucknall was, to transform some rusty relic from its traditional shape into a much-desired tracker which would pass the scrutinous, envious inspection of schoolfriends and have the essential street-wise credentials. The basic idea was to 'bend' the bike frame. This was achieved by hammering the hell out of the top strut until a further angle was added to the triangular norm. A respray was desirable, though hardly essential, and there were constant Saturday forays to the bike shop on Hyde's Market Street to purchase such real essentials as tracking tyres and bull-horn handlebars (these were exceptionally wide so the riders had to assume a position not dissimilar to a travelling version of the crucifixion. And, as the trends of the day dictated, they had to be bull horns as opposed to the more common cow horns, which were less

15

ridiculous and therefore only used by wallies).

Hucknall couldn't afford many of the more expensive items and none of his bikes were ever considered cycle speedway standard. (Cycle speedway was a largely mythical sport, practised by a few, bragged about by many.) He would glean most of his parts, not from the Hyde shop, but from the grubby Peak Forest Canal that ran parallel with the River Tame and stretched from Audenshaw, between Hyde and Denton, and down towards Gee Cross and Woodley. The canal was to play a major role in the dubious recreational activities of the young Hucknall, particularly the area between Hyde and Gee Cross Mill. It was an area, possibly magical in Hucknall's young mind, that offered limitless possibilities for grubby adventure.

Immediately beyond Gee Cross Mill, for example, stood a series of mounds, probably the remains of an old, tiny, long-forgotten quarry. The mounds had been rubbed bare, literally carved into an all too inviting mock tracker-bike track. (Any bike would do. From laughably naive customised 'Choppers' to the aforementioned bull-horned speedway cycles to racing bikes, bullishly 'borrowed' from kids of a less muscular ilk in the playground.)

Hucknall and his apparently constantly fluctuating little gang spent aeons in this muddy metropolis, furiously skidding about, flying over humps and crashing into nettles. The fun was mostly harmless although things did become a little more serious when one of the gang managed to procure a rusty moped. A small consortium was formed, with each gang member regarding himself responsible for 20 per cent of the vehicle and each taking it in turns to buy half a gallon of petrol-oil. In many respects it was a bind, as it would be forever requiring inexpert mechanical attention. However, with an open throttle and a canal towpath devoid of irritating anglers, the very real thrill of motorbiking, albeit in its most modest state, could be experienced. It was also great fun to steer the moped dangerously into the 'mounds' thus apeing Saturday afternoon's televised motocross.

Occasionally, these little glimpses into the world of motor-biking would explode into something rather unsavoury. Hucknall's gang was, of course, just one of many who would use the mounds for precisely the same purpose. Hence, minor territorial warfare would break out. It wouldn't usually be too serious – most fights, after all, were just a series of badly aimed punches resulting in at worst a bloody nose and the instant joy of bonding with the opponent. Nevertheless, the area, which attracted more people from the estates on the Woodley stretch of the canal than Haughton Green, did gain a reputation for nastiness; naturally, the reputation was exaggerated by local folklore. Within this whispery network, the name Mick Hucknall was increasingly making its presence felt.

Hucknall, partly to his own consternation, passed his eleven plus examination. (The Manchester education authority had grimly hung on to the old system and Hucknall was among the very last batch of pupils to take the exam.) Reg, Nell *et al* were naturally delighted but Hucknall's best friends had all failed and would attend the homelier, nearer, less daunting (unless you believed some of the exaggerated tales of bullying that were flying around Haughton Green at the time) Two Trees Secondary School. Two Trees, thought Hucknall, was where he really belonged. The prospect of travelling through Crown Point, the length of Ashton Road to reach Audenshaw Grammar frankly terrified him. What's more, this discomfort was hardly eased when he arrived to discover that the 'posh gits' of Audenshaw didn't play soccer like normal boys. They played rugger. Hucknall would never come to terms with this alien sport.

In fact, it was far worse than that. Rugby was, at least to the mind of the young Hucknall, a method of keeping the working-class boys firmly in their place. The sport was a device, a tool, which the games masters used to, as Hucknall would later say, 'Teach these people how to become soldiers.' From that traumatic first day, as he dragged himself around the classrooms half-heartedly filling in his timetable, he always regarded himself as an outsider.

As the first few terrible weeks passed, Hucknall gained a reputation for rebelliousness. His father, his only true role model, had instilled within him the determination to stand up to unfair treatment whether it came from a teacher or a bullish fellow pupil. He found the system at Audenshaw wholly repressive. Each teacher, apart from the enigmatic music master, Mr Fisher, would leap upon Hucknall's idiosyncrasies and attempt to stamp them out, as if they represented some kind of subversive threat to the other pupils. Hucknall may have been only twelve, but he thought the regime stupid. It was an opinion he was to carry through his school days and remains unchanged to this day.

Hucknall's schooltime was average. His most healthy activity was his ability to come to life suddenly when in the art class. He loved to paint, to draw and to study the lives of classic artists, although nobody can recall him being particularly gifted. However, from a very early age his paintings showed signs of a strong leaning towards the avant-garde, which was certainly unusual for a fifteen-year-old Dentonian. His fellow pupils, arguably more skilled than him, tended to dismiss his wilder efforts, believing them to be a mere cover for his lack of artistic talent. (It was noted that Hucknall's paintings – brash, loud, gaudy and demanding – tended to reflect his personality. The truth is that to overcome the traumatic jolt of moving to Audenshaw Grammar, he had become noticeably more aggressive, and in the eyes of a number of fellow pupils, utterly selfish.)

'I didn't dislike him,' stated one former pupil, now a tax inspector, 'but I never felt comfortable when I was hanging around with him. Most of the time he was very nice, very witty and good fun . . . he seemed to know so much about pop music, even then. He would go into long talks about it, sometimes I found them boring, but mostly I just' couldn't understand where he got his information from. That's one reason why I liked him. Because I knew hardly anything about music or films and he seemed to have all the answers. A few of the other kids knew this, as well.'

Our tax man, like a number of fellow pupils still living in Denton, preferred not to be named (and many more refused to talk at all, but not through any sense of loyalty, rather a prevalent desire *not* to be involved). One pupil named Bob

Kenyon, who shared Hucknall's most noticeable passion, a love of Manchester United (in later life, he produced the Manchester United fanzine, *In League With The Devils*) stated that, 'I can't remember anyone who was "hated" more than Hucknall. Absolutely nobody seemed to like him at all . . . he was always in fights.'

This phrase 'always in fights' seems to be just about everyone's recollection of Hucknall's schoolboy antics. He was recognised as being a rather dangerous character. By hanging about with Hucknall, you were more than likely to end up in some kind of trouble. It wasn't particularly a tendency towards nastiness – although he did have his moments – it was the fact that he would always want to take things one step further than anyone else. He was a ferocious competitor whether in class or playing football in the playground. (Balls were banned, in case of window breakages, and so they improvised by using old, rolled-up socks.) Hucknall would always be the one to take the penalties, to tackle – too hard, too rough – whenever an opponent caught sight of goal. But when fights did break out they were not usually particularly vicious encounters.

One pupil recalls having his ego attacked by an over-zealous Hucknall who thought he had stumbled across an easy target. 'He kept goading me, he kept going on and on about something . . . I can't remember what it was . . . could have been a girl, actually, who I was going out with. It was typical, pathetic schoolboy stuff. But he wouldn't stop . . . I think it went on for weeks. Whenever we would pass in the corridor he would aim a punch, or he would deliberately have a go at me during games. One day, he caught me totally unawares and aimed a peck [stacking the fingers in a pyramid fashion and bringing them down in the middle of the victim's back] at my back. I completely snapped and launched myself at him. I can't recall much else, we rolled around the school corridor and I think we were broken apart by some teacher. I do remember, however, that Hucknall was always really nice to me from that moment on. We didn't become mates, although he seemed to respect me more.'

Chapter 2
Searchin' for the Young Soul Rebels

Even a freckly-faced thirteen-year-old would have gods and these gods would have worshipful names. The names would be scratched on to road signs, spray-painted on the back of corrugated garages, etched into juvenile folklore. SCRAGG RULES OK. PRINCEY IS KING. WIMP OV HYDE. GDR RULE.

GDR. These initials mystified the authorities for years. (Police would regularly hunt for a graffiti artist called something like Graham Desmond Robinson.) In fact, GDR stood, quite simply, for Gorton, Denton, Reddish. It was a tripartite gathering of skinheads, soulboys, smoothies and Crombie kids, all of whom would hang ominously around the corners and squares of the three towns as well as the neighbouring Hyde. In many respects Hyde was the evening magnet, the Mecca towards which every scooterboy, every brogue-wearing soulboy would drift. And in particular, Hyde bus station.

Mick Hucknall was superbly placed to study such early seventies action. After all, it was just a hop out of West Park Road, down Mill Lane before turning right on to Hyde Road. The famous approach to Hyde bus station was where the name lads – the 'faces' – would flirt with pretty girls with feathered hair and tonic two-tone trousers, and intimidate little old ladies in woolly overcoats.

Hucknall adored the fashions. He would dream of wearing Rupert Bear trousers, cherry-red Doc Martens, velvet-collared

Crombie coats, slash-back blazers with red roses adorning the pockets, Prince of Wales check jackets, red socks, tassled leather-soled loafers, patchwork jumpers, Brutus shirts with penny-round collars, Ben Sherman check shirts, bleached Wrangler jackets, black parallels, Burton suits, electric blue twenty-four-inch parallels – it was a virtual minefield of sartorial suss, one which no parent could possibly hope to understand. Mick Hucknall aspired to such things – but they had to be right. He didn't want 'Astronaut' Doc Martens, he *had* to have the sixteen-hole originals. He couldn't be seen in cheap Oxfords, he wanted Stead and Simpson Royals. At thirteen, his true teenage years were yet to come, but he was a very old thirteen.

He resented, for instance, the fact that he would have to wait three years (or four after the new government licence laws) before he too could own a Lambretta GP 200 or LI 150 or SX 200 (these scooters were beautiful, yellow, sky blue or silver affairs, adorned with the names of American cities on the side panels: *Detroit, Los Angeles, Chicago, Des Moines*).

There were fights, of course. They would be, for example, a midnight scuffle outside the Moon disco in Dukinfield between three Crombie lads and four Stalybridge-based 'Grebos' (bikers). In reality it would be nothing more than a few wildly aimed blows and a good deal of shouting. But by the time it had travelled by word of mouth down through the years on the streets of Haughton Green, the incident would attain something approaching Little Big Horn status. After Manchester United footballers, the early heroes of Mick Hucknall were the street gang kids of the GDR.

The early teens, for Hucknall at least, was also the age of the cider party. And there were many in Denton and Hyde. So many nights were spent sitting in the darkened front rooms of Stockport Road terraced houses, fumbling with the blouse buttons of giggly girls behind the sofa, as the floorboards throbbed to the sounds of Motown, of Atlantic soul, of James Brown's *There Was A Time*, Arthur Conley's *Sweet Soul Music*, Bob and Earl's *Harlem Shuffle*, Marvin Gaye's *Little Darlin'*. Soul was the ever-present sound, unless fleetingly replaced with Trojan reggae. The Pioneers' *Long Shot Kick The Bucket* was a particular Hucknall favourite. He purchased, as did practically every non-rocker kid of that era, the Trojan compilation album *Tighten Up Volume Two* at a budget price. He adored reggae but was in truth a little late, a little young for the Trojan/skinhead heyday.

By the time Hucknall had turned fourteen, glam rock had already reached its artless fag end and become commercialised and banal. Parallels had widened into absurdity. The waistband expanded to cope with three buttons. Brogues and loafers were discarded in favour of platforms. It was as if all the style and grace of the Crombie era had been replaced with an outbreak of sheer tackiness.

Hucknall went begrudgingly along with the trend. By the time he was ready to buy his own clothes, he was travelling to Stockport to try on pairs of twenty-six-inch Oxford bags from the glam emporium Othello. At £17 a pair they were far from cheap. Lurex jumpers, long woollen cardigans complete with karate style tie-belts and tiny colourful T-shirts were in. In 1975, standard street fashion had split from the soulboy image of before. The fanatics had latched on to Northern Soul but this was not a movement that Hucknall ever became seriously involved in. He would later dismiss it as a term used to describe a particular beat. It was about speed (amphetamine) and dancing all night. But even at such an early age, Hucknall was getting more and more into beer, and in many respects he still preferred the soul of Motown, Stax, Atlantic and Philadelphia.

Nevertheless, Northern Soul was mushrooming all around him. As a culture, if not musically, it was certainly a strong influence. In later years, nostalgia for the Northern Soul scene would be tainted by multitudinous examples of snobbery. There are those who think that Hucknall, aged fifteen in the mid-seventies, had missed the true thrust of the scene. True enough, he was too young to have been a regular at Chris Burton's club the Torch in Stoke-on-Trent which was considered by many to be *the* seminal club of the early seventies. Manchester's Twisted Wheel, of course, had long gone but the hip chatter on the streets of Manchester was full of tales of wild nights down at the Wigan Casino. The truth is everyone, from every era, from every section, will tell a different story and seem to regard the little scene that *they* attended as the true nucleus. (Every ageing soul fan wishing to retain his or her dignity will claim, for example, to have seen the Major Lance gig which took place at the Torch one Sunday in the early seventies.)

Hucknall entered and enjoyed the greater part of his teens surrounded by the legacy and culture of soul music, be it called Northern or otherwise. It *was* a culture, too. For instance, if you were to travel to any small village weekend disco in darkest Lancashire, you would find a crowd, barely out of school, dancing expertly to *Darkest Days* by Jackie Lee, or *Tainted Love* by Gloria Jones, or *You Don't Want Me No More* by Major Lance. All these 'sounds' were carried about with unabashed pride in ubiquitous plastic singles boxes, the true tell-tale sign of any serious soul fan. It was everywhere and for the young pretender it was scary. Standing beside the dance floor at Wigan Casino, about to launch into dance for the first time on that hallowed floor, was unnerving to say the least. At Blackpool Mecca things were a little more relaxed.

What is important, at least as far as the story of young Hucknall with a growing musical awareness is concerned, is the sheer weight of knowledge that serious soul fanatics were expected to take on board. This was, of course, a product of snobbery and many great records were cruelly ignored simply because they were not obscure enough to merit essential coolness. A man's worth, in some extreme and rather pathetic cases, was estimated by the coolness of his singles box. This became even more ridiculous and to some extent helped to kill off Northern Soul when such collecting mania pushed the prices of soul records through the roof. It is interesting to note – as has been the case with every teen cult since the sixties – that, if something is considered essential then teenagers at school or on the dole will somehow find the money. Nevertheless, when soul rarities – many of them considerably inferior to less desirable discs – were beginning to change hands for £50 a throw, even Mick Hucknall became seriously disillusioned. There was great music around and Hucknall devoured it feverishly, allowing it to soundtrack his teenage adventures continually, but it wasn't necessarily always connected with the heart of Northern Soul. What Mick Hucknall saw was not an entire region revelling in wave upon wave of perfect soul records but a scene which, after being granted too much publicity, twisted away from the music. Suddenly Northern Soul fanatics were not music people at all but crass, posing 'stompers' who loved the idea of 'all nighters' and fell into a downward spiral of macho dancing. This was not anything to do with music and Hucknall recognised this. And it was the music primarily which he loved, right down to the smell of the plastic, the designs on the labels, the pop and crackle of needle upon groove and, of course, the dancing.

One of the social problems for a young, proudly rebellious soulboy during the mid-seventies was the difficulty he faced trying to break the trappings of peer pressure. A soulboy – GDR or otherwise – was supposed to be completely immersed in black music, the more obscure the better. The ultimate crime for any self-respecting soulboy was to buy, listen to or be attracted by a rock or pop record. To be caught carrying Pink Floyd's *Atom Heart Mother*, for example, would be seen as a definite sign of 'going weird'. This was, according to the soulboy's unwritten law, the first step down the slippery slope that would see the hair grow from blow-wave perfection to long, straggly and greasy. It was akin to becoming a social dropout. Embroidered heavy metal symbols – 'Led Zeppelin Zofo' for instance – would appear across the back of Wrangler jackets and the wearer would express curious desires to attend concerts at Manchester's Free Trade Hall.

In Denton, which to be fair was just about the last truly soulboy area left in Manchester, it was extremely difficult for Hucknall to fully express his new found 'weird' leanings. His favourite album – and a record that would still claim such a coveted position many years later – was the Rolling Stones' seminal and zipper-clad beauty, *Sticky Fingers*. As far as Hucknall was concerned, the songs on this record contained just as much 'soul' as anything recorded by Major Lance – more, perhaps. No way would he allow his instinctive love of

Keith Richards' guitar, like his love of Lennon's songwriting, to be tempered by some silly and irrelevant localised prejudices. And so Hucknall, for a while, wavered uneasily between the two extremes. He would attend discos at Tameside Town Hall in Dukinfield or the Concorde Suite in Droylesden, content to dance the night away to the sound of George McCrae's *Rock Your Baby*. He basked, perhaps untrendily, in such glorious pop soul.

These were, by and large, frenetic nights. On one occasion, after heartily downing far too many rum and blacks than the average fifteen-year-old might reasonably be expected to consume, Hucknall found himself drifting alone through the streets of Dukinfield. Somehow, by fluke or divine guidance, he found himself stumbling into a party in a darkened terraced house in Hyde's Lodge Lane. Lying in the centre of the lounge floor, between a Draylon settee and a rather angry cat, Hucknall found himself staring at what was probably a constantly spinning ceiling. Three girls, giggling profusely, danced all around his prostrate body to the sounds of the O'Jays' *Back Stabbers* and Detroit Emeralds' sublime *Feel The Need In Me*. When the stereo's throbbing became too much for him and his face turned ghostly pale, one of the girls, Louise Housley, took him into the back garden and held his hand tightly while he noisily vomited over the prize sunflower.

Although that story might be typical of anyone who at the age of fifteen regarded himself as well and truly 'one of the lads', in Mick's case it was far, far from isolated. Hucknall was a heavy drinker and a fast social developer. At the age of sixteen, he took an evening job waiting on tables at the raucous Broomstair Working Men's Club in Denton. Brian Turner befriended Hucknall at the time. He remembers the wild redhead, 'drinking between ten and fourteen pints during the evening. But the thing is, it wasn't just Mick doing that. Everyone around him was just as totally pissed. The only difference was that Mick was about half the age of most of them. Still, that just didn't seem to matter.'

Broomstair WMC on Linden Road (just off Stockport Road), Denton, was little more than a rectangular scout hut with a stage at one end. It was strangely situated above the sweep of Hyde Road and looked out across the unlovely acres of Dukinfield, Stalybridge and beyond that the Pennines. This exposed situation – although, of course, not in evidence on dark nights – gave the club the unlikely feel of some kind of yacht or golf clubhouse. It was filled each weekend with bad fat comics, hilariously inept Elvis impersonators and standard cabaret crooners. Waiting on, Hucknall effectively became one of the adults. He was admired by his rather more angelic looking mates, who had yet to progress beyond the realm of the obligatory cider parties.

It was during this period that Hucknall truly became a burden to his despairing father. One particular nightly ritual was becoming beyond a joke. Hucknall's machismo-inspired thirst might have impressed his friends and workmates at Broomstair WMC but, once home, it would all too often end in him noisily throwing up into the toilet bowl. A seriously worried Reg Hucknall gave his son a 'good talking to' on many occasions. Mostly, the young Mick would wipe the water from his eyes and mutter a series of 'never agains'. Once in bed, suffering considerable effects of room spin and even having numerous alcohol-inspired nightmares, Hucknall would swear to keep his promise. Until, of course, the very next day when, surrounded by his mates, he would weaken and opt for the glory of the drink.

At first, it was little more than another case of infantile bravado, similar to smoking Park Drives in the junior school playground. But a serious drinking problem was surely beckoning Hucknall. He was incredibly fortunate as two separate routes of escape were opening up before him. His singing, of course, and his intelligence. Some of his friends from that period, understandably wishing to remain nameless here, are still sitting in those same tap rooms but are now older, rounder and redder. They still spend too long bragging about recent drinking binges and, perhaps, thinking winsomely about the fantastic world into which their mate had escaped.

As well as owning, as his mates would constantly jibe, 'hollow legs', Hucknall had certain other attributes.

'I never really understood why but, even at that age, Hucknall was always the first to trap off with the women,' recalls Brian Turner. 'Trapping off' was to be Hucknall's most prodigious mid-teens pastime. The nights spent at Droylesden's Concorde Suite would almost by habit end in, to quote Turner, 'A knee trembler down a back alley.'

Although in retrospect and written here in black and white, his success with girls might seem rather seedy, it was in fact merely indicative of his enormous self confidence. At an age when most boys would be clumsily fumbling with bra straps and attempting sloppy, sexless kisses after half a pint of Woodpecker, Hucknall was consuming more booze than the average Salford docker and eagerly 'chatting up' every girl in sight.

When the Concorde Suite finally gave way to city-centre nightclubs, Hucknall was far from fazed by the surrounding glamour. It was a period of profound hedonism that would, inevitably perhaps, return to haunt Hucknall in the years to come. This 'haunting', courtesy of a hundred press articles, would cast him as some kind of crazed juvenile sex beast. Hucknall was nothing of the sort. During his most voracious period, his sexual exploits would be little more than the clumsy finish to the previous evening's revelry. Many times he would wake up in the morning, sipping tea with some sweet young thing, and ask himself, 'Why did I want to do this in the first place?' Hucknall later stated, 'Usually, it was because I was drunk, she was drunk and we would have this carnal lust and we went off and made shouting noises.' It was a part of growing up, albeit a most extreme and apparently extensive part.

At Pips nightclub, in the famous 'Roxy' room, Hucknall fell into a circle of building society secretaries all on a hen night and high on whisky and lemonade, David Bowie and Cockney Rebel, and passing inebriated males. Hucknall fulfilled the latter role quite splendidly and would, the next day, boast about the secretaries he 'went' with on the previous evening. Although, no doubt, his tale was spiced with teenage bravado, even Hucknall was surprised to find himself waking up in a Swinton bedroom. Swinton was a place that he had actually never even heard of. Further forays into Manchester nightlife yielded similar results.

Both Hucknall and Turner would later admit that these were wild days for these two rumbustious Dentonians, even by the standards they had set themselves throughout their early teens. Most of their after-dark activities would be dubious, to say the least. According to Turner, Mick was particularly fond of stripping lead from house roofs. If one had to pinpoint the lowpoint of Hucknall's life then surely the lead-stripping would come pretty close to winning the prize. It was the ultimate, hopeless ragamuffin tactic. Clad in increasingly filthy clothes, the lead-stripping Hucknall nurtured a Dickensian appearance that would surface strangely in later life as an integral aspect of the initial Simply Red image. Is the man who gazes forlornly from the cover of the *Picture Book* album merely a nod back to such days, or an indication for Hucknall of what he might have become had he continued on the downward spiral? The truth is, as he would later admit, Mick Hucknall observed the golden rule. If you can't be good, don't get caught. 'I don't know what would have happened to me if I did get caught,' he would later state, as if still haunted by that old possibility.

Mostly, Hucknall nicked the lead in order to raise the necessary money to be able to see his beloved Manchester United (to whom the unthinkable was happening. An ironic backheel from Denis Law, then playing for Manchester City, had sent Docherty's Reds stumbling into the Second Division. But the fall was just about the best thing that could have happened to the club. It galvanised the team spirit and, the next season, they won the Second Division championship in style, playing quite the best football seen at Old Trafford for a decade. The drop into the Second Division also tended to refuel the fans' spirit who simply relished the prospect of arriving en masse at a tiny and terrified little ground like, say, York City. It was a bizarre turn around. Manchester United fans loved to boast about the size of their following. They are, they would often shout, the largest football club in the world and nothing, not even footballing failure, could hinder their size. It was to Hucknall and his red comrades an immense source of pride, accentuated by their brief visit into Div Two).

In later life, the red/blue divide would sever Mick Hucknall from the cliquish remainder of the Manchester music scene, and that gulf would persist in the later days of Simply Red. While Hucknall and Turner were donning the red, white and black scarf of Manchester United, the majority of the people who were about to form the nucleus of the Manchester scene were profoundly blue in alliance and attitude (Factory Record boss Tony Wilson and Joy Division's Ian Curtis being the two curious exceptions).

This gulf was not to be sniffed at. Manchester City fans, then as now, regarded the red followers to be rather naff, downbeat and untrendy. The United fans, of course, hotly disputed this notion and would see their City counterparts as the eternal poor relations, whingeing fans who never deserved to taste the glories that should come naturally to Manchester United. The divide is destined to colour Hucknall's life forever.

Back in Denton in the mid-seventies it was in evidence everywhere. He wouldn't think of going into, for example, the Flectures Arms on Ashton Road because of its Manchester City affiliation (which is no more). He was understandably annoyed when a pub in Crown Point, called the Kings Head, sported a sign featuring the king of Manchester football, Denis Law, wearing a *City* strip. It was absurd, of course, and still is. Come Saturday morning, friends of his would become vicious enemies when scarved and booted. Naturally, this rivalry was at its most intense during the legendary Manchester derby matches between City and United. On such days, Hucknall would 'lose' himself in the overwhelming passion of it all. Contrary to popular belief, the rivalry was rarely 'healthy'.

'You can always tell whether someone is a City fan,' stated Hucknall in 1975. To some extent that is correct and can be levelled equally at those with red affections. Mick Hucknall, as every Mancunian would testify, could never be anything other than a Manchester United fan. There is something about his manner. It is not easily definable but it was, and still is, there although, in 1990, when Dave Wallace, the creator of the Manchester City fanzine *King Of The Kippax*, went along to interview the City supporting manager of Simply Red, his most pertinent question was, 'How can someone who sings like that be a Manchester United supporter?'

Saturday afternoons were spent catching the 210 bus into Manchester and then the train, from Piccadilly's platform thirteen, to Warwick Road. The frantic scurry between Warwick Road Station and Old Trafford Football Ground would be punctuated with menacing chants and heavy taunts directed at coaches ferrying terrified away-team fans and endless jibes at the policemen who uneasily lined the roads. Old Trafford was a release for Hucknall, and as Tommy Docherty transformed a devastated sham of a football club into a fast-flowing dream team – League Championship failures aside – a surge of pride flowed back into the red half of the city and into Hucknall.

Although Hucknall was not known to everyone by the nickname 'Red', it was beginning to stick at least in certain company. It was, after all, a most fitting and not altogether unattractive monicker, and carried with it a three-way connotation. Firstly, and most importantly as far as Hucknall was concerned, it made it absolutely clear just what his footballing allegiance was. Hucknall had no objection whatsoever to this becoming public knowledge. Secondly, and most obviously, it was a reference to his hair colour and general complexion. This was the rather derogatory schoolboyish angle and as such didn't exactly please Hucknall. But thirdly, it referred to Hucknall's political leaning. Although barely obvious in his teens, Reg Hucknall had instilled in his son a profound sense of left-wing sensibility. This was a natural stance for a youth who tramped the streets of Haughton Green, and Hucknall would often naively take it a step further, telling his mates how one day he would do something fantastic, something which would help redress the social imbalance in Great Britain. The Tories, needless to say, were quite simply the enemy and his animosity would spill over into juvenile exploits come election time, be it local or otherwise. The few blue placards that were to be found in the gardens of Denton, mainly on the Dane Bank side of town, would be indignantly ripped from their rose beds, snapped in two and thrown across

31

the road. Usually, the purple-faced householder would scream obscenities at Hucknall and the gang who would scamper away in search of the next blue garden.

Hucknall would never lose his political affiliation. Indeed, on various occasions in later life he would drag it out, dust it off and air it in song. When his father admitted, in the mid-eighties, that he had lost faith in the Labour Party and had voted SDP, before then deciding not to vote at all, Hucknall was genuinely horrified and pleaded with Reg to rethink his allegiance.

Chapter 3
The First Flush of Punk

Mick Hucknall made an inconspicuous debut in the pages of the *Manchester Evening News* on Thursday 26 August 1976. Buried deep within a slab of Audenshaw Grammar School O'level results, M.J. Hucknall was credited with three passes. As expected, and especially in the context of the considerable successes of his fellow pupils, it was a distinctly modest result. In 1976, when most slightly above-average pupils could reasonably expect, with a good deal of application, a return of four or five passes, the Audenshaw results would generally sparkle. Sevens, eights and nines shouted from the page.

Hucknall, however, was far from distraught. Two new worlds, parallel in his mind, had already begun to beckon. The two-year arts course at Tameside College of Further Education was, by this time, a looming reality. Set adrift from the closeted camaraderie of the schoolyard gangs, and probably a little disturbed by his lack of sheer brilliance at O'level, it was beginning to dawn on him that everything would not simply fall into his lap once out in the real world. He felt the burn of ambition. More though, he felt himself strongly attracted to notions of Bohemia. 'Soon,' he would boast, and as loudly as possible, 'I will be an art student.'

'Art student' had a welcome ring to it. It made him feel special. At sixteen years of age he found himself going through a period of transition. The streets of Haughton Green after dark had lost their romance. No longer did it seem to Hucknall's raging imagination like a little New Jersey, like a Springsteen scenario. None of that was real. The records in his bedroom would still be an escape but there had to be more and it had to be real. What was real was the Mill Lane chip shop, the gossip in the shop next door, the few remaining scooter boys, all now ageing unglamorously into courtship if not marriage, and the sheer parochial lack of ambition surrounded and terrified him. Even the big lads, the local heroes of 1974, the United hooligans, had somehow lost their charisma. Seeing them now in the Whitegates, the King's Head or the Top, playing pool, darts or swapping tales from the Sunday football leagues saddened him deeply.

It would have been easy, at this point, to snap off any possible career plans and drift into inebriated obscurity. To Hucknall's mind, surging with all the naivety that goes with impending studenthood, the lives of these lads seemed small, pathetic even. After all their swank and swagger what were they now? On the dole? Working in the local print works or down the market? On their backs, changing the oil in rusty Cortinas? Oh, how he had once worshipped these boys. Even their much-prized nicknames, Scragg, Wimp, Princey – all still etched on to local road signs prefixing the obligatory 'Rules OK' – had completely lost their power.

Hucknall was no longer the small-time teenage rebel, the soulboy. Even the old geezers in Haughton Green would have to respect him now. Say it loud. Say it again. Mick Hucknall was an art student – well, nearly. And he knew full well that art students were pretty thin on the ground in Haughton Green.

For the precocious teenager, the first half of 1976 had been a musical nightmare. Such a person could not live on Thin Lizzy alone and the pop charts, which seemed so important at that age, were simply brimming with uninspiring bile. Safe in his freezing bedroom, Hucknall would experiment with the likes of Little Feat and Led Zeppelin. Once outside and exposed to the blaring mass of transistors and local discos, his head would be invaded by the likes of *SSSSS Single Bed, Fernando, Jeans On, Convoy*. From his father's television, Telly Savalas, Demis Roussos and bloody David Soul would leer at him. Even his precious Beatles had grown hideously soft – well, Paul had. How the hell could someone so great, thought Hucknall, churn out something like *Silly Love Songs*?

But mercifully something else had happened in 1976, though admittedly not in Denton. It happened in New York and then in London and then just five miles away in Manchester city centre. It was called punk. An embryonic punk scene had begun to form. A tiny, oft-inebriated élite were beginning to meet regularly, to hang out in the Ranch Bar on Dale Street. Soon their numbers would swell.

On Tuesday 20 July, at Manchester's Lesser Free Trade Hall (a small, plain concert lounge adjoining the ostentatious grandeur of the main hall) a rock gig took place that, even to the present day, remains the most famous and cataclysmic event in Manchester's illustrious rock history. This was the day the Sex Pistols returned to Manchester. (Rock historians have often been confused by this date. The Sex Pistols had performed at the same venue on Friday 4 June. Morrissey, as it happened, attended the first date and subsequently wrote a curious letter to the *NME* comparing the Sex Pistols to his true heroes, the bands that formed the American New Wave. At this point, Howard Trafford – who, as Howard Devoto, had established himself as the dry intellectual singer from Manchester band, Buzzcocks – acted as unofficial publicist for the Pistols, effectively setting up the second gig. And it was the second gig, on 20 July, that effectively changed the course of Manchester music.)

It would be easier, of course, to provide a list of Mancunian luminaries who haven't claimed attendance at this gig and the real truth lies lost in the mists of nostalgia. Nevertheless, something happened. Many careers were forged in the fire of that evening.

The inspiration flowed, quite definitely, from the sardonic leer of Johnny Rotten. To stumble across this manic figure for the first time was to experience something truly stimulating. Writer Paul Morley stood quaking in the aisles as the Pistols launched into their first live rendition of *Anarchy in the UK*. That was the precise moment when Morley knew, for definite, that a writing career beckoned. Photographer Kevin Cummins snapped away gleefully. Before the gig he had been a struggling snapper, happy to sell colour shots of David Bowie to Wythenshaw glam band Slaughter and the Dogs – also on this bill – but from this point onwards he was a 'punk' photographer. He was right in there at the epicentre, revelling in the chaos.

How many bands were conceived that night? It is well known that Bernard Sumner and Peter Hook both went out the very next morning and bought 'Play In A Day' guitar books. Soon, tentatively from their bedrooms, they would form Stiff Kittens, who became Warsaw, who became Joy Division, who became New Order.

Mick Hucknall was also in attendance. Wide-eyed and shaking with disbelief, he gazed admiringly into the scorching eyes of J. Rotten. The eyes said everything. They had cynicism, intelligence, rebelliousness, wryness, urgency, pride, indignation and fear. They were brooding, enigmatic eyes. Mick Hucknall had never seen such a character before. He had never seen such a display of self belief so great, in fact, that it wholly overcame the musical ineptness of the Sex Pistols who, without Rotten's charisma, were little more than a mediocre heavy metal outfit.

"'Ow many of you lot like the 'Ot Rods?" sneered Rotten, in full flow, jibing at the Essex R'n'B outfit, Eddie and the Hot Rods, who had attempted to steal the punk mantle from the Pistols and, Rotten knew, had already been booked to play the Free Trade Hall proper. 'Our imitators, they are . . . the 'Ot Rods.'

What Rotten so effectively sold that night, if not throughout his career, was attitude. This wasn't some high-flying, coke-snorting superstar fresh out of the back of a limo. This was a working-class Londoner, no richer and quite possibly considerably poorer than most of the audience.

Mick Hucknall couldn't believe his eyes. Shuffling noisily out of the Lesser Free Trade Hall he knew that something had changed inside. As corny as it may sound, Hucknall felt inwardly invincible, as did the rest of the crowd. His reticence towards the punk hype had evaporated and, quite possibly, the seed of musical ambition had been sown. If Rotten could do it so could he. Hucknall was almost disappointed to remember that, unlike Rotten, he could sing, even if his voice had only thus far been unleashed amid the cacophonies of school assemblies or to produce sub-standard versions of *All Right Now*. Travelling home on the late-night bus, Hucknall felt, perhaps for the first time, truly alive.

Chapter 4
The Art School Dance

Mick Hucknall, art student, burgeoning punk of Haughton Green, alighted onto the unlovely concrete bus station at Ashton-under-Lyne on 3 September 1976. The precinct immediately behind him – one of the most hideous ever built – sprawled horribly around the remains of the Birdcage, the once infamous soul venue. Ashton-under-Lyne, perhaps more than any other Lancashire town, had suffered terribly at the hands of crazed developers. The once teeming, glamorous Stamford Street at the town's very heart had been reduced to ghostly, inconsequential desolation. The lovely Woolworth's with its dark floorboards had gone the way of most local shops. It now stood boarded and lonely. The shopping axis of the town had been shunted, literally, towards that terrible precinct. The town, never the quietest of places on Saturday night, had been drained of character.

Even an anxious first-day college student with a head full of punky bravado couldn't fail to sense this. Hucknall wandered up the length of Penny Meadow which rose from Ashton's ferocious centre to the leafier, gentler climes of Higher Hurst. On Beaufort Road, stumbling past the row of semi-circular engineering classrooms, Hucknall stopped to catch his breath. Wandering into the college proved to be nerve-racking. A gang of lads – a collection of would-be mechanics, turners and fitters – stood around the entrance making disparaging remarks at the 'Poncy types from the other side of the college.' These, 'poncy types' would be the students from the celebrated catering block, or from the

37

general studies unit, or the art students. This banter, albeit harmless, was always present in the college, spicing the atmosphere a little and serving to keep the feet of the art block aesthetes firmly on the ground. It wasn't quite what Hucknall had expected.

The main building of Tameside College rose five storeys high (A to E floors) and was in essence a thoroughly typical further education establishment, perhaps with a more disparate blend of students than most. The refectory, in Hucknall's day situated across the courtyard in the catering block, was the college's true nucleus. And in particular, whether the lecturers cared to admit it or not, all college life seemed to be magnetically attracted to the two bar football tables which were in continuous and cacophonous action, swamped by feverish hands and bullish yelling. Hucknall loved the sheer noise and vivacity of the place. It was quite the antithesis, he often thought, of the comparatively oppressive regime at Audenshaw Grammar. What's more, once past the howling imbeciles at the gate he could relax into his beloved new role. He was an art student.

He also had plenty to prove. He did feel rather embittered. It wasn't so much the fact that three O'levels was somewhat less than stunning. It was the sheer fact that nobody even expected him to do any better. He would, he believed, be treated with a good deal more respect at Tameside. 'Misunderstood!' That was the word he often used and, quite naturally, he found solace in the equally misunderstood punk movement. Audenshaw Grammar and the world had failed to come to terms with Mick Hucknall. The system wasn't right for him. Yet he knew – *he knew* just how special he was. What's more, he would prove it some day.

What Hucknall failed to understand, which was quite natural for any bright sixteen-year-old, was that practically every other student and indeed, every other person on the planet felt exactly the same way. But as a student one tends to exaggerate such feelings. Hucknall had become a naive existentialist. He would enthusiastically soak up the world of Kerouac, Sartre, Camus and Burroughs. Even at night, in his bedroom with *Sticky Fingers* on the turntable, he would flick through his copy of Camus' *Outsider*. He was, at last, beginning to feel like an intellectual.

It was also a fantastic release to be able to dress in whatever he wished. This was often a creation, a mish-mash of cultural cross dressing, so bizarre that it wasn't just his aghast father and Nell, but the lecturers too who would shake their heads in disapproval. A punky relationship with a dog collar was thankfully not to last too long. The odd thing was that Hucknall, with his shock of red hair, cut such a distinctive figure that even the slightest deviation from normal attire would seem greatly exaggerated. People had started to look at Mick Hucknall. He wasn't the kind of greyish student who would merge into the back of classrooms never to be picked out. He was fundamentally up front, in the thick of the action. Out of the three hundred students who walked up Penny Meadow each morning and back down Stamford Street in the evening, the often tastelessly garbed Hucknall, with his forthright colour sense, was the one most people remembered. Although, when asked he would still regard himself as shy, he loved and possibly craved the attention.

But at Tameside he still failed to shine. His art lecturers saw nothing exceptional in the boy. 'He just wasn't talented in the arts,' one of them told me. The weeks passed by and still Hucknall remained mostly unexceptional. Even his personality – although fleetingly tempestuous and hugely distinctive – still failed to make much of an academic impact, and the rest of the class largely treated him with mild contempt.

But one strange thing did happen. Mike Rooke, a teacher and local poet of repute with an unashamedly progressive approach to teaching, held mixed media sessions on Friday afternoons. (In latter years, Mike Rooke would become Head of Performing Arts. In Hucknall's day, he merely took care of the drama aspects. He was not an arts teacher.)

Friday afternoons were seen by some as something of a joke. But not by Mike Rooke or, so it transpired, by Mick Hucknall. The mixed media sessions would include students from arts courses, drama, dance and music. It was simply a gathering of all the more sophisticated college students. And Mike Rooke just loved to experiment with this intellectual cocktail. It was in the context of these gatherings that Mick Hucknall finally began to show signs of his true potential. 'As soon as he wandered through the door,' claimed Mike Rooke, 'he would visibly change. I believe he was quite sullen in the arts classes, but he was quite the opposite with me. You could sense the enthusiasm welling up within him as our sessions began.'

Initially, within this freeform environment, Hucknall would indulge his own boisterous leanings, gleefully assuming mannerisms of a profoundly laddish nature. He would brag and tell endless jokes. He swiftly became class leader. Stray art teachers wandering inquisitively into Rooke's rooms would find themselves totally astonished by the new, brash, ultra-confident Hucknall. Something very strange was going on. Rooke's technique was to 'organise giant games'. This would mean that an extraordinary, practically avant-garde atmosphere would prevail. Casual passers-by would be stunned by the apparent anarchy of the sessions. Of course, to Hucknall this all seemed to fit in perfectly with his new-found punky leanings. The more anarchistic the better. Any teacher like Rooke who showed a fervent desire for innovation simply had to be a good thing. It was the way things were in 1976. It was extremely exciting.

'For many of the students,' states Rooke, 'this was like opening the door to a wonderful new world. A world with no scholarly pressure. Some hated it. But many, and especially Hucknall, saw it as a wonderful opportunity to experiment and show off. It may sound arrogant, but I knew almost straight away that this lad would do something in the performing arts field. It was blatantly obvious.'

Hucknall revelled in a variety of drama exercises during that first year. He also dabbled in video and just occasionally in music. Rooke, encouraged by what he regarded as a genuine talent, pushed Hucknall to the full. Hucknall's fellow students, however, were less than enthralled with this teacher/pupil relationship.

'It became more and more obvious that this boy had a big ego. What's more, it was getting bigger week by week. It was extraordinary, you really could sense a power in him.' Naturally, a great deal of friction surrounded this precocious redhead. Most of the girls, being the highly sophisticated types one tends to find in art schools, regarded him as a rather vulgar individual. They did not enjoy his jokes or, for that matter, his laddish swagger. As far as they were concerned Hucknall was on another planet and they openly rejected him. But Hucknall seemed to thrive on such notoriety. 'It was as if he enjoyed being disliked,' states Rooke.

One morning he turned up for class simply glowing with pride. His face was something of a mess. A black eye, a swollen lip and a bulbous nose. The previous night, returning on a late-night bus from a punk gig in town, he had encountered the downside of the punk phenomenon. A spate of punk bashing had broken out. Anyone sporting mildly punk gear – drainpipe trousers might be enough – were considered fair game by a section of society who would at other times engage in gay bashing, Paki bashing, or bashing anyone not wearing the accepted football colours.

Hucknall had fought back apparently, but had taken a severe beating. This, he thought, was quite wonderful. It gave him a licence. It was now official. Hucknall was a punk. As for the distaste of his fellow students, he practically nurtured it. He would tell rude jokes with added gusto whenever one of the more sensitive females happened to be within earshot. He didn't want to upset, he wanted to shock, to be disliked even. It was a punk thing.

At college, emboldened by his battle scars, he spent each week looking forward to Friday afternoons when his artistic nature could be truly unleashed. One day, Rooke set a task for the students to explore the nature of commercial culture. The class was split into groups of three or four. Between them they had to come up with what they considered might be a hit record. Mick's group, perhaps not surprisingly, came up with the most interesting tape. It was a song, a ballad, complete with Mick's voice and lyrics. As the rest of the class sat and listened it became apparent, at least according to Rooke, that this boy had a distinct and unusual talent. Rooke would call it 'special'. The rest of the class would prefer 'strange'. Unfortunately the tape was wiped in readiness for another session. 'You've no idea how we wished we had not wiped that tape,'

41

stated Rooke. 'It would have been a perfect example of talent in the raw stage.'

This was the very first song that Mick Hucknall wrote on an acoustic guitar. It was an instrument on which he could play about with basic chord structures and experiment, in an incredibly naive way, with songwriting. Copying his heroes, John Lennon in particular, was quite impossible. As Hucknall practised, he realised just how incredibly difficult it would be to write something of simple beauty like McCartney's *Yesterday*, or the song he associated with 'sheer gorgeousness' – John Lennon's celebrated *Imagine*. He did notice though, flicking through his old record collection, just how the Beatles had progressed in public from a state of simplistic and clumsy naivety to their sublime peak circa *Sergeant Pepper*.

It was not a time when the average seventeen-year-old, spiced by punk's glorious push, would take time to appreciate the Beatles. In fact nothing could be less hip. But Hucknall managed to see beyond such a narrow viewpoint, indeed he could see the punkiness in the early Beatles. He also noted that despite the musical failings and horrific clichés of that early material, the talent, the originality, still lurked. Until this point he had decided to wait at least until his musicality had attained a certain degree of deftness before venturing into songwriting. However, probably because of the Beatles he changed his mind.

The second song Mick Hucknall ever wrote on an acoustic guitar, sitting in his icy bedroom in Haughton Green, was indeed simple and naive. Hucknall hoped that some originality might shine through. It was a long shot really and, after writing it, he filed it away. He probably went downstairs to watch 'Coronation Street' or, more likely put another James Brown record on his bedroom turntable. Whatever, the song remained unfinished. He had written the verses, the words and the melodies. The song wouldn't be finished with the chorus added until he finally dug it out seven years later. The song was called *Holding Back The Years*.

'I sensed something,' said Rooke. 'But you wouldn't necessarily define it as talent. Students who have left this place and have gone on to do better things have got there because of drive, ego and determination. Hucknall had all those things in abundance.' Hucknall was also creative, inventive. One test – and one of Rooke's strangest – was for everyone in the class to go out and learn a dance. A week later the students would return to face the arduous task of teaching the dance to the rest of the class. Most students failed to take Rooke's eccentric testers at all seriously and returned with clumsy examples of Northern Soul 'footsie' or the rocker dance, 'Hell'. Hucknall, however, had a different attitude. He went to the library and took out a book on ballroom dancing. The following Friday the rest of the class were somewhat stunned to see Hucknall dragging a slide projector into the classroom. Armed with this and blacked-out windows he projected the foot positions on to the ceiling and turned the entire exercise into an event, a parody, an entertainment.

'It was a complete spoof,' explained Rooke. 'But he could do that, you see. He was, especially in his second year, kind of inspirational. Even if Mick ended up as a bank clerk, I would have remembered him. Distinctive students like that are not uncommon, but some of them end up in nut houses, some of them become winners. The only thing you can be certain of is that wherever they ended up they would still be kind of inspirational to the people around them.'

Hucknall was a good attender – quite rare for an arts student – and appeared to revel in college social life, often nipping round to the local pub, the Swan, at lunch time for games of darts with the bewildered locals. Or he simply hung around the canteen with his first girlfriend, Catherine Gearey. In year two, under the expert guidance of art teacher Bill Clarke, his potential as an artist became a little clearer. Nevertheless, none of his achievements in the art class could possibly match his sense of the anarchic which surfaced, stunningly, on certain Friday afternoons.

He was attracted to the performing arts and simply adored Rooke's wild scams. On one particularly memorable occasion Rooke had split the class up into groups. Each group would elect a leader and try to project a 'happening'. Rooke's brief was as ambiguous as that and most of the groups acted out rather staid rituals – witches around a cauldron, the sacrificing of a virgin, that kind of thing. Hucknall, however, seized the opportunity to show off and jumped out of the window, two storeys up, and shuffled along a six-inch ledge before coming back into the room through another window. Outside on the tarmac three members of staff and a gaggle of first-year catering students craned their necks in total disbelief and terror.

'I think,' stated Rooke in a casual manner, 'that proved that Mick Hucknall was prepared to go a little further than anyone else . . . it showed that, whatever it might take to break through he would, at least, go for it. I respected him for that. I also admired his capacity to not give a damn about what anyone else would think. That's quite a rare thing and a good measure of someone's self confidence. He wasn't easily fazed . . . I suppose he was quite dangerous. He wasn't the sort of guy you would lightly invite to your party. You never quite knew what he was going to do. For my Friday sessions he was the most perfect catalyst I've ever encountered.'

Chapter 5
The Electric Circus

Back in Stockport in the latter half of 1976 stood a second-hand bookshop run, at first glance, by an unassuming, middle-aged and rather bookish woman. The woman would smile – she smiled to all her customers – and only her cardigan, a little too garishly coloured, hinted at the kind of eccentricity only found in shops of a dustier nature. One thing seemed very strange. Seeping from downstairs there would be a distinctive noise, say the Patti Smith Group's anarchic debut album, *Horses*. This hard noise – a noise which Hucknall had become dutifully well acquainted with during the months which transformed the summer of 1976, the hottest summer in living memory, into a violently freezing autumn – clashed mightily with the racks filled with frayed Margaret Drabble paperbacks. Good-natured arguments took place downstairs. Beneath the violence of the music, the following conversation would be typical.

'How can you kids listen to this rubbish – it's dreadful, dreadful.'

'No it's not – it's wonderful.' The lisping voice continued, 'Wearly, wearly intelligent.'

The first voice might well belong to another middle-aged woman who would then rush upstairs and, shaking her head, stride out of the shop in the manner of Barbara Woodhouse. The second voice belonged to a thin, long-haired young man who was sitting amongst racks of second-hand Wishbone Ash and Henry Cow albums. His name was Paul Morley. He had shown a certain entrepreneurial flair by setting up this

45

somewhat austere, poster-lined record cellar.

Someone had told Hucknall that this curious figure – who had become known to just about everyone who found themselves edging nervously into the Manchester new wave fraternity – had starting writing for the *NME*. Could this be true? Inside the shop, one's eyes would be drawn to a notice which read, 'Buy *Out There* a magazine for people who know, not just teen whimsies'. This was expertly produced, unlike all the other scruffily produced punk fanzines (Morley had borrowed £75 from his dad to pay for the printing). The writing style was odd – unashamedly pretentious. Hucknall bought it. After all it did include the words, 'Buzzcocks, support your local band!' He was in on the scene. He had even met Paul Morley.

The nucleus – the Morley set – had been formed and met in the Ranch Bar, a former gay disco on Dale Street (next door to infamous drag revue bar, Foo Foo's Palace). In this tiny dive, bands were formed and often interviewed by fanzine writers – *Out There*, *Shy Talk* and *Ghast Up* were the leading titles – before a note had been played. There were times when the music hardly seemed to matter at all. It was a tiny, ferociously cliquish social circle, hardened into gang mentality by occasional attacks from the teds. The Ranch was raided on one occasion by six heavily inebriated teds. They rushed down the club's stairs wielding blunt instruments, and one could be forgiven for anticipating the kind of vicious fracas that tabloid hacks dream about. What ensued was rather different. The teds began to chat with the punks and joined forces. Their leader, a huge guy named Dave, later became a familiar figure on punk Sundays down at Manchester's most famous venue of the time, the Electric Circus. He was seen one night staggering out of the Circus's eternally waterlogged toilets proudly carrying a toilet pan, complete with seat, above his head. That was a typical sight in the Electric Circus, and Hucknall just fell in love with the seediness of the place and, indeed, of the entire scene.

The Electric Circus stood cornily, from a punk point of view, amid waste ground. No American film director hoping to find a location for some dreadful post-apocalyptic punk flick could possibly stumble across a more perfect scene. It was once a beautiful picture house but by 1976 it had decayed horribly into a slab of ornate Victorian frivolity. This was Collyhurst Street, two miles to the north of Manchester city centre. Spanning the twin arteries of Rochdale Road and Oldham Road, it cut across a triangle of land that was, even in the picture house's heyday, a somewhat unwelcoming area – as it was in 1976 and as it certainly is today.

It was a Sunday in March 1977. The Manchester punk scene, a mere six months old, had already been declared bankrupt by the handful of purists who had attended the Lesser Free Trade Hall. By now, thanks to acres of tabloid exposure and four solid months of erratic though ever intriguing new wave single releases, the scene had mushroomed. Representatives from the *Sun* and the *News of the World* – fat men with safety pins stuck through their lapels – mingled with the crowds, searching for minor incidents to blow out of all recognition.

The Stranglers were to play on this occasion. By 9p.m., the Circus's grubby interior was filled to dangerous capacity with hot, wet bodies in black T-shirts. Outside, like the six preceding Sundays, a queue snaked around the corner and alongside the Circus's crumbling side wall. As it happened, this crowd were not so punky at all, at least not by the standards of later eras. If you looked hard you might have glimpsed tartan bondage trousers purchased on some wild tourist foray to London. The odd ear sported a razor blade or safety pin, which would be hastily removed before the wearers returned home to tabloid-believing parents. On the other hand, you might notice half-caste Paul with bleached yellow hair, bizarrely swathed head to toe in bandages and with a light bulb dangling uncomfortably from his left ear. But apart from that the regular clientele at the Electric Circus, possibly the most notorious punk venue of all time, were a pretty conservative if ungainly rabble.

Paul Morley bobbed about, as only Paul Morley could. 'Everyone who *is* anyone is already in there,' he bragged to the hapless queue before disappearing back inside. Another writer, named Nicholls, gushed embarrassingly over a non-plussed bouncer.

'But I'm from the music press,' he pleaded. 'You've just got to let me in.' He wasn't at all happy when Tony Parsons and publicist Alan Edwards from London pushed past, disappearing without paying into the Circus's hellish interior. And then it happened.

'It's the teds . . . it's the teds . . . it's the teds!' screamed one young buck with 'Sten guns in Wilmslow' stencilled across the back of his jacket. *'The teds are in the flats . . . the teds are in the flats.'*

But wherever the teds were that evening, they were not in the flats opposite the Electric Circus. However, seven half bricks that rained down on the queue were enough to carve a gash into the head of one fishnet stocking-clad punkette, cause considerable panic outside and in the Circus, and provide the tabloid hacks with a glorious story.

Mick Hucknall was standing in that queue. He was annoyed – not at the brats who had thrown the bricks but at himself. If he had arrived at the venue earlier he would have been wallowing in glory with the sweaty folks on the inside. He was incensed by Morley's arrogant remarks. He felt insignificant, on the periphery, uninvolved. He knew the Morley set well. He knew the Buzzcocks, the fanzine writers, the Worst, the Drones and Slaughter and the Dogs. The only trouble was they didn't know him. There was no reason, of course, why they should have known him, or of him. Nevertheless, his lack of success in penetrating that clique irked him considerably. Indeed, this was the very spark that fired the spirit of his soon to be formed band . . . the Frantic Elevators.

Although he was in at the beginning at the Lesser Free Trade Hall, the Manchester punk scene had blossomed very nicely with minimal contributions from the red-headed Dentonian. He was stunned by the bizarre, rather anti-punk image of Buzzcocks, pre and post Howard Devoto. They sang love songs derived from an intellectual edge that was hardly widespread in the punk scene.

Buying the Buzzcocks' cheaply made, self financed (the sleeves were physically stuck together and the discs inserted in manager Richard Boon's front room) EP *Spiral Scratch* proved to be a symbolic turning point in Hucknall's life. It demonstrated that there was a little more involved in this whole punk thing than merely the tales of a few reprobates from Finsbury Park throwing up in airports. This was a genuinely local band, who Hucknall had actually seen about town on many occasions, producing cheaply made music that carried genuine – and as time would prove lasting – quality.

Howard Devoto's manic voice sounded like a speed freak northern Captain Beefheart – even though Hucknall had never heard Captain Beefheart he understood the reference. It was scum music with an intellectual edge and topped by lyrics which were stratospherically beyond the scope of most of the dole queue gush that was beginning to pour from the mouths of most young punk pretenders. One song in particular fully captured the spirit of Manchester in 1976–1977. Oddly enough it was far from vivacious. It was a nihilist whinge aimed just as much against their new waves as society in general. Hucknall devoured it, allowing it to soundtrack his every moment. Around and around in his head it went. 'You know the scene is very humdrum . . . You know me I'm acting dumb dumb . . . Boredom, boredom, boredom . . . B'dum b'dum.'

Boredom, this scruffy little ditty, catapulted itself to the top of Hucknall's private hit parade and has remained there. Years later, when asked to list his top ten influences, he would dig it out and proudly place it alongside the likes of Miles Davis's seminal *Kind Of Blue*, John Lennon's *Instant Karma* or Cole Porter's *Love For Sale*. *Boredom* just seemed to be the most beautifully succinct twenty-year-old angst song ever written. And it was from Manchester. What's more, it had been produced by a penniless and musically naive crowd who used their ineptness to great advantage.

'That guitar solo just changed the way I thought about youth,' Hucknall said, referring to Pete Shelley's parodical two-note guitar part performed on a £20 broken Woolworth's guitar. This two-note solo wouldn't have worked in any other era. It was the perfect, pathetic punk reply to all the musical pomp and grandiose gesturing typical of the progressive rock era of the early seventies. Pete Shelley's laboured and repetitive plucking of those two notes reminded people of the real point of young, rebellious music. It was about passion and excitement, cheap thrills and laughs. It was not about sitting in the Free Trade Hall watching the ludicrous sub-classical posturing of the likes of Emerson, Lake and Palmer. They had been overruled by two notes. Shelley's two notes supported pop rather than rock, Marc Bolan rather than Bad Company, the Kinks rather than Cream, or Tamla Motown rather than Dandelion. It was a lesson that Hucknall didn't really need, despite owning the odd Deep Purple album. Just as he had despised the soul snobs, so he had loathed the progressive bores. Sitting around cross-legged, smoking dope and listening to Hawkwind had never been his bag.

Hucknall's final conversion to punk came about during a brief sojourn to the unlikely, although suitably greying town of Barrow-in-Furness. Sitting on the beach there, he ritualistically cut his hair to something at least approaching the kind of spikiness characteristic of the era. It was a mildly crazed pastiche of a scene from the Who's *Quadrophenia* (a homage-to-mod concept album, yet to be ruined on film).

The closure of the Electric Circus was shrouded in controversy. The police, deciding that the venue was unsafe – which, in retrospect, it was and the authorities' only failure was to not close the damn place earlier – used the age-old excuse of the food licence to force the aggrieved owners to nail the doors firmly shut. Before this significant nailing took place, a full weekend celebration was held at the venue featuring just about anybody and everybody from Manchester, and quite a few more besides. Buzzcocks, Slaughter and the Dogs, the Drones, V2, Warsaw, Steel Pulse (reggae from Birmingham), John Cooper Clarke, the Fall and, of course, the ever-present Jon the Postman (was this an act or an orgy of ad lib inebriation? No Manchester punk gig would be complete without Jon – an actual postie – clambering onstage to deliver a version of *Louie Louie* clutching a brown ale bottle). The entire event was celebrated, warts'n'all, on a Virgin mini EP more notable for Paul Morley's sleeve notes than the actual music it contained.

Mick Hucknall felt, like everyone else, thoroughly down-hearted by the Circus's closure. He regarded the Monday evening sessions at the Band On The Wall, watching poor-quality hippy bands grunge their way through hastily written dirges, as a poor substitute. He did attend a scattering of city centre gigs, most notably at the ex-folk club, Rafters, where he witnessed spirited performances by Elvis Costello, Rich Kids and Wayne County. But perhaps Hucknall's most famous outing, as a plain old punter, was to the old Elizabethan Suite which stood inside the rapidly decaying complex called Belle Vue. Belle Vue was the legendary Manchester fairground/zoo/ boating lake/circus and speedway, which had boomed in the mid-twentieth century as *the* natural magnet for Manches-ter's Sunday trippers and Bank Holiday crowds. During the early sixties it became an integral part of Manchester's thriving nightlife and music scene. The infamous Zooby Doo Disco played host there to most of the bands of Merseybeat. In the early seventies, by now a dying beast, Belle Vue enjoyed one last flutter of fame as the fairground in *That'll Be The Day* and *Stardust*. Belle Vue's circus venue, the King's Hall, also challenged the Free Trade Hall as Manchester's premier rock venue with appearances from the likes of Deep Purple, the Who and the Rolling Stones. It also played fleeting parts in the early life of Hucknall. As a boy, naturally, he visited the fairground. As a teenager he became remarkably bored dur-ing a trip to the speedway.

Hucknall's punk excursion to the Elizabethan Suite, much to his later embarrassment, saw him well and truly captured, mid-pogo, by the cameras of Granada Televison. To this day, every time Granada decides to wheel out a nostalgic look at the punk era the same footage is shown, and the entire region seems to join together in an impromptu spot-the-Hucknall competition. And there he is eerily and jerkily in freeze frame, his instantly recognisable features amid a seething audience, the crazed, sweaty faces leering, screaming and unfortunately spitting at the black-clad figure of Joe Strummer from the Clash.

The Belle Vue gig was a punk showcase, organised specifi-cally with the Granada film in mind. The film would be cut into fractured segments and scattered through the second anarchic series of Tony Wilson's groundbreaking 'So It Goes' show. The first series had featured the Sex Pistols for the first time live in the studio. This time around, Wilson dragged his complaining camera crew to a number of Manchester live gigs – Elvis Costello at Rafters for example – and attempted to force Granada to bolster the budget (which they didn't do. Although 'So It Goes' attained legendary status because of perfect timing and attitude, it angered the bosses at Granada who plainly despised anything that could be regarded as punk rock, and the ensuing argument almost cost Wilson his job).

The evening that Hucknall attended featured the Clash, Siouxsie and the Banshees and Penetration. It proved to be a suitably riotous occasion, not least because a large proportion of the crowd, not including Hucknall, had succeeded in breaking down the doors at the rear of the rather staid ballroom and had gained admission for free, much to the embarrassment of the security. The Clash's Joe Strummer, onstage and in near hysterics, screamed, 'And this one's called . . . *Geeetttinngg in feer Nuthin!*'

It was seen as a small punk victory. The joyous crowd slam danced the evening away, first falling to one side of the stage and then the other. In the middle, pushing, shoving and simply screaming with laughter was Mick Hucknall.

'I think I've discovered who the true star of this show is,' drawled Siouxsie Sue dryly, before pointing towards the television camera and continuing, ''cos that's where all the eyes are pointing. You want to be on the telly do yer?'

'YEEEEEESSSSS!' screamed Hucknall, punching the air before falling to the floor and scrambling around in the dust and the fag ends and the plastic pint pots.

Chapter 6
Voices in the Dark

Brian Turner, who had for some time drifted out of the Hucknall circle, began an engineering course at Tameside College in September 1977. Indeed, he had become one of the vociferous hordes who gathered menacingly around the college's entrance.

Brian was sharp, witty and brash. Like Hucknall, he was profoundly working class and, also like Hucknall, he came from a family with absolutely no musical leanings whatsoever. However, a music fanatic, he decided to stay in and learn bass guitar rather than spend every evening in the local pub. He kept a keen eye on the minuscule Manchester music scene and wasn't particularly surprised to learn that his old mate and fellow Tameside student, Mick Hucknall, had started to front a ramshackle punk band called the Frantic Elevators.

'I simply blagged my way into that band,' he says. 'I knew that Mick's band would be good and when I saw him rehearsing with his co-songwriter, Neil Moss, one night down in Chorlton, I instantly thought the band would evolve into something very special.'

However, to describe the band as 'ramshackle' is, if anything, rather kind. It was a chaotic and flexible unit, adrift from any Manchester cliques – the way it would stay – and included its fair share of eccentrically gifted characters. Mick and Brian were nothing if not upfront, while Neil could be insular to the point of rudeness. There were other 'interesting' members. One early drummer, Steve Tansley, was proud to be a fully fledged heavy metal sticksman, happily displaying all the clichés that – post Spinal Tap, post Bad News – go with such a position. Subtlety was not his forte. He would sit and hammer the drum kit and the tune into a state of wilting submission, more often than not leaving the rest of the band exchanging silent, concerned looks. Mick and Neil should have known he would be unsuitable when they first saw him eating his way through a bag of granulated sugar.

'This guy's just too loud,' said Mick one night in the Angel Inn in Denton. 'We are going to have to let him go.' 'Letting him go' wasn't at all easy, in fact it was embarrassing in the extreme. It was the first time that Hucknall had realised that there is far more to running a band than merely organising weekly convivial practice sessions. In that respect the harmony that existed in the Beatles, the band that he had most closely studied was a lie, that is until their legendary cracks began to appear. The all-encompassing gang mentality was practically impossible to maintain, especially with four separate egos each with different ideas of how a band should sound or look, and each with differing standards of musicianship, let alone aspirations. The impossibility of maintaining band happiness caused Hucknall considerable anguish and was tempered only by his punkish belief in camaraderie.

'We are not in this band to make great music,' he once pompously proclaimed. 'We are here to share a lifestyle, to be part of a team . . . for fun!'

On drums, once the heavy-handed Steve Tansley had exited, came in Kevin Williams, a far more sedate and controllable prospect from Chadderton. Another early member, a bass player called Mark Reeder, left the band for Germany (where he still lives and where he played an active role in Nena's number one hit *99 Red Balloons*). These fluctuations were matched by the band's over-ambitious attempts to steal from too many musical styles, most of which were way beyond their abilities, anyway. The sound of early Frantic Elevators was typical of the noise that could be heard seeping from beneath many practice room doors in 1978. It was the sound of ambition being pinned down by lack of ability – a dull, uninspiring, seemingly hopeless sound. Nevertheless, the huge majority of bands who evolved into lucrative glory during the eighties had once made the very same deadening noise.

By mid-1978, the definitive Frantic Elevators had been formed and as their hastily photocopied biog would boast the line up had settled on Mick Hucknall – guitar/vocals; Neil Smith (sometimes called Neil Moss) – guitar; Brian Turner – keyboards/bass; and Kevin Williams – drums. Rehearsals, be they in Denton or at Manchester Art College, had about them a distinctive aura of anarchy although they were impressively regular. If the band were not able to make an impression on the disparate and messy small band network of the era, and if they really weren't in the business of writing classic songs that would transform their respective lifestyles into a glamorous, popstar whole, then at least they would be able to have fun. This might seem to be a rather less than original attitude, but most bands of the time – especially in Manchester – attempted to peddle an attitude of humourless self importance. Such wholly pretentious nonsense rarely worked. In fact, and this was blatantly obvious at the time, it would be the cause of considerable future embarrassment to all concerned.

The Frantic Elevators, much to their later credit, made a conscious decision that rehearsing, gigging, writing even would relate not to pretentions of high art but a Saturday spree down at Old Trafford – however untrendy that might be. Their angle, their image would be one of working-class honesty; of HP sauce, Boddingtons bitter, darts and pool, trips to Blackpool, caravans in Rhyl, football matches and quiz shows, union meetings and bingo, working men's clubs and travelling fairs. It was attitude, not imagery. It was working-class pride. It was anti-aesthetic – which cut a little against the grain of Hucknall's daytime activities at Tameside College – and a direct assault on the kind of dour posing clichés that were just beginning to affect many aspiring Manchester bands of the time.

One early Elevators song more than any other seemed to be the embodiment of this spirit. It was a simplistic, catchy little ditty with lyrics that rather lacked any sense of poetic mystique. The song, arguably inspired by a similar number by New York's premier punk drag queen, Wayne/Jayne County, was called *Fuck Off*. Hucknall had scribbled the lyrics on the back of a beer mat after four lunchtime pints of bitter in the Angel Inn – not, of course, that inebriation was any excuse. The song's punchline went as follows: 'No spittin' . . . No smokin' . . . No shaggin' . . . Fuck off . . . No pissin' . . . No shaggin' . . . No smokin' . . . Fuck off.'

This piece of profoundly juvenile minimalism never made it, thankfully, into their stage set. It did, however, enjoy one moment of glory. At one early rehearsal in Denton, the band were delighted to hear the approaching sounds of a marching brass band in full angelic flow. As the brass band came nearer and nearer, Hucknall opened all the windows on the road side of the rehearsal room. The brass band were not, reportedly, overtly amused to be drowned out by such a ramshackle punk din topped by Hucknall's vulgar lyric line. A cheap shot, it must be said, but the Frantic Elevators laughed all the way to the nearest Banks pub.

Although it soon became apparent that the Frantic Elevators would have trouble fitting into any of the Manchester cliques, they did manage to secure a number of early city centre gigs. 'Actually, we had no idea whatsoever about how to get gigs,' admitted Brian Turner, before adding, 'but we would seem to get them by some form of osmosis. Somebody's brother would know someone who knew someone who ran a venue. It just happened. I think we were incredibly naive in that respect. We expected the music business, the attention, the audience, the credibility – everything really – just to come to us. I know it sounds hilarious, but we didn't even really feel that we would have to play gigs. We thought that if we just carried on in the practice room someone would come and see us – fate would take its course.'

One gig that did take place in mid-1978 was at the musicianly venue the Band On The Wall on Swan Street. Steve Forster, rock writer for the local listings magazine, *New Manchester Review*, and part-time Band On The Wall sound engineer, encouraged local musicians by organising a weekly three band showcase, taking place on Tuesdays. It made good if not wildly lucrative sense. Three bands would bring with them three lots of thirsty mates. How else could one manage to get thirty hearty drinkers in one pub on a dead Tuesday? Nevertheless, it was a fine venue run by musicians for musicians. Just occasionally one had the feeling that such evenings were nothing more than mass insular jam sessions. Practice sessions with a bar. It was not, as has been reported, the hub of the Manchester scene at all. But it was, with its Georgian atmosphere more typical of London than Manchester, a nice place to meet, talk deals and bullshit (the rest of the week, it returned to its most preferred role of downbeat jazz venue).

As well as the Elevators, the gig in question included a gang of rampant schoolboy scruffs from Burnley called Not Sensible (latterly the Not Sensibles) and a band called Unit who had formed just three days prior to the gig – and it showed. The gig was actually reviewed by me for *Sounds*. Forgive, if you will, the somewhat naive rock journalist vernacular, typical of the fanzine-like style of *Sounds*.

. . . Finally come Frantic Elevators who are typical of those 1977 bands who survived the year and finally proved that they really do have something to say. The problem is finding out what it is. They crashed through a very competent set and gave me little to criticise but, at the same time, showed little or no originality. A great band to dance to on a drunken stage night, a kind of sub Status Quo with a touch of humour. Their first number was the best of the night. It was not unlike *Wire* and proved quite haunting, being based around a slow drumbeat and chanting lyric. If only the rest of the set showed the same promise.

Through that murky journalese and my equally murky memory of the evening one can infer that the Frantic Elevators were a spirited, if rather derivative combo. But at least they displayed an ability to enjoy themselves and, quite rare for the time, even expressed a desire to entertain. I recall Mick Hucknall screaming violently while showing the outstretched palms of his hands à la Al Jolson. Paul Morley, hovering around with a triple vodka and orange, exclaimed, 'I can't stand this bunch. They remind me of . . . of . . . my least favourite early seventies band . . . Slade.'

Watching Hucknall straining his vocal chords to the limit, while the band wavered between out-and-out cacophony and clumsy thudding pop, one could sympathise with Morley's astute reference to Holder and Co. After all, they had an uncanny lack of pretension – which is probably why Morley, who was thundering against anything that wasn't crippled by hipness at the time, disliked them so much – and a tendency to perform in a manner which suggested artlessness. They were anti-style. As the gig crumbled to a halt, to rippling applause, Brian Turner's bass guitar was first raised and then crashed down on to an unfortunate amplifier. Nobody seemed to understand why.

In 1979, Manchester was in post-punk-pre-Hacienda limbo. It was a beautiful era – the very *best* era, at least for those with a sense of involvement. Beneath the daunting shadows of the Hulme estate – four crescents teeming with despair . . . and students – sat the Russell Club on Royce Road. Tony Wilson, after striking a deal with local businessman Don Tonay, secured the club for Friday evenings. On such occasions it was called the Factory, to be anarchically run by Wilson's partner, Durutti Column manager and ex-actor, Alan Erasmus.

It was a time of small audiences, enjoyable pretension, intense hipness and occasionally great music. The lad who broke his arm outside the Factory club one night and refused to go to hospital until he had seen the blistering set by Joy Division typified the feel of the time.

In Manchester at that time, unlike later years, a solidarity prevailed caused mainly by the stunning stupidity of the London-based music press. As Manchester correspondent for *Sounds* at the time I had the finest, most innovative and (to lapse into rockspeak) most happening bands in the world sitting around the pubs of the North-west yawning and begging to be interviewed. Yet gaining space for these artists was never easy. True enough, the likes of Joy Division, Durutti Column, the Distractions, the Fall, and their brash Liverpool cousins, Teardrop Explodes, Rainbows Over

Nagasaki, Echo and the Bunnymen, Wah Heat (later to become Wah!) did gain media attention, but after the coverage had been begrudgingly allotted there followed a hollow anticlimax. There wasn't a backlash, there was just nothing. A lonely void. The London press, obviously believing that Manchester had had its day, moved on – to Bristol or somewhere. This left a huge mass of bands – all excited to be so near the action and all believing that the aforementioned bands had broken through – thinking gaining press attention would from now on be easy. But, of course, as they made their weekly phone calls to disinterested hacks in London, it didn't take long to dawn on them that things were going to be far from easy.

To be in a band, queueing up in the gargantuan wave behind these front-runners, was to be almost totally ignored. And the Frantic Elevators (take it from me – from one who was there) were about fiftieth in line for press exposure. It is with no sense of pride, that I sit here penning this warped retrospective and recalling the disembodied voice of Mick Hucknall one Saturday morning, calling from his Haughton Green living room. 'A feature on us would be really good,' he pleaded. 'We are the best . . . we *are* the best band in Manchester.'

They weren't the best as it happened, but Hucknall's indignation was justified. If, to the Manchester élite – the Joy Divisions, the Distractions, Morley shortly before his defection to mediaville – if to these people, the Frantic Elevators were non-starters, then what chance did they stand with the London media? The Frantic Elevators were about as hip as a clog dance troupe in Whittle-le-woods.

There were other cliques in Manchester and they wouldn't give valuable time to some precocious Dentonian redhead, to some *United* fan. After all, with this guy Hucknall you were talking *working class*. He wasn't some dressed down student in a band, slumming in some Didsbury taproom. Hucknall even went to working men's clubs.

New Hormones, a record label set up in 1976 and natural home of the Buzzcocks, was run by ex-Reading art student Richard

Boon. It was based in evocative Victorian warehouse offices in Newton Street and already it had progressed to a state of indignant pretension. New Hormones was also the record label of Ludus, formed by the brilliant Arthur Kadmon and fronted by the beautiful Linder. They were attempting an avant-garde sub-jazz stance, a stance which worked in the cosy confines of the Factory club but nowhere else. It was strange. New Hormones was a label founded on the Buzzcocks, a band who believed so strongly in the power of the song. Yet it was also seeking artists of a freeform ilk. Biting Tongues soon happened along. They too had ideas above and beyond their abilities, although their dreams would one day be realised in the form of 808 State. But the New Hormones crowd tended to concentrate their energies on drinking cappuccinos as artistically as possible. The label, although well intentioned, mirrored Factory Records in the sense that it was run on an absolutely 'matesy' level. It didn't have ears for out-of-town talent – talent that preferred milky coffee in mugs.

One boy, a dreamer, who sat in the corner at the Factory club would send self-made demo tapes to New Hormones. He was a strange boy, forever seen in corners at gigs or wandering gormlessly through Piccadilly gardens. He was the kind of boy who you knew, you just knew, would sit in a room penning bloody awful poetry to a girl on the Woolworth's checkout. His name was Steven Patrick Morrissey. One day he would be a huge star. He is mentioned here because his path crossed, on more than one occasion, with the gig-going singer from the Frantic Elevators. Steven Morrissey and Mick Hucknall, who didn't know each other, sank a beer together upstairs at the Factory club (during a Ludus set, I think). This minute event is recalled here for two reasons. One is that I had just eaten one of the Factory's famous goat curries and rushed past the pair to throw up in the Factory's equally famous and equally disgusting toilets. The second reason is that, to be honest, if one had to pick the two people most unlikely to achieve pop success from the hordes who hung around the Manchester music periphery at that time, then Hucknall and Morrissey would both immediately spring to mind. It really is quite weird and worth thinking about. Mick Hucknall and Steven Morrissey were both anti-charismatic. Although opposites, they were generally regarded as mere hangers on, hopeless cases. This might speak volumes about the stupidity of the sycophantic circle to which I belonged. But the fact is that everyone knew that someone, somewhere, hanging around that scene would make it really big. It was a pity that everyone happened to be looking in the wrong direction.

Morrissey, at least, seemed to know the right people. Legend now has it that he was besotted with Linder and so had found a route into New Hormones. As for the Frantic Elevators, they didn't even have hipness on their side. The Elevators couldn't even consider Factory (they didn't sup Guinness with Joy Division manager Rob Gretton, or roll joints with Tony Wilson). If they rang New Hormones, New Hormones wouldn't speak to them. Where else could the Frantic Elevators turn? Who in Manchester, a city simmering with insular artiness, would be prepared to give a break to a gawky working-class band with no manners, no essential middle-class aloofness and as far as many were concerned no style? The answer, at least for a while, was quite simple.

Tony (TJ) Davidson was Manchester's strangest music business entrepreneur. An angelic-faced soulboy, he lived in a smart mock Georgian cottage in the leafy suburbs of Marple. Few people in an area bubbling with twentysomething newlyweds like Tony paid him much attention. Quite possibly, as they sponged down their Honda Civics on Sunday mornings, they would cast envious glances in Davidson's direction as he reversed his pristine Lotus Europa on to Church Lane and roared off to catch one of his bands running up huge expenses in a Stockport recording studio.

The son of a diamond merchant, Tony was in fact an endearingly flash Wythenshawian Manchester United fan. His first link with the music business had been as a hooligan buddy of Slaughter and the Dogs, often, come Saturday, setting off on wild sprees to faraway towns. This habit had not subsided even when Tony moved into respectable suburbia, ran a practice studio complex and gathered a bunch of the most itinerant Manchester bands together for his label, TJM.

'I remember once being rounded up by the police – in Derby I think – and I was sitting in the police station surrounded by United fans who were bricklayers and plumbers. None of them could believe me when I told them that I owned a record label, even a small record label.'

TJM was, indeed, small but it was also entertainingly maverick. It provided the first recording step for bands such as the Distractions. They were a Stockport soul pop outfit fronted by Mike Finney, a ginger-headed, bespectacled, profoundly unglamorous soulboy from, of all places, Reddish. Finney had been an active member of GDR, in his youth. Although not a football fan, he was essentially working class. The parallel was not lost on Hucknall who nurtured a distinct dislike of the Distractions. He was particularly irked by the way they had moved from TJM to Factory, and had been granted a considerable amount of hip kudos by accepting support spots with Joy Division. When Paul Morley wrote in the *NME*, 'Joy Division are the perfect rock band for the eighties and the Distractions are the perfect pop band for the eighties', Hucknall's sense of indignation began to boil over. 'Why is it that all of Manchester is in love with the Distractions?' he once asked, perhaps with a degree of envy, 'when all they do is play crappy little pop songs.' The Frantic Elevators, of course, had their sights set on a higher musical plane than that.

The Distractions were the one true jewel in a TJM back catalogue that was, frankly, rather stodgy and tarnished by Davidson's mateyness, although Tony Davidson probably didn't realise it. His top band, V2, were an hilarious glam rock outfit from Gorton who attempted to emulate Bowie and the New York Dolls but strongly resembled the 'brickie-in-lipstick' look of the Sweet circa *Blockbuster*. He also financed the migration of promising Belfast band, Victim – who once topped a bill which included both the Undertones and Stiff Little Fingers – from their Ulster base and implanted them into the Manchester bedsit land of Whalley Range. Victim never managed to catch the attention of the Manchester élite and slowly lost their teenage edge, finally embarking on a career playing for beer on Manchester's pub circuit. Their one claim to fame was the fact that one of their latterday drummers, Mike Joyce, later joined the Smiths.

Many other bands fluttered around the flickering lamp of TJM hoping that a slab of Davidson vinyl would lead to better things, as it had with the Distractions. The Frantic Elevators, indignant at a Manchester scene that didn't care a jot about them and desperate to achieve the status of a band armed with genuine product, nervously wandered down Little Peter Street, inwardly praying that the planned meeting with Davidson would prove fruitful. In a sense it did. In 1978 the Elevators moved into the basement of TJ's rehearsal complex.

There was a strange hierarchical system operating within the rehearsal complex. Tony would sit in a central office abetted by his secretary, Veronica, and hold court while a seemingly endless parade of hapless musicians spewed forth their frustrations. New Hormones' brightest hope, Ludus – famously fronted by Linder, the ex-girlfriend of Howard Devoto, who seemed to have successfully bewitched most of the predominantly male Manchester music inner circle – could be found next door. Davidson's most famous lodgers, Joy Division, held their intense practice sessions upstairs amid layers of dust, discarded crisp bags, cigarette packets and the prevailing ghostly ambience, enhanced by dour brickwork and ribcage industrial radiators.

For Joy Division and, indeed, for the Factory organisation, it was a hugely important atmosphere. For it was in this evocative room that the dour video for *Love Will Tear Us Apart* was filmed, effectively stigmatising the entire scope of modern Manchester music with an image of industrial greyness, sallow expressions and introversion. Tony Davidson's building, a cavernous ex-grain warehouse, became the manifestation of this damaging image. Interestingly enough, the area in which it was situated – Knott Mill or Little Ireland depending on the era – would play a curiously large role in Manchester music in the years which followed. The marina around the corner, for instance, would become the Hacienda. The building on the next corner to Davidson's would one day be purchased by enterprising geography graduate Colin Sinclair who transformed it into the Boardwalk, an essential venue and rehearsal room complex that would play a signifi-

cant role in nurturing the talent that generated the Madchester explosion of the mid-eighties. Tony Davidson's plans,
which never reached fruition, predated Sinclair's by six years.
Davidson even had plans to place a venue in the complex
called Powerpoint. Unfortunately, it never appeared.

The Frantic Elevators enjoyed the atmosphere of TJ's
rehearsal rooms (quite cheap, too, at £20 per week even
though it had no light and was upon entering noticeably
damp). Although loath to admit it they also enjoyed the
prevailing bonhomie of the bands. At last, if only fleetingly,
they felt part of the scene. Many times after rehearsals they
would join the other musicians in the local pub, the Gaythorn,
which became something of a classic Manchester music pub.

If the gruff streetwise suss of the Frantic Elevators prevented them from falling for Davidson's fast talk, they had to
admit that, compared to the negative responses they had
received elsewhere, at least this man seemed enthusiastic.
Hucknall would spend many hours in Davidson's office, chatting mainly about his plans for the Elevators. Davidson was
particularly struck by Hucknall's approach towards his songwriting. It was, after all, fairly unusual to see a young left-field
musician show so much respect for the likes of John Lennon.

'He was Lennon mad,' Davidson later said. 'He would dissect
Lennon songs and attempt to find out how they had been
written. I must admit, at times, I thought he was being a little
over ambitious and, much as I liked some of his songs, they
still seemed light years away from the Beatles.'

But there were other noticeable differences between Hucknall and most of the other budding musicians who gathered in
that dusty atmosphere. Despite college commitments, Hucknall seemed to be an ever-present fixture. It became something of a standing joke among the other acts. Whether it was
merely his work ethic beginning to show through remains
unclear, but his attitude was noticeably different to the bands
who would use the complex as a stepping stone between home
and the pub. It soon became obvious to Davidson that Hucknall was angling for some kind of recording deal for the
Elevators. (This was always on the cards. Davidson had scored

minor success with Slaughter and the Dogs who had surprised the distributors, Rough Trade and Red Rhino, by achieving reasonably healthy sales. The two distributors, reservedly pleased, made it quite plain that they would be willing to handle more TJM product.)

Hucknall approached Davidson initially with a view to the Frantic Elevators covering a soul classic. This was a tactic, although fairly unconventional within the indie sector of the day, that did appeal to Davidson who shared if not the singer's encyclopaedic knowledge of R'n'B then certainly his enthusiasm. (Even the label design of TJM had been lovingly copied from an old, obscure soul label, plucked from Davidson's black singles box.) 'You know,' stated Hucknall, 'I really think we could do a great cover version of something old . . . something black . . . I really think we have got that feel.'

There clearly existed a gulf between the sound in Hucknall's head and the actual sound the Elevators produced, which most people regarded as fairly standard indie thrash. Although a sideways move into a soulful feel would seem, from the outside, totally unexpected and probably beyond their abilities, Hucknall and Moss were clearly viewing it as a natural progression.

It wasn't to be, although one Elevators' song in particular, *Hunchback Of Notre Dame*, employed a distinctly Northern Soul style attack. Other Elevators' songs of the era were not so lively. Far from it. Too often they fell too neatly into the 'dour' image that had attached itself arguably unfairly to the Manchester élite. One song in particular became something of a standing joke within the TJM complex. Entitled *Everyday I Die*, it contained a repetitive lyric surviving, just about, on top of an equally repetitive backbeat.

'I often thought,' stated Davidson, 'when I heard that song that perhaps they should paint the walls of the rehearsal room white – perhaps they should liven it up a bit. They were getting too influenced by their grey industrial setting. Honestly, I thought brighter walls might inspire brighter lyrics.'

Every Day I Die was the one tune that would bring back a nostalgic yearning for Davidson's studios, if played to most of those musicians today. For the Elevators always seemed to be

65

trudging through it. It was a song that seeped into the walls, penetrated into the corridors. It even seemed to escape upstairs – literally along the pipes – to the most desirable practice rooms inhabited by the Joy Divisions and V2s. The part-time caretaker, Michael, would often be heard complaining, 'They are playing that bloody death song again – is that the only bleeding song they know?'

Ironically enough, Michael was not the only person who developed a comical loathing of the song. It was Joy Divison – whose image was as grey as a Scunthorpe Wednesday but who, in reality, were an endearingly lighthearted crowd – who most vociferously aired their irritation. 'God, the doomy bastards,' screamed the bass player, Hookey. 'Can't they play something with a little more umph!'

Despite this unbecoming reputation for dowdiness, Davidson remained excited about the prospect of recording and working with the Elevators and his standard contract was drawn up. (Basically Davidson, who would pay for the recordings, would retain all rights. The publishing was a fifty-fifty split.) The deal was struck, perhaps all too swiftly, and it was with gleeful anticipation that they entered into a tiny recording studio in Chorlton to record three tracks, *Voice In The Dark*, *Passion* and *Every Day I Die*. The three songs surfaced on a TJM single (TJM 5) in June 1979 and, due to a little sharp prodding from me, reached the dizzy though dubiously contrived heights of number eight in the *Sounds* independent charts.

Voice In The Dark was a typical indie song. A sprightly tune, scratchy in delivery but not without melody and not without hooks either. If played, say, late in a set down at the Band On The Wall, and if listened to through ears dulled by Guinness, it might sound like a hit record. On vinyl, however, it lacked power and certainly finesse. The two songs on the flip side certainly told a rather different story. *Every Day I Die* featured Hucknall shouting over a marching drum beat while on *Passion* the vocals are speeded up and slowed to a halt, with little regard for the casual listener. They were both simply the result of a band who had been reading too many *NME*s, listening to too much John Peel, too much Fall, too much

Throbbing Gristle. It was a case of innovation at all costs, which although suiting the spirit of the times, would like all trends soon fade horribly into cliché. (There was a second Frantic Elevators single on TJM, comprising three songs, *The Hunchback Of Notre Dame, I See Nothing And Everything* and *Don't Judge Me* although it never surfaced in anything more than demo form with a limited number of just twenty copies in plain white labels. Legend also has it, and Davidson would confirm this, that Hucknall approached TJM with a view to releasing *Holding Back The Years*. However, the song was knocked back by Davidson who didn't believe it to be of sufficient quality.)

If the single did little to improve their state of aloofness, it certainly fired the band with a new spirit and they began to gig with impressive regularity. Within the band, a new-found confidence prevailed and was, if anything, heightened considerably by the continuing indifference of the rest of the Manchester scene. Even within Tony Davidson's tight little circle of young hopefuls, a rather bitchy hierarchy served to spoil much of the proceedings. V2, Victim and the Elevators all fought for attention, all harangued Davidson, who despite his Lotus Europa and flash boy reputation, was hardly made of money for further investment. The small-time label owner often takes a good deal of stick for not having the muscle necessary to break a band. But this was the time when it was impossible to make a quality recording without booking into a reasonable standard recording studio. The costs were enormous and the prospect of returns slim, and a good many classic independent recordings of the late seventies existed only because of the commercial naivety of the smaller independent label owners. A little more research into the distribution system, if not into human nature, would surely have put them off. In producing an indie single, in effect all they were making was a vinyl demo, a tester. Any band who would pledge, hand on heart, everlasting allegiance to the likes of Tony Davidson would naturally hope to progress to a larger scale operation, a major perhaps, at the first decent opportunity.

The fact that the Elevators didn't split under a variety of pressures says a great deal about their strength of spirit, if not self belief. But there were problems. Neil and Brian were languishing on the dole, both hoping, praying, that something positive would come from the music and neither particularly wanting to take the day jobs that they felt would not have justified their prowess. Mick, of course, was enjoying college and simply revelling in the glories of art studenthood while Kevin Williams had a wife, a mortgage and a messy job in printing. The fact that he could not simply down tools – although he often did – and set off in the obligatory Transit van for some God-forsaken dive in Edinburgh was another source of tension for a band who, to a man, believed that the Elevators were the most fantastically important musical unit on the planet. Naively, perhaps stupidly, they believed as many such bands do that the hand of fate would reach down and miraculously hurtle them on to the road to superstardom. They tended lazily to let Davidson do the talking, the dealing. Not once did it occur to them that the best plan might be to approach the London record companies themselves. Even Hucknall, for all his brashness, never thought to pick up the telephone and bullshit some hapless A & R talent scout.

It was an indie thing, a sense of indie pride. Nevertheless, the names of most A & R men were often on the lips of most of the bands in that rehearsal complex. Furthermore, A & R men would frequently be deposited in the corner of the room while a band ran nervously through their set, no doubt under the outrageous impression that the scouts would be suitably impressed and indeed empowered to begin talking contracts. Unfortunately it didn't work that way. But no A & R man ever sat in the corner of the room occupied by the Frantic Elevators. And for no reason other than the odd fact that they never even thought about it.

Hucknall had taken a shine to Davidson by this time, and could see that once past the fast talking he was in fact quite an endearing personality. After all, they had much in common. In the Little Peter Street greasy spoon café, slumped over sodden breakfasts and pints of tea, Davidson and Hucknall would chat about soul music, Manchester United and plans for both band and label. World domination would always be on the agenda, although financially just out of reach, over the horizon. Occasionally, the talk would become a little more personal.

'I remember once,' recalls Davidson, 'we were sitting on the steps outside the rehearsal rooms on Little Peter Street and Hucknall suddenly began to pour his heart out. It was odd because I'd always known him as quite a confident person, certainly not the kind to disclose too many heartfelt secrets. But this time he did. He told me all about, and I vividly remember this, how he resented the fact that his mother wasn't around during his childhood and how much he loved and admired his dad for bringing him up in the correct way. It wasn't a particularly rock'n'roll conversation, that one, and it was unusual because most of the bands were only interested in furthering their careers. At that point, I think, I realised that perhaps there was more to Mick Hucknall than most of the others. Not as a musician but as a person. I certainly gained considerable respect for him.'

Tony Davidson, wishing to promote his loose record label, TJM, arranged a nationwide tour – Identity Parade – which would showcase his acts in rotation. It was, he stated, his version of the Stiff Tour of late 1979 (featuring Costello, Dury and Lowe) or the oft-celebrated Chrysalis budget priced revue of the early seventies (which showcased Van Der Graaf Generator, more than ably supported by Genesis and Lindisfarne). At least, thought the fast-talking Davidson, this would put TJM on a level with his Wythenshawian contemporaries – Rabid/Absurd, if not Factory – who seemed to have the monopoly on music press hipness. Davidson, to his credit, did seduce certain sections of the music press (even taking me to his club, the decidedly un-rock'n'roll Playboy Club on Manchester's Canal Street. Like George Best, Davidson had been known to fritter away rather large amounts of dosh within that neon-lit palace).

The tour, despite a good deal of hard graft on Davidson's part – sweet talking dodgy venue owners and pleading with local journalists to attend the events – had about it more than an air of sheer unglamorous anarchy. It was the kind of tour that could have easily been transformed by a clever writer into a BBC 2 'Play For Today'. The bands – the glam rock thrashers V2, Belfast hopefuls Victim and loud-mouthed working classers the Frantic Elevators – all pushed for the spotlight. In truth, the Frantic Elevators, through sheer force of commitment and Hucknall's budding talent, blasted their way to the top of the less-than-impressive billing. Davidson, in particular, seemed most impressed.

'It was hard for me to put it to V2 who were supposed to be the name band,' states Davidson, 'but it soon became obvious that Hucknall was the real star. Everybody on that tour, whether they cared to admit it or not, recognised Hucknall's star quality. The band were not up to much . . . in fact they were all over the place, but Hucknall had this power within him. It was definitely there . . . I knew it, everyone did.'

Arriving at one gig in Birmingham, the Frantic Elevators were depressed to discover that the venue was, in the words of Brian Turner, 'a venue behind a venue – behind a venue.' None of the Elevators had been near Birmingham before and there was much mimicking of Brummy twang. Indeed, as punky looking pedestrians tried to help them defeat Birmingham's insane one way systems, the Elevators were left to exchange silent, non-plussed glances – the silence broken with the standard, 'What the hell was he talking about?'

They were surprised to find that this particular venue, with a capacity of four hundred, had in fact sold out. This confused the Elevators for, surely, neither they nor V2 nor Victim had even the most minuscule following in this strange, alien city? However, unbeknown to any of the TJM bands, Davidson also had non-political connections with the notorious skinhead National Front supporting band, Screwdriver, and had put out an EP by them. It was not an association that Davidson readily bandied about, especially when in the presence of the music press.

Nevertheless, the gig was obviously big news in Birmingham. The Frantic Elevators performed a more speedily paced set than usual in front of four hundred tattooed foreheads. Even Hucknall, normally the most aggressive of performers, felt relieved when they wandered back into their dressing room, limbs still intact. To the Elevators' extreme amusement V2, who would top the bill, had upon sizing up the audience hastily scraped off all their make-up, dropped the glam image and careered through a set which would not have disgraced the thrash metal idiom of the late eighties.

At another gig in Derby the trio of bands found themselves in an arena which strongly resembled an old-time music hall, albeit with a curiously multi-racial clientele. The gig was good for all the bands and a rare aura of post-gig camaraderie replaced the usual outbreak of bitching. Suddenly, and much to everyone's utter amazement, a large cine screen came down from the ceiling in the corner of the room and the bands were delighted to find themselves watching a selection of hard-core porn flicks while being absurdly served piping hot potato scallops.

The finest gig on the tour, according to Tony Davidson, was at the Middlesbrough Rock Garden when 700 sweat- and blood-stained punks stopped their pathetic ritualistic spitting mid-set and cheered the Frantic Elevators with all the fervour of the Kop or, more fittingly, the Stretford End.

'At this point,' stated Davidson, 'I knew that Hucknall really had the potential to become something very special.'

The Frantic Elevators, unabashed by lack of critical interest, at least managed to scrape together a furiously parochial and often rather unnerving following. This mainly Dentonian crew would be assembled largely from friends of friends and never really comprised standard gig-goers, let alone the student fraternity who patronised the Factory bands. If they did read music papers, then the more fanzine-like *Sounds* would be their first choice. Of the bands they might take an interest in, it would be the Not Sensibles or Splodgenessabounds rather than Joy Division or the Gang of Four.

The only other Manchester band considerably more successful than the Elevators, but equally aloof from the Manchester mafia, was the Fall whose ungainly following were, and still are, culled from the most disparate sections of society. The similarities did not end with the following. The Fall, a highly intelligent unit, were resolutely a tap room outfit. They believed, as did Hucknall, that the working class were quite capable of appreciating music forms which had an intellectual

angle and certainly didn't need middle-class hacks on the
NME to show them the way. On the odd occasion when the
Frantic Elevators supported the Fall the bill always seemed
perfectly balanced, even if the clashing egos of the two band
leaders, Mark E. Smith and Hucknall, would have prevented
any true comradely bonds forming.

The Fall had become Hucknall's favourite band at this
point. He very much admired Mark E. Smith's benevolent
despotism and would have loved to impose the same thing on
the Elevators. Unfortunately, at least for Hucknall, it was
rather too late for that. He also admired the constant evolution of the Fall's set and their absolute refusal to play to the
whims of audiences, music press or record labels. The Fall
radiated a strength, a sense of supreme self confidence. It was
incredible, Hucknall often remarked, just how many wonderful songs the Fall recorded only to hide them away mid-album,
on B-sides or mid-set. The fact that the Fall's live set was
always an album ahead of the expectations of the live audience wasn't a popular tactic, in fact it was virtual suicide. But
it clearly displayed the Fall's fantastic, unparalleled, powerful
aloofness. Hucknall believed that no band in the country came
close to the Fall – apart, of course, from the Frantic Elevators.
That was the kind of genius he was striving for while paradox-
ically moving the music more towards an R'n'B feel.

The Elevators were pleased to see their small but intense
following trooping to the cavernous Leeds Queen's Hall for the
optimistically named Futurama 1979 event. This three-day
affair was subtitled – for reasons which never became apparent to anyone – 'The world's first sci-fi music festival'. It wasn't
sci-fi at all, not even remotely. But it was, as Green from
Scritti Politti perceptively noted, 'Like Reading without the
mud and different badges.' Quite. Futurama 1979 was a pop
festival. It did, however, provide the smaller bands of the day
with a glorious opportunity to play in front of a large audience,
even if most of them would be asleep at the time. Filmed by
Granada and condensed into a one-hour late-night special,
Futurama did at least give early television exposure to the
likes of Altered Images – and Frantic Elevators.

The Frantic Elevators came on to an audience who had

travelled from across Britain and beyond to catch such heroes as the seriously blasé Public Image, the off-form Joy Division and on-form A Certain Ratio, Altered Images and the Young Marble Giants. The Frantics went on at 5p.m., a notoriously bad time for any band. Despite Granada filming the worst song of the set ('I don't even want to talk about it . . . we played a blistering set and all they could film was that!' – Brian Turner) the Frantic Elevators effectively woke the huge Futurama crowd from mass late-afternoon slumber causing 'dancing' to break out in the ranks of the decidedly cool raincoated hordes. At Leeds, much to the crowd's amusement, the Elevators encored with a rumbustious and cheeky version of *Give Peace a Chance*. One sight not easy to forget was a wave of parodical two-fingered 'peace' signs. It was a glorious moment in an event all but ruined by the superstar notions of a few of the top bands. 'I think we were the best band in the entire event,' said Turner and for once his conceit was entirely justified. What a pity though that the potential so clearly on display at Futurama wasn't picked up by a major record label. 'Well, you can't completely blame the A & R men,' states Turner. 'Every time one got near us we would shower him with abuse.'

The performance of *Give Peace a Chance*, although most definitely against the grain of the era, was not untypical of the Frantic Elevators. They had grown to enjoy performing unlikely cover versions and Mick, in particular, relished the chance of emulating his heroes. Soon, in live sets, spirited versions of the Beatles' *Don't Bring Me Down*, Iggy Pop's *I Wanna Be Your Dog* or Howlin' Wolf's *(She Gave Me) Gasolene* would creep in. More often than not this was to the annoyance of a crowd who, having studiously read their pompous *NME*s, regarded cover versions as being the ultimate symbol of naffness. The Elevators, however, were beginning to understand the true sense and the power of song. Their Beefheartian pretensions were beginning to fade and the band's set, to be honest, became all the better for it.

If the Elevators were going to go anywhere, other than to more seedy, blackened venues with dubious money-shy managers, some kind of break would have to happen. Quite what it would be and where and how it might happen remained a total mystery. In fact, despite their new-found niche within Davidson's organisation, the Elevators began to feel more and more that the world would forever pass them by. They were given and to some extent they thoroughly deserved a reputation as 'existentialists' – a band who were quite happy to remain in their own little world. In many circles, this defensive image was seen as arrogant and there is no doubt that Hucknall especially thoroughly enjoyed the idea of casting two fingers at the entire planet.

'People always try to pin this existentialist thing on us,' he would later say to *Melody Maker*'s Steve Sutherland (one of the few writers, incidentally, who actually fell for Hucknall's voice and sensed something special *before* it was obvious through later success). Hucknall continued, 'In many ways I think we defy that, but I suppose in many other ways that's the nearest you can get. I suppose we're existentialists.' Not an uncommon remark for an art student with an obligatory chip on shoulder. It is also difficult to believe that existentialism means *not* going down the Factory but staying firmly aloof, if half inebriated, in the tap room of the Whitegates and indulging in a frighteningly serious debate about the complex ins and outs of Beatles records like *Let It Be* or *Sergeant Pepper*.

And then, in unspectacular fashion, something did happen. Booked to play the legendary Liverpudlian watering hole, Eric's, the Elevators found themselves in the kind of quandary that to this day typifies the practical problems facing struggling bands. They didn't have a van. Brian Turner, forever the agitator, wandered out of Davidson's, across Little Peter Street and into the somewhat menacing café which was always filled with taxi drivers biting into greasy bacon butties, slurping pints of tea, scanning the *Sun* and making general disparaging remarks about the odd-looking characters who kept carrying guitars into the building across the road. Turner, already quite practised in the art of convincing people to do something they might not be too keen on, cajoled a cabby with the promise of £20 and managed to secure a lift to and from the gig in Liverpool. It wasn't the most comfortable of rides though. With the drummer sitting up front holding two drum sticks, Brian and Neil squashed behind their guitars and Mick proudly holding the coveted mike stand, it was pure bad news. A quite pathetic sight. Halfway down the M62 an unusually silent Hucknall turned to the others and solemnly remarked, 'Do you think we are completely wasting our time in this business?' The short silence which followed provided Hucknall with more honesty than he really wanted.

However, he didn't know – how could he – that awaiting the arrival of this gawky unfashionable Mancunian combo was a gentleman, housed in Eric's, of considerable influence and perception. Roger Eagle.

Chapter 7
The Guru

If you take the A6 out of Manchester and continue through Stockport for twenty miles, you will find yourself nudging into Derbyshire. At the village called Whalley Bridge, stop and look around. Unless it is Saturday night, it is a dull, somnolent place, lined with dark hills, peppered with stone cottages mostly inhabited, you would think, with smiling little old ladies drinking tea. You might catch sight of a bus stop swarmed over by a gang of local teenagers, scruffily parochial, red faced and rudely spoken. It is a place of profound ordinariness. Or so it might seem.

If you are very lucky, you might catch sight of a tall, lumbering, middle-aged, briefcase-carrying man filtering his way from the station to one of the stone cottages. If, like me, you are one of those folk who waste large amounts of time trying to guess the occupations of passing strangers, you would certainly fail on this occasion. You might, reasonably, pin him down as an accountant or insurance salesman. No doubt you'd be mightily surprised to discover that this man, so perfectly at home amid the dour Derbyshire stone, has remained an unprecedented influence on the Manchester music scene for a full three decades – ignoring his mid-career defection to, of all places, Liverpool. For it was this man, Roger Eagle, who was the hugely influential R'n'B disc jockey at Manchester's legendary club, the Twisted Wheel, in the early sixties. The same man provided the platform for the city's punk explosion in Liverpool. And it was this man whose inexhaustible enthusiasm for R'n'B and encyclopaedic knowledge of same combined to pick a disillusioned Hucknall up from the floor and, quite literally, pump him full of confidence and vivacity. When the whole world, or so it seemed to Hucknall, had shrugged and turned the other way it was Eagle, and Eagle alone, who spotted the true potential of the singer.

Should you visit Roger Eagle in his quaint Derbyshire stone cottage, you will, as you drift through the door, see his veneer of ordinariness peel away as his endearing eccentricities are allowed to spring to the fore. He is quite simply a rock'n'roll obsessive. His living room is effectively lined with records and CDs. Anyone with even a passing interest in the music of the past forty years will find it impossible to resist flicking through this vast collection. If it is worth hearing, Roger Eagle not only has it in triplicate, in all known formats, he will in all probability know more about the recording than the artists themselves. His general rock knowledge is also encyclopaedic.

Above his mantelpiece, a black and white photograph depicts a familiar blues guitarist. Scrawled across it is the message, 'To my friend Roger . . . Happy Birthday from John Lee Hooker.' As you sit down, Roger Eagle will also sit, his massive silhouette framed by the window. He will rant, laugh and enthuse madly. His conversational direction will be constantly broken by comments about the music pumping from the hi-fi, 'Oooh did you hear the push on that?' or, 'This is the definitive James Brown . . . no one has ever come close to this. You must ring the record company and get them to send you a copy, really. How can anyone live without it?'

Occasionally the phone will ring and Eagle, this marvellously affable man, will snap back into his persona of hard-line rock promoter albeit, in latter days, a somewhat aloof one. Recently he has busied himself promoting rather eccentric blues concerts and festivals. That said, he is just as capable of chatting about, say, Inspiral Carpets or James as he is about Little Richard or Captain Beefheart. If Eagle doesn't know about it, it probably isn't worth knowing.

It is difficult to leave Roger Eagle's house without some of his obsession rubbing off on you. Chatting with him *is* an inspiring experience, even for non-musicians, even, I guess, for those who believe that Ray Charles is a ventriloquist with an oafish dummy.

Roger Eagle hails, not from Manchester but unlikely as it may seem, from Oxford. His rock'n'roll life began in the mid-fifties when as a schoolboy he stumbled – Van Morrison like – across the magical world of radio. He began listening to Al Freed on AM Frankfurt and Gus Goodwin on Luxembourg. Almost instantly he found himself well and truly hooked and would regularly blow his dinner money on 78s carefully studied, smelled, listened to and bought from the local record shop. It soon became clear, to Eagle if not to anyone else, that this was no shallow teenage pop infatuation. The already incredibly well-informed Eagle cared not for the lightweight pop dirges which clogged up the pop charts and recognised in 1958 that rock'n'roll was more or less finished as an innovative, creative force. He began to grow mildly disillusioned – and the possibility of a career in or around the fragmented music business seemed remote, if not absurd.

Then along came Ray Charles. In particular, the live at Newport album, *Ray Charles In Person*. The record's effect on Eagle was profound and thirty-two years later he would still regard it as, amongst other things, 'The greatest record ever made.'

'That was the record which changed my life ... it had everything. The raw excitement of rock'n'roll ... but also gospel and blues, as well. It was a ferocious album ... and the musicianship absolutely stunning. It was also the base for much of what was the best in popular music over the next three decades. Ray Charles on electric piano. A new instrument of the day. It was a transitional album of soul and jazz. You can hear that album in the background even today ... even in the music of Simply Red.'

Eagle, after taping the album on a rather dodgy Grundig reel-to-reel recorder, began to take it around the Oxford parties of the day. It was his first tentative step into what had yet to be defined as the role of disc jockey. Although he didn't know it at the time, he was already making a name for himself, albeit locally, as a music expert.

In the early sixties, practically by accident, he came to
Manchester in search of 'some kind of work'. Quite naturally
he began to hang dreamily around the pustulating mess of jazz
clubs and coffee bars in the city centre, using what spare
money he had to buy rare Chuck Berry and Bo Diddley
albums from the States (mainly filtering through the Liverpool docks). If anything, it was a somewhat directionless
period – or so he thought – made bearable only by his feverish
escapism into music.

One typical day, sitting amid the hiss and chatter of a coffee
bar, Eagle began instinctively to flip through his huge bag of
prized records when he was approached by two brothers who
recklessly asked him if he owned any R'n'B records. Once
engulfed by Eagle's hyperactive, unstoppable rhetoric, they
asked him to become resident disc jockey at their recently
opened nightclub, the Twisted Wheel. Although not quite
knowing what a disc jockey was, Eagle couldn't believe his
luck.

What he didn't know, and couldn't possibly foretell, was that
this rather dowdy, multi-roomed cellar club would still be
spoken about in lasting awe twenty-five years after its eventual closure. What's more, its legendary status would in no
small way be attributed to the hugely innovative prowess of
this heavy-featured man who would stand behind the Garrard
record decks (situated behind a tangled mass of welded bicycle
wheels) for seven hours each evening. (His fee, incidentally,
was £1 per night.)

Eagle would bring a new dimension to nightclubbing. He
sifted not just the obligatory 'in-vogue' R'n'B but also blue beat
and jazz. It was a gradually evolving fusion which neatly
streamlined itself into an identifiable whole a couple of years
later. This was the precise start of the mid-sixties soul movement which, years later, would become 'Northen Soul'.

Eagle also had a talent for chatting up top artists and
persuading them that the Wheel was the place to play.
Everybody seeking a certain hipness would play there: John
Mayall (from Macclesfield), T. Bone Walker, Screaming Jay
Hawkins, Jimmy Reid, John Lee Hooker. Although coinciding
with Merseybeat, the definite rock'n'roll angle was rather less

pronounced at the Wheel. This made the Manchester scene arguably more open minded. Without doubt, the furious debate which raged thirty years later about whether it was Manchester rather than Liverpool that housed the true Merseybeat explosion – a rather futile argument – was certainly due to Eagle's energetic activities.

But Eagle's thirst for new product was satisfied by Liverpool. Merseyside seamen, returning from stints on the celebrated Liverpool/New York run, would return with literally sackfuls of vinyl. They were odd, thick, black discs of staunch, aggressive R'n'B like Barret Strong's *Money* or Ritchie Barrett's *Some Other Guy* and, perhaps the most important of all, the hugely influential records of Arthur Alexander.

After three years of crazed disc spinning, Eagle had been transformed into a veritable 'walking jukebox'. The age of the all-nighter had dawned and it was Eagle's rather unenviable task to keep the kids frenetically dancing until at least 7a.m. (after which they might travel to, say the Bone Yard *All Dayer* in Bolton). Unfortunately, as the scene grew in size if not in stature, a menacing tension began to creep in. Even Eagle's enthusiasm began to wane when faced with what looked like a particularly unsavoury soul revolution. As with most youth movements, the initial rush, the endearing naivety, the simple joyous bonhomie, slowly faded to be replaced by a viciously snobbish hierarchy. And, of course, the pills began to flow. 'Most of those kids were totally smashed out of their heads,' admits Eagle. 'It became very nasty indeed and there were, at the end, a few tragic incidents.'

The beginning of the end came with the Twisted Wheel's move from Brazennose Street to new premises in Whitworth Street. On one occasion and directly in front of Eagle's DJ booth, a girl collapsed. Eagle, despite protests from the girl's friends, called security and the girl was eventually taken to hospital to face the necessary torture of the stomach pump.

'I just didn't like it any more,' he states, 'The feel had gone completely. All that was left was a nasty emptiness. It was very strange but I felt I was in the wrong place at the wrong time. What's more, the music was no longer what I wanted to play. So I left. It wasn't worth putting up with all that for £3 a night.'

Eagle moved to another club, the Blue Note, where freed from the chains of the soul scene he took great delight in spinning all kinds of music. Jazz, blues and the new wave of American West Coast bands. It was 1967 and the first signs of what was to become known as 'underground' began to seep from Eagle's speakers.

Eagle's underground phase took place mainly in Manchester's Magic Village. This was a trippy den featuring liquid light shows by the score and, of course, the brash, young innovative talents of Tyrannosaurus Rex, John Mayall, Tim Rose, the Savoy Brown Blues Band and Edgar Broughton. However, the transformation from innovation to stale pretension was fairly swift, especially as the progressive era ushered forth a level of self indulgence never previously experienced by the music of the twentieth century. The Magic Village, in sync with the hippy movement, became a drab meeting place for sexually repressed young males in dirty combat jackets. The place mercifully closed at the end of the sixties. Eagle fortuitously fled to Liverpool. By accident, again, he heard about a venue called the Stadium and, against the odds, secured a deal whereby he would present rock concerts on Saturday nights. Although artistically dull, the next three years proved to be the most financially successful of his career. It was the era of the rock giants and fairly soon he found himself promoting the likes of Mott the Hoople, Led Zeppelin, Black Sabbath, Captain Beefheart, Can, Love, Steve Miller, Rod Stewart and Roy Buchanan. The fans of the day were noticeably undemanding and quite often desired nothing more than a lengthy drum solo, an over-priced programme and a black tour T-shirt. It was the beginning of the mid-seventies slump into pomp rock – an aesthetically barren mush of introversion. Eagle's boredom was contained only by the trappings of his runaway success.

In 1976, in Liverpool as in Manchester as in London, the prevailing feel was one of excitement and rapid change. Eagle met up with Roy Adams, the owner of a small, empty club which, frankly, wasn't doing much at all. Eagle began putting bands on upstairs. It was immaculate timing whether Eagle realised it or not. The punk boom flourished, as was only right and proper, in seedy clubs. Soon, Eagle was booking the likes of the Sex Pistols, the Runaways and the Stranglers. The club was called Gatsby's. Unfortunately, it was pub hours only. After the gigs, Eagle and Adams would wander across the street to the club that had optimistically been called Cavern Two. Noticing that this would be a far more fitting home to house Liverpool's punk bands – it was, in effect, strangely similar to London's Roxy Club, heart of the English new wave – they promptly bought it, named it Eric's, and invited the overtly wacky locals to swarm into it. The Eric's scene had begun.

Eagle, to his delight, soon found himself surrounded by an explosive gathering of youthful talent. Big in Japan, Yachts, the Crucial Three who evolved into the Teardrop Explodes, Wah Heat and Echo and the Bunnymen, and Holly Johnson, Margi Clarke, Pete Burns, Ian Brodie – the raw thrust of punk providing the impetus for a whole mass of careers.

Once again, Roger Eagle had found himself in precisely the right place to oversee an embryonic and, eventually, highly influential scene. For two years, Eric's prospered. After a while, following the first flush of punk, things did settle down. Bands, no doubt blowing publishing advances, became accustomed to using rather sophisticated equipment. PAs became powerful once more and musicianship – as punk metamorphosed into new wave/power pop/arty introversion – became something to be proud of again. This was not necessarily a bad thing but Eagle knew full well that self indulgence would, most likely, be the next step. This time around, the cycle from raw innovation to staid posturing had been completed with record speed. It was very depressing which is probably why his face lit up when the unpromising Mancunian combo, known to a few as the Frantic Elevators, turned up, *sans* decent equipment, in a taxi driven by a bemused cabbie. Here, thought Eagle, was a bunch of lads who were refreshingly unpretentious. A gaggle of gawky no-hopers they may have been, but he loved the way Hucknall watched the Cabaret Voltaire soundcheck before remarking, 'Boring buggers, ain't they?'

Eagle and Hucknall hit it off immediately. Before the end of the evening they had fallen into deep, impenetrable conversation, swapping R'n'B stories and exchanging ecstatic references to their favourite artists and albums. This instant friendship was cemented the moment Hucknall visited Eagle's flat and fell head over heels in love – with his record collection. Hucknall excitedly sniffed the sleeves and scanned the sleeve notes intently. Here, he thought, lay his true education – a living room university complete with his own hyper-enthusiastic professor.

Eagle began to take over the management of the Elevators with his partner, Pete Fulwell, and Mick took the position of regular DJ at Eric's. For the second time, Hucknall had stumbled into a scene which, although all but over in Eagle's eyes, he thought capable of amounting to something.

After Eric's had closed, at Eagle's next venture called Adams he and Hucknall would spend many drunken nights kipping on Eagle's floor after, of course, the obligatory lengthy two-man musical seminars. But Eagle's fondness for Hucknall went beyond mere bonding. 'Nobody else seemed to notice,' he said later, 'but even then, Hucknall was a phenomenal singer. It was so obvious, well, at least to me. My favourite Hucknall was when he was jamming, very loosely, to the blues. The Elevators did a series of support slots to the Teardrop Explodes and it was during these that they would start this jam. Suddenly Hucknall would cut loose and just blast into this wild blues. Absolutely fantastic. Here was this funny looking lad, fronting a definitely out-of-vogue Mancunian band – no-hopers really – and yet I couldn't stop comparing him to the greatest black singers in rock'n'roll history. Even I thought it was absurd at the time and often had to pinch myself. But still nobody liked him. Record companies wouldn't come within a mile of him. Hucknall had this supreme self confidence, which I saw as an attribute, but I think it would serve to wind a lot of people up.'

Chapter 8
Holding Back The Years

The mutual respect and understanding between Hucknall and Eagle seemed destined to evolve into a professional relationship, and so it did with Hucknall initially taking up residence on the Eric's DJ desk. It was important to Eagle that any disc jockey in his club would arrive armed, not only with a black box full of records, but with the knowledge to back this up should a punter pursue a particularly awkward or obscure line of enquiry. This stemmed from his days at the Twisted Wheel where he had virtually transformed the DJ box from mere record deck into a centre of knowledge, a place of worship even. A good DJ also had to have an understanding of the basic power of the records, for instance whether a record would fill a dance floor or, alternatively, ease the tension. It wasn't merely a question of a record's popularity. In effect, the DJ was in total control of the mood and atmosphere of a venue. It was, and still is, a highly skilled job despite its (largely deserved) reputation for tackiness.

Who better then than Mick Hucknall, who had all but taken up residence in Eagle's flat and had started to significantly impress the old trooper with his barrage of Frantic Elevators' tapes. It seemed equally obvious that a professional relationship between Eagle's Eric's Records and the Elevators would evolve and absolutely nobody in Liverpool was surprised to hear that plans were being laid.

In the autumn of 1980, perhaps to catch the glamour of the odd nightclubbing footballer, be he red or blue, Mick Hucknall started to attend Sandpipers disco regularly. Maybe it was to harangue the regular record company receptions which took place every weekend. The place – soft lights, hard bouncers – was a veritable haven for minor Manchester celebrities, many of whom would clumsily attempt to catch the attention of sharp-eyed *Manchester Evening News* diarists and therefore reap the rewards of local notoriety. Not, alas, being a local celebrity, Hucknall couldn't latch on to this somewhat pathetic circus, not that he would want to. His interest, footballers aside, was in the music. It was a strangely tasteful blending of soul, more often than not spun by DJ Barry Neale (who would progress, via a stint on the precocious pirate radio station, KFM, to becoming a presenter on Manchester's excellent, though ever struggling ethnic station, Sunset Radio). Neale, through sheer hard work and suss, had gained a reputation for spinning the very best soul imports of the time, hence the attentions of Hucknall and soul-crazy cohorts. Neale was the only DJ in town who could effectively satisfy Hucknall's thirst for rare groove tunes. One record in particular became synonymous with the scene at Sandpipers. Neale played it to death and he later remembered it was a particular favourite with the Hucknall entourage. It was, of course, the Valentine Brothers' *Money's Too Tight To Mention*. It was one of the few records that contained the message and the power to make someone living a dole queue existence actually feel rather good. 'I love that record, you know,' stated Hucknall at the time. 'It has a certain power.'

Hucknall, who was still tied to the deal with Tony Davidson, had already started talking about the possibility of the Frantic Elevators leaving TJM.

'Are you going to release any more material?' he asked Davidson in a hopeful but amiable manner. Davidson, unfortunately, couldn't summon up the enthusiasm or, for that matter, the finance. Even though a second Frantic Elevators EP had been recorded it had remained firmly in the can, much to Hucknall's dismay. Davidson, however, couldn't possibly justify another release. The independent market had become worryingly unfashionable and had been drying up for some

Mick Hucknall at a Frantic Elevators rehearsal session in Brian Turner's flat. (*Richard Watt* (*RW*))

Mick entertaining a few friends: *left to right* Brian Turner, Gwynn Jones, Steve Cummings. (*RW*)

Bleary, beery days in Hulme, 1980. (*RW*)

Moss and Hucknall at The Gallery, Manchester, 1981. (*RW*)

Boys will be yobs. Mick and friends frolicking outside the Salutation
pub, Manchester. (Heavily censored!) (*RW*)

The sartorially elegant Elevators. Hucknall and Moss in 1981. (*RW*)

Mick Hucknall and Kevin Williams at the Checkmate club,
Liverpool, 1981. *(RW)*

Mick as party DJ. *(RW)*

Mick Hucknall and Brian Turner during the recording of *Holding Back The Years,* Stockport, 1982. (*RW*)

The last-ever Frantic Elevators concert, at the Band On The Wall, 1982. (*RW*)

Cracking open the ale. (*RW*)

Mick and Mog at Manchester Poly, 1983. Note Mog's CND sticker – soon to be banned by Elliot Rashman. (*RW*)

All budding acts loved to play at the raucous Trades Club, Hebden Bridge. (*RW*)

Pre-gig anxiety at the
Manchester IYY festival,
2 August 1985.
(*Karen Middles*)

The confident,
accomplished artist,
1993-style.
(*Universal Pictorial
Press & Agency Ltd*)

time. Davidson – fending off the naive enquiries from his entire roster, all of whom were beginning to blame him for their lack of true success – felt as if he had been simply pouring money down a hole. It had to stop. He was even considering moving out of the Little Peter Street building. TJM Records was about to go to sleep. Sensing this, and excited by his new-found Liverpudlian connections, Hucknall wanted out.

The parting arrangement seemed amiable enough. Davidson typed up a simple letter to the effect that although Hucknall would be free to record elsewhere, Davidson would retain the rights to the Frantic Elevators' back catalogue as well as fifty per cent of the back publishing.

In 1987, Tony Davidson released all six TJM Frantic Elevator tracks on an LP entitled *The Early Years*. Although this immediately ran into legal problems and had to be withdrawn, Davidson was later granted the right to release the material. *The Early Years* LP was rare and became even rarer when 400 copies (only 1,000 were pressed) were stolen from the back of Davidson's car. The tracks did resurface, however, on a Receiver CD.

'I felt vindicated,' said Davidson. 'I had every right to release the material. I never made any money out of the Frantics and I took a lot of chances for them. Trying to stop *The Early Years* from being sold was a simple case of the big man trying to stamp the little man out. Thankfully, this time, the little man won.'

Cargo Studios in Rochdale were arguably the most favoured studios in the North-west, at least as far as independent labels were concerned. It was perfect – a comparatively cheap eight track which still managed to churn out wave after wave of quality demos and, as Joy Division, A Certain Ratio and much of the disparate Factory roster would testify, which was quite capable of producing singles of invigorating rawness. What's more, the sound which would appear tinny and insubstantial in later years actually managed to define the feel and pace of the late seventies indie boom.

It was a strange time. In production terms it was certainly a period when quality of sound counted for little. As far as innovation, passion and commitment were concerned, it was practically a golden era and never before or since has Radio One's John Peel show – the natural home of indie music – sounded so perfectly in tune with the times. At the top of the tree were the Fall – also clients of Cargo – who typified an era when innovation overshadowed musicianship.

The Frantic Elevators' second single, *You Know What You Told Me/Production Prevention* appeared in November 1980, six months after its recording on Roger Eagle's Eric's Records. It was nothing if not a typical indie single – feeble but feeling, spirited but devoid of genuine inspiration. It was a record which would be bought and enjoyed by friends and followers, all of whom would believe that the band were destined for greater things, but it was not a record that in any way could turn heads. It had no spark. When sent to a music paper for review it would arrive accompanied by about another hundred records, all similar in every respect, all equally deserving, all carrying the weight of expectancy of their respective composers. To stand out from the pack, it would be necessary either to produce something absolutely extraordinary or gain media exposure by some other method. *You Know What You Told Me*, being standard indie fare, was simply not good enough. Worse still, it wasn't even truly representative of the Frantic Elevators' slow climb into areas of R'n'B. Even Roger Eagle was aware of this.

The irony was that Eagle had actually recorded a Frantic Elevators live album, a furious slab of raw R'n'B which, for the first time, actually managed to display the magnificence of Hucknall's rapidly developing vocal skills. Eagle was planning to release the material but due to lack of available finance, and the fact that the band were most definitely unsure about such a prospect, he kept it on ice. It was a great shame, for had it surfaced it would surely have been the vinyl proof that the Frantic Elevators really were a band capable of soaring to considerable heights. It would have pinned down the band in their finest moment, in live performance, blasting away from the standard indie sound and hurtling into the realms of R'n'B and being fronted by the increasingly dominant vocals of Mick

Hucknall. But it was not to be. (In later years, the recording would be locked tightly away by the Simply Red management.) Significantly, if Eagle's recollection of that recording is accurate, it would have been good enough to rank as one of the truly great English R'n'B albums. Even if it hardly compared with the fifties American albums in Eagle's collection, it certainly reached the kind of level attained by Canvey Island's Dr Feelgood on the evergreen *Stupidity*.

'It was a shame,' Eagle later admitted, 'because I really did feel that the Frantic Elevators were capable of kickstarting some kind of R'n'B boom. But they never quite managed to get their act together and were always too dragged down by the pressure to be like the Factory artists. I think that by the time the Elevators realised just what the potential was it was already too late.'

The third Elevators' single, *Searchin' For The Only One Hunchback Of Notre Dame*, appeared on another ersatz label, Crackin' Up, in April 1981. Yet again it was a disc high in spirit and low in true inspiration. Like both its predecessors it failed to fully capture either Hucknall's improved vocals or songwriting prowess. That said, the Northern Soul edge to *Hunchback Of Notre Dame* not only made it worth a second listen, but also hinted at glories to come. In a sense, and Hucknall was begining to understand this, the disc was dragged down by the band's conflicting musical aspirations. The spark of originality which powered the A side was too easily dulled, either by the band's lack of ability to expand a theme, or the cheap production techniques available. It was clear that if the Frantic Elevators were going to prosper, then someone somewhere would have to inject a good deal of money. Equally, it was apparent that the Elevators would simply have to sort themselves out. Jamming with Liverpudlian bands like the Lawnmower and providing the odd furious live set was simply not going to be good enough. Back home in Manchester, the Frantic Elevators were all but forgotten, long since cast as parochial also-rans, unhip, unloved and unhappy.

As 1982 brought forth wave upon wave of stupendous pop

gush, a genuine 'golden era' dawned, effectively and thankfully killing off the solemn tones and self-indulgent posturing of the indie scene, circa Futurama, circa Joy Division. It was from the unpalatable remains of this 'scene with no name' that much of the bright, optimistic pop talent of 1982 was born.

Perhaps the explosion was entirely record company inspired. Perhaps the A & R men realised that gigging around, performing unlistenable trash in the name of yawn-inspiring heartfelt art, was no use at all – not to the bored inebriated artists, the bored inebriated audiences or the bored inebriated record company scouts. Even the brisk naivety of the *NME* had begun to wane. It had dawned on people – even the most sullen, raincoated dullard who carried his Bunnymen LPs around as if they contained divine wisdom rather than mildly poetic whimsicality – that life could be more fun than this. And it was.

The very writers who had lionised the likes of Joy Division and the Gang of Four and despised the pop charts with murderous venom, actually began writing complimentary articles about, gasp, even the likes of Dollar. The *NME* singles page, always good for a laugh, suddenly began to feature fewer and fewer records of the scratchy indie ilk. Trevor Horn was emerging quite rightly as the most influential record producer in the country. Trevor Horn! The man responsible for Buggles? Far from being mocked by arrogant writers, he suddenly found himself being interrogated and championed by them.

Manchester's indie scene had waned and slipped from fashion. When Richard Boon, boss of the largely avant-garde New Hormones label, asked Paul Morley what he thought of the recent New Hormones material, Morley burst into laughter and began talking about Trevor Horn and ABC and Dollar. Times had changed indeed.

Horn's work with ABC during the spring of 1982 would produce the seminal early eighties recording, *Lexicon of Love*, destined to become one of the finest pop albums ever produced – and boy, was a record ever so 'produced'. It was lush, lavish, unforgettable, and backed up with a year of incredible pop music from the likes of Soft Cell, Haircut One Hundred,

Culture Club, Tears for Fears, the Associates, Malcolm MacLaren. The age of pop sensibility had begun. No more exposure for scratchy indie bands – well, not much. Even Factory Records, despite New Order's very clever transition from atmospheric rock to slick dance music had grown quite staggeringly unfashionable. All the pop kids wanted, after all, was a bit of fun. The rather overblown New Romantic phase left a thirst for lightweight fashion, glossy magazines, haircuts and yellow shirts, sockless legs and string vests, toothy smiles and hair streaks, *The Face* and *Smash Hits*.

So where did all this leave the Frantic Elevators? Where did this leave Mick Hucknall, last seen onstage wearing a frayed tank-top and kipper tie? He had so carefully nurtured a styleless, jumbled look. Downbeat and downcast, he liked to mix colours haphazardly. He was quite the embodiment of anti-fashion and was in looks as in musical aspiration just about as far away from Nick Heyward as it was possible to get.

Surprisingly, considering his future success in playing the system, he didn't even notice the changes. He did not see the transition of, say, ABC from stolid Sheffield art funksters to one of the most joyous pop outfits of all time. It just didn't happen inside Hucknall's world. In Manchester, Factory had opened the Hacienda, a cold, cavernous, all too often empty but gorgeously designed purpose-built rock venue and night-club, pledged to providing plentiful opportunities for the city's burgeoning acts to perform live.

The Frantic Elevators, once rejected by Hacienda booker Mike Pickering, never tried again. Hucknall even stayed away from the club during its first year of opening. He had become more and more isolated. Having moved to a Whalley Range flat, he proceeded to stay in it with the radio off, the television off and little but his bottomless pit of ancient soul and blues recordings for comfort. For a full eighteen months, since 1980, Hucknall had barely noticed the charts, hardly glanced at a copy of *NME* or *Sounds*, and had been content to remain sadly aloof. The fact that he almost completely missed the most interesting period of pop music since the mid-sixties is testimony to his appalling state of isolation.

How bizarre then to note that the Frantic Elevators actually recorded *Holding Back The Years*, the one song that would seem to be perfectly suited to the mood of the day. *Holding Back The Years* was released in October 1982 backed with *Pistols In My Brain* on No Waiting Records. The tasteless nature of the B side was pictorially represented on the single's dreadful sleeve, which depicted the Fair Isle tank-top-clad Hucknall placing his mouth over a cocked pistol (the idea was nothing more than a feeble throwback to the sleeve of Eddie and the Hot Rods' 1976 single, *Woolly Bully*). The most noticeable fact about this was the quite unbridgeable gulf, in terms of style and production, between the Frantic Elevators and the trend of the day. Record company A & R men were still, by and large, on the lookout for glamour, albeit of a cheap and rather transient ilk. A shirtless but tank-topped Hucknall was not even a remotely glamorous image.

Holding Back The Years was placed, hopelessly, by Hucknall on the jukebox at the Whitegates pub. It was a rather sad thing to do, for a person who wished to see his record back to back with the Beatles and Queen did invite a certain amount of local ridicule. The locals knew little of the pop industry, but they had to admit the chances of their boy attaining popstardom were pretty remote. After all, his era had been the punk era, had it not? His time was past. But most of them had to admit that the song was not at all bad for a local band. Their lethargy should not be mocked. As Roger Eagle continually pointed out, here was a great singer with a great song, but unless he managed somehow to manoeuvre himself into the right position at the right time, nobody – not even the so-called experts in the music business – would be able to see it. By 1982, A & R scouting had become a predominantly sheep-like activity and it still is. Raw talent would never be enough. Somehow the fuse must be lit, the game must be played.

Mick Hucknall's flat was raided twice in six months by thieves who, apparently, boasted a high musical awareness. Much to Hucknall's almost suicidal dismay, they managed to pilfer his rare and extremely valuable collection of James Brown live tapes. The possibility that the thieves might be recording Abba's *Arrival* over the top of them terrified Hucknall, who used the experience as an excuse to break his isolation and get back in touch with the real world.

He was astonished to discover, for example, that the Associates were now a chart band. And Dexy's Midnight Runners, who he remembered as a rather pathetic bunch of soul pretenders, were the number one band in the country.

Emerging from the dusty gloom of Whalley Range, he gleefully accepted an invitation to London – on his own as the rest of the band couldn't afford it – to be interviewed by the *Melody Maker*'s highly perceptive Steve Sutherland. Much to his credit, the *Maker* writer had noticed something special when the Elevators had supported Wah Heat at London's 100 Club two years previously. 'The sheer crazy joy of that performance is a memory that vividly sticks,' wrote Sutherland, although few people would believe him.

When challenged about the sincerity of the Elevators, which is possibly the one charge one could not level at the band, Hucknall responded venomously, 'We are *totally* sincere. *Totally*, and I don't think that anyone who sees us knows that because we are not really successful in terms of record sales or massive audiences, but the people who do come are absolutely astonished that we are not enormous.'

'My major description of my stuff is that it is just completely me,' he stated. 'Basically I think one of the things that might relate to people is that I don't know anything about anything. I can't do anything about anything. I write about virtually nothing, about being nothing, about having absolutely no power over anything. You see these ridiculous atrocities going on and what can you do about them? I mean, what was that ridiculous man in Israel doing with all those people in Beirut? Carnage! There's no other word for it. He's just murdering people when he doesn't need to and I just feel sick when I see things like that. This doesn't represent what we do but one of our songs says, "All there is to do is live". I don't really agree with that because it's an absolute cop out but I don't feel capable of fighting this revolting system, this absolutely obscene system.'

Was this a man who was, quite naturally, sick to the back teeth of feeling utterly powerless? Had he already decided that, should a break happen along, he would go for it, regardless of the consequences?

'We could be popstars,' he mused, somewhat wearily, 'but I find it very difficult to stand there and be a star and look at them all looking at this star who is nothing, who goes and has a shit once a day and does exactly the same as they do and is being revered for being something outstanding. When all it is, is that he happens to be interested in music and plays and writes songs. Success is not something I'm striving for. I mean why, *why* do people have to know what you have got to say? If I can sell records and remain reclusive then that's my ideal. I'm quite happy to sit in a pub somewhere, get bevvied and then go home and maybe the next morning write a song, record it and put it out, simple as that.'

It is interesting that this period preceded Hucknall's departure from the band by a couple of short months. And yet there was a resilience in his tone that suggested a rather greater unity existed.

The last tortuous year of the Frantic Elevators was 1982. After five years of fluctuating solidarity the cracks began to widen. World weary and indignant, they exited their practice sessions early too many times, and became embroiled in heated debates in the nearest pub. The debates differed from the arguments suffered by every band that ever attempted to break into the music business in just one way. Although fuelled by alcohol they were no longer fired by hope. The band were slowly but most definitely sliding into an apathetic grave. Gathered around a table one evening in the Whitegates pub they did actually split up for twenty minutes, before falling back together after a verbal attack from a cynical local. The Frantic Elevators had been around for too long and their differences, marginal in their first years, were now vast.

'It was like being in Led Zeppelin without any of the success,' Brian Turner said, referring to the conflicting forces which were tearing away at the band's solidarity, and creativity. Turner, who had begun life in the Elevators practically as a novice, had started to open up musically. His practice session contributions became more and more adventurous. Kevin

Williams, although a trier, was somewhat limited. But the major unbridgeable gulf was between Hucknall and Moss. Hucknall's songwriting had, post *Holding Back The Years*, experienced a remarkable surge of creativity. Moss, on the other hand, had all but closed down. 'Neil was definitely shutting down,' stated Turner. 'He was a nice guy, but very reserved and I certainly had the feeling that all the fire had gone out of him. His partnership with Mick seemed all but finished.'

Securing a gig at Manchester Polytechnic's Mandela Building was quite a coup. Hucknall had blagged the gig from social secretary Elliot Rashman who had uncharacteristically wilted in the face of Hucknall's gall.

The gig was not untypical of the Poly. The crowd was mainly semi-interested students, immersed in alcoholic relief who hardly noticed the band onstage. Elliot Rashman, however, was 'gob-smacked'. His friend, Tony Bowers, had told him to watch out for the singer of the Elevators. His interest had been aroused but he had never expected this. Sidling closer to the stage he just couldn't tear his eyes away. The singer was phenomenal.

Rashman's naturally Machiavellian mind kicked into gear. He had been looking hard for a new band to manage, a new career to guide ever since his rather over-ambitious plans for the Mothmen had imploded in unspectacular fashion. Rashman saw his future flash before his eyes. Plans unfolded before him – deals, talks, debates, arguments – never before had he seen such enormous talent so modestly packaged and so clumsily backed. The band, he felt, were falling all around the singer who had clearly developed way beyond the capabilities of the rest of them. They would have to go. But Mick Hucknall was a star. Of this, Rashman was totally sure. Nobody else seemed to see it. Not the crowd, not even the band as far as he could see. But Hucknall was a star and it was only a matter of time.

A rollercoaster would begin and Rashman intended to be on it, guiding it. It was a ridiculous notion, of course, as he hadn't even spoken to Hucknall in this light. Nor did he have any real idea about what plans Hucknall had for the Frantic Elevators. He vaguely knew Hucknall, for Rashman was a Manchester Polytechnic graduate, but he had had absolutely no idea that the precocious ginger-headed scruff was in command of such formidable talent. Before the end of the gig, Elliot Rashman's plans for his own future had changed drastically. It would be a marriage of sorts – all he had to do was tell the other party the news.

Chapter 9
Stepping Out

The transition from Tameside College to Manchester Polytechnic, where Hucknall embarked on a four-year course in
fine art, was a natural one. Although grateful for the scope
and vision of the Ashton-based college, Hucknall had long
since wanted to work at the heart of Manchester's cosmopolitan student land. Suddenly, Hucknall's axis had shifted both
geographically and culturally.

The second-hand clothes he chose to wear, a striking mish-
mash at times, would no longer seem so bizarre. There was a
vast difference between wandering down Oxford Road, garbed
in all manner of frayed garishness among others of equally
Bohemian apparel, and stalking the backstreets and tap
rooms of Denton and Ashton. To his delight, Hucknall also
discovered that there was more to Indian food than a quick
vindaloo takeaway after seven pints of Guinness down the
Whitegates. Hucknall discovered the delights of Rusholme – a
thronging, multi-racial strip boasting the finest Indian restaurants in the city. What's more, as the clientele was mainly
students and Indians, they tended to be cheap – basically half
the price of the city-centre establishments.

Rusholme opened up a whole new sub-culture for Hucknall,
who basked in the cosmopolitan glory of it all. His favourite
restaurant, The Sanam Sweet Centre, was to instil the profound love of Indian food that would never leave him. He
would never eat the same thing twice. He would experiment,
learn the ingredients and would marvel over a plethora of
exotic, ugly fruits and vegetables in the shops along Wilmslow

Road. This was the period when Hucknall became a gastronome. It was as though a veil had been lifted from his eyes, a muffle from his tongue. Thanks to his father, he had always been very well fed and would repeatedly express his gratitude in later lafe. However, the time had come when the essential diet of beans and fish fingers would be well and truly eclipsed. Even simple food, he discovered, could be sexy, sophisticated, stylish and luxurious. Cracking a bread roll in half and eating with cheese and red wine, could be a stylish, sumptuous, loving act. Hucknall was taking his first true steps towards sophistication.

This period, of course, was influenced by his life at Manchester Polytechnic. Even the comparatively loose atmosphere at Tameside hadn't prepared him for this. Contrary to his expectations of a four-year block of intense graft, the course seemed unreasonably laid-back. It would have been all too easy to have slowed down and treated the course, as many did, as a four-year stint of hedonism and relaxation. Although hardly lacking as far as hedonism was concerned, Hucknall never lost sight of the fact he was at college for himself and not to appease the system.

'I had a healthy respect for *myself*,' he would later stress. 'I wanted to get on and do things. At Manchester Poly they really treated you like an adult. They earned my respect, and I respected them.' Nevertheless, speaking to Q magazine, fellow student Richard Watt recalled the entire course being nothing more than, 'A piss up, a three-year holiday.'

Hucknall was popular at the Poly. At last he had the confidence to consider himself the equal to the same kind of girls who snubbed him at Tameside. He even tempered his outlandishness a little, and the rough Denton edges to his speech and general attitude were showing signs of becoming, if not highly polished, then certainly 'rubbed over'.

The course, however, didn't have the most studious of reputations. Richard Watt, once again, expressed the feeling of general apathy to Q magazine's Lloyd Bradley: 'Not many of the painters there took anything seriously. As long as you did the minimum amount of work you could scrape by with a second-class honours degree. There was a great deal of drinking and not going in. There was a general air of rebellion among that course because they had a right bastard of a director who wanted everyone to paint Jasper Johns-type paintings with splattered paint everywhere and hated it if you painted figuratively. Mick painted figuratively all the time and was in deep shit for it. He wasn't the only one but he was always doing drawings of his bicycle.'

His bicycle, which had increasingly become an integral part of his lifestyle, wasn't his only artistic eccentricity. One painting, which he laboured over for aeons, had the word 'fuck' written all over it. Needless to say the tutors exploded when they saw this. One day, Hucknall wandered into the class and, whether out of remorse or sheer frustration at a system which still failed to understand him, smashed the painting to bits.

But Brian Turner thought very highly of Hucknall's art – and still does. 'There were some really classic paintings, you know,' he said. 'Mick was a great artist and nobody ever seems to pick up on this point. In fact there was a time when I really could see the art side to him taking over. It's weird to think of it now, but as the Elevators began to struggle it just seemed that Mick was getting more and more into his painting. He was getting better and better too. I just thought he might go places.'

But had Turner confronted Hucknall over this issue, he would surely have been reassured. Hucknall was certainly not about to give up his music. In fact his experiences at the Poly actually served to reinforce his love of music and heightened his desire to turn this love into a career. Far from being a natural painter, he found toiling behind a canvas very hard work indeed. As he later put it, he had to 'Think and think and think'. Painting drained him. With application, he could certainly have pushed himself towards considerable artistic achievements but he didn't have the necessary talent to coast through. Although he knew he would achieve his degree – failure in that sense never entered his head – it did not seem right for him to be pursuing a career in a field where he would have to really labour just to keep up with his peers.

It was halfway through his Poly days that Hucknall finally decided that music would be his vocation. He was in no doubt that he was a much better singer than painter and he knew he had no real choice but to follow the path which came most naturally to him. Not that his artistic education was in any way a hindrance. On the contrary, he found that it actually inspired his musicality. He became fascinated, not just with his own art, but with art history. He loved to research the background of artists and find out how they came to do a particular painting: what kind of artistic influences they grew up with, how their work changed over the years, how they adopted certain influences and adapted their own work accordingly. He loved to see what happened when, for instance, two opposing aesthetic cultures clashed and how things progressed or not as a result.

He couldn't see any difference between his study of the history and evolution of art and his night-time study – with the help of a growing mass of vinyl – of music. In this unstructured way he traced musical influences from the twenties, if not earlier, to the present day. He pondered over facts, almost in train-spotter fashion. He learned how to answer rhetorical questions. Would there be a Led Zeppelin, for example, if Muddy Waters had never existed?

This would, in time, lead to another obsession – the study of people's careers. Hucknall's naive punkish loathing of the likes of Eric Clapton and Elton John began to be replaced by a good deal of respect. He studied their career paths quite closely and attempted to ascertain the secret of their survival. He became aware that they were more than just dated popsters. They were people who had understood how to survive shifting trends, how to adapt their music and change, if not in sync with the more superficial pop fads, then certainly with similar haste. This was an important lesson for Hucknall, and a fine example of how his education extended way beyond the barriers of university or qualifications. He learned a good deal from his degree course, but he also learned to appreciate its limitations. How not to become trapped in one specialist area. He noticed in class the artists who made mistakes. It was somewhat easier for him to apply the same critical eye to pop music. He noticed how the best in the dire progressive era of the late sixties – Clapton, Fleetwood Mac perhaps – understood the need to evolve, and how many exciting young talents had faded and sunk. It was all filed away. The knowledge would come in useful – one day.

Having said that, Hucknall's musical tastes were far from broadening at this stage, as one would expect. In fact, his deep personal study, his true passion and intensive listening could be narrowed down to just four artists. Firstly the Beatles who retained, even through the punk period, almost religious status for Hucknall. And then his big three almost divinely inspirational artists: Duke Ellington, James Brown and Miles Davis. Davis was arguably the most unusual. Although most musically minded students would, sooner or later, find themselves sitting in smoky rooms listening to *A Kind of Blue*, it was rare for anyone to delve too deeply into the vast expanse of Davis's career. Hucknall devoured everything, even Davis's least celebrated works from the jazz rock stage of the late sixties. Hucknall could talk with considerable authority about the multitudinous musicians who had accompanied Davis during all the stages of his career.

He knew the big four inside out. They formed the central core of his true education. Everything else, however esteemed, would be peripheral for him. That is not to say he restricted his knowledge to them. A friend of mine once spent a full two hours arguing about the relative merits of the many John Coltrane albums with Hucknall in Manchester's Sawyers Arms. Emerging from this alcoholic ordeal the friend remarked, 'He is the most arrogant, opinionated, mad, crazy, self-important bugger I've ever crossed swords with . . . he knows his stuff though . . . he sure knows his stuff.'

Hucknall's garish dress sense and personality reached their expressive peak on graduation day. Not for him the dull robes of academia. Hucknall was an art student, right to the wire. As the remainder of the gathering remained firmly within the bounds of tradition, if not respectability, Hucknall took great delight in collecting his degree dressed in a lurid mohair jumper and equally noisy trousers. It was not a particularly stylish approach, merely an extension of the Frantic Elevators' philosophy of mad clothes, mad music, mad lifestyle.

After all, reasoned Hucknall, what was the point of attending art college if at the very end you have to bow to tradition. It might well have been a naive viewpoint, but it was certainly honest. Hucknall became known around town by his dress sense, in particular his big, black hat.

Throughout his Polytechnic days, Hucknall had become genuinely sophisticated. What he never did, however, was to allow that sophistication to flow over into affectation which is what happens to so many art students, let alone art students with a foot in the music business door. In this sense Hucknall remained most profoundly a Northerner. It was only as he was on the verge of leaving the Poly that he woke up to the very real differences which separate North from South (differences which, however, would be exaggerated beyond belief in the oncoming mythical North/South divide). Hucknall was horrified when he met art students from the London scene. 'The greeting in the London scene is to fuckin' kiss each other,' he said, sounding more like a Collyhurst coal merchant than an arts graduate. 'If someone kissed me like that I'd fuckin' hit 'em. It drives me mad.'

Chapter 10
The Management

The journey from Manchester to the Yorkshire town of Hebden Bridge is short and more often than not greyly uninspiring. Superficially, this would seem to be the case during the early to mid-eighties when each and every trip, be it by rail or road, would merely see the steady transformation from inner city decay to the kind of depression one feels when entering a mill town in a post mill town era.

Hebden Bridge is handsome when approached on a sunny autumnal day when the Pennines assume a yellowish hue and are ravished by grey-haired, big-booted walkers of the Wainwright ilk. But it can be, with respect, one hell of an ugly town too, especially when overcast and drizzled upon rather than storm swept. On days like these, the Pennines stand like black foreboding shadows and the mills really do live up to their satanic image.

For Mancunians, Hebden Bridge town is foreign soil. It is, after all, situated just within the clutches of Yorkshire and Lancastrians from a couple of miles down the road are traditionally made to feel slightly uneasy when entering the tap rooms intent on buying pints of 'real' Yorkshire Tetley Bitter. There always existed in Hebden Bridge a faint sense of a clashing of neighbouring cultures. The town has always nurtured a feeling of 'edginess' and it wasn't by accident that, come the mid-eighties, many of the aspiring Manchester bands (who would go on to great things in the oncoming Madchester boom) would openly cite Hebden Bridge as their favourite, most responsive small-time gig.

In the seventies, Hebden Bridge had acquired a new role which, one always sensed, was not entirely welcome within the closed ranks of the true locals. The so-called 'alternative society' created by mid-sixties studenthood, especially in Manchester, had thrown up a crazed cottage industry. A mass of bearded, rainbow-jumper-clad Bohemians had embarked upon lives of simple artisanship rather than following their peers into the teaching profession. They might be wood carvers, potters, painters, sculptors, knitters and many of them left their degrees, their ambitions and their belongings behind them to head for the hills. Corny as it may well seem, Hebden Bridge was the first real hill town they found. They revelled in its stark remoteness and its industrial heritage. They fell in love with and to some extent took control of local folklore, and used their university training to research the background of local customs to such a disproportionate extent that many of the genuine locals would feel strangely alienated in their own back garden. Hebden Bridge was and remains a proud town, worried by the possibility of appearing 'twee'.

Hebden Bridge had played a uniquely innovative role in the Industrial Revolution, so it seemed natural for it to play a similarly forward role in the kind of 'theming' which would sweep the North-west during the eighties, when towns would become hands-on museums reflecting the period. Hebden Bridge would unfortunately become heavily stigmatised in Manchester. In its role as Mecca for those intent on opting out, the town would all too often be tainted by the following, simplistic image: 'Hebden Bridge was the place where hippies went. It was a place where people wore green shoes, dungarees, tea-pot hats and ginger beards.' This was hardly a fair image although, it must be said, it wasn't totally without foundation.

Elliot Rashman went to Hebden Bridge. It seemed the natural place for him to go and I do not mean to mock. Rashman, in his role as social secretary of Manchester Polytechnic and in his time as a student before that, had grown synonymous with the so-called 'Didsbury set'. Didsbury was part opulence, part Bohemian, and the one place in Manchester where people would most easily make the transition from being a student to a media person. It is a district of grand old houses, now fading and split into bedsits. It is both the Hampstead and the Camden of Manchester, a place nourished by media and rockbiz gossip. Needless to say, Factory Records were based in Didsbury.

One close acquaintance of Rashman agreed that the progression from Didsbury to Hebden Bridge would seem to be a perfectly natural one and noted, 'Most of Elliot's friends would be into macrobiotic food and hanging upside down.' At this point, in 1983, Rashman already had close links with the music fraternity who tended to reside in Didsbury and, in many respects, were the controlling force in Manchester music – people like the wonderful, flamboyant, besuited, bow-tied and huggable Bruce Mitchell. Mitchell had gained infamy as the eccentric drummer in the Manchester seventies' anarchic comic combo Alberto Y Los Trios Paranoias. After this Python-esque team had committed a suitably anarchic musical suicide, Mitchell – a good friend of Roger Eagle's incidentally, the two of them would forever love to swap Orson Welles stories – joined Vini Rielly's Durutti Column as percussionist. It was a logical arrangement. Mitchell lodged in Rielly's band, Rielly lodged in Mitchell's house.

Another member of the Didsbury set was Tony Bowers, the bassist with the Rashman-managed Mothmen and later the unmanageable Durutti Column. He and his girlfriend, Penny Henry (another budding social secretary) and in their wake a plethora of folk were, unwittingly perhaps, laying the foundation stones for the oncoming rush of the Madchester youth culture explosion.

It seemed fitting that Rashman should head, hippy style, for the hills. He bought a stone woodland cottage nestling by a river valley. The cottage was a weekend haven, not just for Rashman but for his many friends, including Hucknall. Although it contained no hot water, no adequate heating, no bathroom and only sported an outside toilet, it also housed something that would seem irresistible, especially to the young Hucknall. This was a truly gigantic record collection which included everything from sad, frayed, Gentle Giant albums to an extensive James Brown collection. Yet again

Hucknall thought he had died and gone to heaven. The cottage must have seemed every bit as naturally inspiring as Eagle's Liverpudlian flat. The fact that Rashman had installed an enormous set of speakers before even thinking about installing hot water, spoke volumes. It perhaps even reminded Hucknall of his Denton youth.

Rashman was a man whom Hucknall could really trust. He was a music lover and here was the proof, the manifestation. It was during these days that the relationship became cemented into something more than even manager/artist. It would have to be as solid as a family link.

Rashman had fallen head over heels in love with the idea of managing Mick Hucknall the singer from that famous moment with the Frantic Elevators onstage at Manchester Polytechnic. He knew, from that moment on, that he would form a future partnership with Hucknall. Pretty soon Hucknall knew this as well. It was swiftly recognised, initially by Rashman and fairly soon by a number of record company A & R men – including Sire Records boss Seymour Stein, the man most responsible for plucking Madonna out of her nightmarish poverty – that the one great asset of the Frantic Elevators was Hucknall's voice. Down the years, unknown to Hucknall even, a good many influential folk had been making mental notes about the singer with the Frantic Elevators. The band as a whole remained an unattractive proposition to the end. No record company particularly relished the task of trying to steer a bunch of hot-headed, left-field, scratchy Mancunians with absurd aspirations towards playing funk. If the comparatively pretty Orange Juice, armed with good songs, a good front-loaded budget, a polished, well-produced sound *and* a huge amount of music press credibility still failed to gain any notable success, what chance had a band who made the Fall look like Duran Duran? (And if some of the demos were to be believed, made the Fall *sound* like Duran Duran as well.) Nobody, not even the strangely impressed Seymour Stein, really came to terms with the fact that the singer, wearing a kipper tie over a Frank Spencer tank-top, owned a voice that could span five-and-a-half octaves with a little training. Nevertheless, the boy could sing and good singers, with an eye for soul, were not exactly thick on the ground.

Rashman and Hucknall held many often impromptu meetings, interrupted by an endless stream of phone calls from irate managers attempting to secure Polytechnic gigs. Between them, the pair slowly came to realise that if their relationship was to form the base for a new career, then a fresh start was needed. The Frantic Elevators had run their course. Hucknall had been a friend of Neil Moss since the age of three and a friend of Turner's for many years as well, but good sense told him to follow Rashman's advice.

The impact Rashman made on Hucknall during this period was immense, although it is not difficult to understand why. Hucknall still felt a mite indignant about the failure of the Elevators to break through on any tangible level other than gaining a small following of vociferous Scousers. Perhaps a Rashman-style figure would be the missing ingredient? Sure enough, Rashman was hardly the type to shy away from difficult tasks, awkward tactics, verbal bullying, even. It could have been an extremely naive judgement. After all, although Rashman certainly had about him an aura of authority, his managerial experience was practically nil. His brief stint with the Mothmen had amounted to little more than a rarely heard twelve-inch issued by Didsbury's post Rabid Records, the Absurd Label. Nevertheless, it was enough. The outrage that Hucknall felt when he first discovered that record companies were tentatively interested in the voice but not the band began to subside. He would have to change his reliance on musicianly camaraderie in favour of a more selfish approach. From now on his voice, his career, would always have to come first. He was going to go for it, somehow – perhaps assemble a group of more serious musicians. The punk days, for Hucknall, were effectively and finally over.

Wandering nervously into the Frantic Elevators' rehearsal room one day, he broke the news that he was leaving the band. Shell-shocked, Turner, Williams and especially Moss fell silent and departed for the comfort of the nearest tap room. Curiously enough, though surely fired more by indignant bravado than genuine self confidence, the band decided to continue without Hucknall. This lasted for about six months and was a curious period indeed, especially as Hucknall would continue to attend practice sessions. He would sit on the amps, casting faintly guilty glances as the band ran through their set with steadily decreasing vigour. Finally, Turner upped and left, although he continued to stay in the Hucknall/Rashman circle. That, needless to say, really was the end.

Elliot Rashman is, as previously mentioned, Machiavellian by nature. Although generally regarded as a 'nice guy', all his friends would agree that he would always seem to be operating on different levels with greater depth than the norm. As such, it was sometimes rather difficult to assess his motives. He owns a furiously active mind. Certainly, when he first saw Hucknall perform, the next few years of his life didn't just 'flash before him' as he stated. But he had started, semi-consciously perhaps, to plan a future for himself and Hucknall, perhaps even including subsidiary roles for his friends Tony Bowers and drummer Chris Joyce, another Durutti Column member. Even Hucknall, one tentatively states, wasn't fully operating on a par with Rashman.

Rashman is the kind of person who is interested in everything. Friends who visited his Hebden Bridge cottage would later state that they often felt overwhelmed by their host's 'endlessly enquiring mind'. One of his cottage guests, local photographer Steve Wright, spent many a weekend sojourn in that distinctive Rashman cottage.

'We'd go up on a Friday night,' said Wright, 'and proceed to get bombed out of our minds, just lying down, listening to music. It was a very hippyish atmosphere. We'd smoke and drink a lot. Elliot was very into trying out new experiences . . . in a healthy way. He just wanted to explore the possibilities . . . of just about everything. I've never known anyone who seemed so active, so enquiring, all the time. Even when in a state of intoxication, which we often were, Elliot would always be asking questions.

'I liked him a lot although I often regarded him as a hippy carpenter, which is what he was, really. A lot of things went down . . . yeah, he was definitely into a hippyish lifestyle. There were records and things scattered everywhere . . . it was like . . . you really were going back to basics . . . but it was good fun and Rashman was always a most lively and entertaining host. I remember thinking to myself that too many people tended to underestimate him. Once you got to know him you began to realise just how bright he was. Sometimes he would unveil some of his future plans. He really thought things out in depth. Even in the early days, when he would play initial Simply Red demos over and over again and would say to me, "How far do you think this will go?" I could tell that he wasn't going to fail, like so many prospective managers. Elliot was nothing, really, just a social sec – just an "ents man" . . . yet you always felt that he was at the start of a big journey.'

Rashman's interests, be they in vegetarian food or music or the occult, tended to provide him with a curiosity value. Even his car, a garish yellow, customised VW buggy, became a local talking point. People warmed to him or perhaps were intrigued by him.

Even when I was immersed rather stupidly in the role of ersatz manager of hopeless Manchester featherweight pop group, Secret Seven – ironically enough, a frivolous offshoot of the Distractions – I experienced Rashman's unnerving capacity to seem totally in control, even if in the reality known only to himself he was floundering along like the rest of us. I can remember him in the Mandela office, filled with hangers-on – Hucknall, Turner, Bowers, Joe Strong (who, like Hucknall, was a Poly DJ) – making a mess of things by offering Secret Seven an unreasonably good deal for a Freshers appearance while making a lesser offer for Stockport rock band, Syncopation. This little imbalance resulted in a drunken bawl out in the Hacienda dressing room between Rashman and Syncopation manager John Barratt. Turning to yours truly after Barratt had stormed off, Rashman simply shrugged and offered, 'I get that kind of shit all the time . . . John's a good guy, really . . . but he was wrong to blame me. It's a really hassle-intensive job this . . . it's not just a breeze . . . you've no idea of how much bloody arguing I have to get through . . . you've no idea at all.'

Rashman had a little more hassle on the night that the Secret Seven played the Mandela Building. Another mix up meant that the cheque for the band had to be sent via the agency rather than direct to the manager, i.e., me. It was a volatile end to a volatile evening which included one minor audience riot, a series of explosions at a nearby chemical factory and, across the road, the famous final gig of the Teardrop Explodes.

'I'm in the wrong job . . . maybe all this shit will come in handy one day . . . maybe,' he said, his pony tail flapping comically across his collar as he spun round and, in a mock camp walk, disappeared to the safety of his beloved office. It was this office that was to become the hub of the embryonic Simply Red empire. Hucknall would hang around endlessly chatting to Rashman, Joe Strong, Brian Turner, Tony Bowers, Penny Henry, even occasionally Bruce Mitchell, discussing possible band members, a band name even, and methods of prising demo money from record company A & R men. It was quite a hangout, but probably no different from any other social secretary's office. But if, during these early months, the very concept of Hucknall's future band would remain loose, hazy and far too reliant on penniless musicians with too many differing ideas, one thing would certainly crystallise. The friendship formed between Rashman and Hucknall, built on dreams really, became the true foundation of Simply Red.

Chapter 11
Ghost Shirt

In 1983, projecting and showcasing the career of a prospective solo singer, without the benefit of huge amounts of cash or influence, was a practical impossibility. The record companies were interested in Hucknall as a solo artist but if this interest was to go any further they would want to see Hucknall work as part of a unit, both in the studio and live. Rashman, for all his guile, couldn't avoid this paradox. In short, Hucknall needed a band.

At least this time the musicians could be, to a certain extent, hand picked. Rashman had enough quality musicians floating about hungry for a gig that it shouldn't be too difficult. But quite where the individual band members would stand should a recording contract emerge was never made clear. It did begin to dawn on Hucknall, however, that he would have to work within a reasonably stable unit once again. It was probably a little rushed, a little too easily formed, but a group was gathered together, of sorts.

The initial rehearsals of the as yet unnamed band went fairly well. A unit of sorts had begun to gel although there was the kind of confused musical undertone, typical of the problems one has to confront when a group of schooled musicians, each with distinct egos and aspirations set firmly in different directions, finally gets together and attempts to become 'a band'. The punk ethic, beautifully typified by the Frantic Elevators – all mates, learning, bonding, stumbling together – more often than not produced bands of a more interesting, if significantly less musically adept, nature. The very point of punk, then as now, was to create something of note regardless of musical value or longevity.

Once past that, and once the songwriter/singer has decided to take his songs to the limit, to the very peak of their potential, then he has no option other than to make a pact with himself and his work. The work must take absolute precedence. Mick Hucknall knew, back in 1983, that if the future was to be as successful as his dreams told him it would be, then a considerable amount of pain would have to be endured, partly by himself but mainly by the stream of people who would be left floundering by the wayside. It's a terrifying prospect but if Hucknall's talent really was as mighty as he truly believed, then his greatest ally, other than his manager, would be the music industry itself – an industry which thrived on a quite horrible winner-take-all hierarchy. Record companies are famous for their 'sifting system' and one of the major roles of any good A & R man would be to cunningly force an act to shed any dead wood, especially in times of industry recession where the most feared word in the world would be 'passenger'.

When a new act of genuine potential is discovered, the very first task of an A & R man is to separate mentally the wheat from the chaff. A plodding rhythm section, for example, might well be the most vociferous and ambitious part of a young band, but if the company decides the true talent lies with the singer then sooner or later that singer will be taken aside and the proverbial 'let's have a drink and a chat' would ensue.

Mick Hucknall had been around musicians for long enough to be fully aware of this situation. He was also more than weary of the chummy existentialism of a unit like the Frantic Elevators. He had already decided back in 1983 that if he ever managed to get some kind of snowball rolling again, then absolutely nothing would ever stand in his way. The problem is, of course, that it is impossible to admit this to the people one is attempting to seduce into some kind of band. Total honesty would be absurd. This is not how one forms a band capable of attracting the serious attentions of record companies. The paradox deepens at this point. The companies, at least in 1983, always wanted to see a fully developed working unit, before they would start to dismantle it and start again with the raw material. This is one reason why dole queue or bottom rung session musicians are, more often than not, completely paranoid. Pick any one of them – a sax player or drummer perhaps – and they would reel off tale after tale of missed chances, of in-band backbiting, of being unceremoniously dumped in favour of someone who, they would always tell you, 'Couldn't play for toffee'.

Furthermore, the only true currency that Mick Hucknall and Elliot Rashman could offer would be a kind of hazy hope that this ungainly meeting, in a practice room lined with crisp packets and beer cans, might just lead to something that would change their life. But as the practice sessions progressed, this man Hucknall began to show that he really did have a fabulous voice – maybe it would go somewhere. Rehearsals began to flow with comparative ease.

A new songwriting partnership had begun to flourish. Guitarist Dave Rowbotham had replaced Neil Moss, and Mick could often be heard speaking highly of the new Hucknall/ Rowbotham partnership. Although Rowbotham's style had rocky edges that must have worried the singer a little, Hucknall seemed more than willing to write the lyrics to Rowbotham's tunes and, in some cases, even incorporate Rowbotham's complete songs into the set. The rest of the band had lesser roles to play. It comprised bassist Tony Doyle (from Liverpool and a band called Lawnmower), drummer Chris Joyce (a close friend of Elliot's) and a keyboard player, from Todmorden, called Kate Crabtree. Kate was arguably the most talented and the one member of the band who was least affected by the lure of popstardom. A classically trained musician, she was far from enamoured of rock'n'roll and saw no glamour at all in trudging around in dirty Transit vans. At one point, after she had flitted in a pique of disinterest, Elliot travelled to her parents' home in Todmorden to plead for her return. Unfortunately, her father took an instant dislike to this pushy young would-be manager.

But as the songs began to gel in the rehearsal room, the band began to think about the possibilities of recording a

demo. The problem, as always, was one of finance. The measly
few pounds that Elliot could gather together would only
manage to sink the band into some subterranean eight-track
studio from which they would undoubtedly emerge with something that sounded as if it had been recorded in a canal. In
short, if Hucknall really wanted to show off his voice and his
part-written songs in their best light then, somehow, they
would have to book into a few cheap-rate night sessions in one
of Manchester's first-class studios – Strawberry perhaps, or
Revolution.

Dave Rowbotham, like most musicians, had connections. He
was a good friend of infamous record producer Martin Hannett. Hannett was a legendary Manchester figure, internationally famous for his hugely inspirational and innovative
work with Joy Division. Locally he was a god-like figure,
especially among the legions of knob twiddling small studio
engineers who all longed to emulate Hannett. They would
speak in awe of Hannett's legendary 'ear'. It was said he could
spend an entire session lying on his back in the Strawberry
Studios storeroom reading the *Beano* and only occasionally
emerging to make an adjustment to the mixing desk.

There were many such stories in circulation around
Manchester and, when coupled with the producer's tendency
towards reckless hedonism, the phrase 'tortured genius' would
most readily spring to mind. The reality, of course, was very
different. Hannett wasn't a genius at all. He was, however, an
extremely bright and likeable if obviously troubled man.
Nevertheless, his 'ear' extended beyond the mundane task of
finding the perfect drum sound. In his formative years he was
uncannily gifted in the art of seeking out the real talent, no
matter in which unlikely corners it might be hiding. He was
also gifted in the apparently complex art of squeezing genuinely emotive songs out of a twenty-four track recording
system. At the end of a Hannett session, the artist's initial feel
would not have been dismantled. And that is the ultimate
compliment.

Rowbotham told Rashman about his friendship with Hannett. What's more he suggested he might be able to persuade
Hannett to do something for them. Hannett had been working

extensively out of Strawberry Studios in Stockport. In many respects he was Strawberry's top client, often procuring important sessions for them. Hannett liked Strawberry. It was, for him, a mere taxi ride away. He understood the desk, felt perfectly at home in there and also enjoyed the fact that a hop across the street stood the Wellington pub. This is not as frivolous as it might sound. So many mid-session tensions – some of them involving recordings that would become regarded as classics – had been resolved in that rather dour lounge bar. The task of soothing the injured pride of some bass player, whose inadequacies had been blatantly displayed by a studio of Strawberry's quality, with a pint of bitter and a couple of fags was something that Hannett was curiously adept at. As Hannett would later state, 'I did most of my best work sitting in that pub.'

Peter Tattersall, then studio manager, had promised Hannett in repayment for the work the producer had brought in, a large bank full of studio time (albeit during hours of darkness). Knowing this, Dave Rowbotham took Rashman to meet Hannett who listened impassively as tales of the untried band's greatness unfolded. The meeting took place in Hannett's flat. The only other person present was Martin's then wife, Susan O'Hara. The deal they allegedly offered Hannett was simple and verbal. If Hannett took the band into the studio and recorded a full four tracks at no cost, then if these songs resulted in the band achieving some kind of deal, Hannett would produce a single at least.

It was, in truth, a loose agreement and Hannett was fully aware that, despite his reputation, most record company agreements would include a clause insisting that the band would have to engage the work of a highly skilled and professional producer, to be agreed by the company. That was a typical clause to cover the company just in case they had signed a bunch of duffers who were incapable of producing the goods in a top-level studio, as is often the case. This is not to say that Hannett wasn't capable of capturing the work of a Manchester light soul band and wrapping it in enough commercial sheen to make it a genuinely marketable product. He was, but to make any such agreement at such an early stage, based on nothing more than a handshake was, at best, naive on Hannett's behalf, at worst, downright lazy.

However, in July 1983, Hucknall's band went nameless into Strawberry Studios. Hannett did suggest a name for the band, but thankfully both Hucknall and Rashman winced noticeably when confronted with the name, 'Ghost Shirt'. It was a reasonably relaxed session, with many tiny ego clashes being fought over games of pool, a cup of coffee and a video run of the perennial studio favourite, the Comic Strip's Bad News Tour.

The result of three nights of hard work could be found on a four-track demo which sounded not dissimilar to many other demos made at Strawberry at that time. There was a distinctive Strawberry sound – rough edges, glossed over – which wasn't unattractive and certainly preferable to many of the alternatives. The problem was that record companies, venue managers and local press all became rather used to hearing mundane songs dressed up by the sheen of Strawberry sound. Hannett had, however, managed to lift Hucknall's voice above this sound. Although the songs were far from great, the voice, if only on occasion, soared majestically free from the backing. It has been said that this was the tape that re-alerted Seymour Stein to the possibilities of Hucknall's voice, his much quoted, 'I want the singer without a band', being evidence of his interest.

As for the songs, they varied from interesting to completely forgettable. The first track, *Hell From You* (music Rowbotham, lyrics Hucknall), bounces into action a little too energetically for its own good. When Hucknall's vocals surge in (a little late, as it happens, but *just* in time to prevent the A & R man's finger from flicking the 'off' switch) they effectively carry the song out of its rock-based mundanity.

The lyrics, in accordance with the melody, are fairly dull: 'Had enough of the hell from you . . . All the peasants climb back on board . . . Cheerful misery takes the overload . . . No hell from you, no postcards or letters . . . No hell from you, no toenails or fingers . . .!' Not the most overtly inspiring of Hucknall lyrics and somewhat feeble when unfairly compared, as everything new and Mancunian was at the time, to the rising sloganeering talents of Morrissey. Hucknall, however, was not too concerned with the earnestness of his Mancunian counterpart. His voice alone, he thought, would be capable of turning heads. He may well have been right.

The second track, *All Through The Day*, combined minimalist lyrics with an R'n'B feel, the most memorable being, 'Eye eye eye yeye eye eye eye yay yay yeahhhhh'. Perhaps this hinted that the singer was prepared to test his voice to unusual effect with a standard R'n'B tune, heavily reminiscent of the Frantic Elevators. Dave Rowbotham remarked at the time that the song carried the ghost of Neil Moss.

Take A Look was of far more interest and surely only a lack of objectivity prevented the band from placing it at the top of the demo. It was a pretty tune with a maudlin feel, complete with a mid-song instrumental break combining a bass and guitar interplay, a curious nod towards New Order in one of their occasional reflective moods. The song's slow pace perfectly suited Mick's impassioned vocals. 'I wonder what I've done wroooong,' he sang, the line towering over the more prophetic, 'An echo still of things to come.' *Take A Look* displayed considerable and rare potential. It was, however, rather underplayed by Hucknall – perhaps because the song, both music *and* lyrics, was entirely the work of Dave Rowbotham.

The final song of the demo, *Make Me Feel Good*, was a disappointing and probably unintentional echo of the Doors classic, *Hello, I Love You*. Hucknall's vocal power was brilliantly displayed by the repetition of the adamant line, 'I believe in principles.'

It is interesting to note that this initial Simply Red line up became lost in the misty memories of the band's fluctuating membership. Even in profoundly investigative articles, messrs Rowbotham, Doyle and Crabtree would fail to surface. The same could most definitely be said of Hannett who had effectively provided the starting blocks for so many bands, most of whom promptly forgot about him after discovering success elsewhere. Rashman never forgot though and was reportedly mightily relieved when an impoverished Hannett turned up at his office, as Christmas 1989 approached, offering to sell back the masters of this session. An agreement was struck, leaving Hannett gratefully clutching a £1,000 cheque.

Chapter 12
Red and the Dancing Dead

The Mancunians busked beneath the neon of Montmartre back in 1977. There were two of them at first, called Simon and Neil. The intention had been to travel around the world but the allure of Parisian delights proved too much. Soon they were joined by a third Mancunian, an old school friend called Mog.

Returning to Manchester, full of tales, the three saw the Clash at Belle Vue's Elizabethan Suite. For them it proved to be a turning point, every bit as poignant as the Sex Pistols at the Lesser Free Trade Hall had been for so many other musicians back in 1976. Cornily, the next day they went out and bought electric guitars and a band of sorts was formed. Called the Smirks, they spent the next two years attempting, and failing drastically, to shake off the unfortunate and thoroughly undeserved tag of 'power pop'. The truth was that Simon, the most prolific and dominant songwriter, was gifted in the old-fashioned way, and could instigate the odd good tune. This ability belied the tiny local following and, after a couple of numbing twists of fate, they were signed to the unlikely Beserkley label, the West Coast home of Jonathon Richman. This somewhat fairytale ascendancy soon soured, however, when Beserkley, weakened by the appalling fact that the general public did not fall for Richman's sarcastic tweeness, ran out of money. This left a mythical Smirks album locked in the vaults and the band stunned, disillusioned, penniless and once again back in Manchester. Nevertheless they fought on, releasing three spirited EPs (most notably the excellent *American Patriots*) before eventually amalgamating with straggling remains of Manchester anarcho-lunatic band, Alberto Y Los Trios Paranoias, to form one strangely incoherent unit, the Charlie Parkers.

When the Albertos – who had always swerved unsteadily between the two incompatible extremes of Pythonesque comedy and straightforward rock – re-formed to take up residence in New York and feature in a short television series, they asked Mog from the Smirks to replace their original bassist, Tony Bowers. Not surprisingly, the talented Bowers was hardly ecstatic about missing out on the journey Stateside.

Mog spent two years with the Albertos. Back in England, their relative fame meant that they could command decent fees on the college circuit. What they couldn't command, however, was decent-sized audiences. Slowly, steadily and not without considerable resistance from this hard-working and by now musicianly unit, they faded from public view.

Nevertheless, from his work with the Albertos, Mog had managed to gain himself a much-prized Equity card. Before opting for music he had been involved in youth theatre, so he naturally decided to shop around and put his card to good use – or at least try. At this point, and just as Mog's aspirations were beginning to crumble, fate intervened. Attending an Undertones gig at the Hacienda in 1983, Mog ran into the casting director for 'Brookside' who he had known from youth theatre. Motivated by desperation, he cheekily asked for some 'extra' work. To his amazement, the cliché, 'I've got just the perfect part for you', solidified into an audition and then immediately into a two-episode part. This soon swelled to twelves episodes. Mog famously brought a touch of hip glamour to 'Brookside', wearing leather jackets, reading the *NME* and leading the dull, naive Gordon Collins astray, ironically into the dubious world of local pop music. It would end in tears when Mog's precocious character was head-butted by Damon Grant.

For the first time in his career Mog felt the lovely pressure of fame, albeit of a minor soap celeb variety. He also found himself afloat in the readies, earning an unprecedented £600 a week from his 'Brookside' stint. Not surprisingly, in the anti-climactic void which followed, Mog decided to try for an agent and opted for a precarious acting career against his true love, music. His double bass would remain unused and alone in the hallway.

By Christmas 1983, the Dave Rowbotham/Mick Hucknall band had begun to disintegrate in predictable fashion. This was despite considerable record company interest, most specifically from a young A & R man called Saul Galpern who was inexplicably excited by Hannett's Strawberry demos. Rowbotham had never really taken to Rashman or his meticulous method of management (his openly sarcastic nickname for Rashman was 'Harry Paranoid, top rock manager'). The situation had grown intolerable and Rowbotham found himself replaced by another guitarist, Dave Fryman. It had not been easy to lure the talents of Fryman into the band. After hearing the Strawberry demos he had pronounced, 'No way are this bunch ever going to get anywhere.' Nevertheless, Fryman soon became an integral part of the band, slotting neatly and to all intents and purposes amiably next to Hucknall's dominant ego.

Musically, it was a strange period for Hucknall. The soul overtones of the first band, Ghost Shirt if you like, had been temporarily put on a back burner, in favour of a rockabilly approach. Hucknall, sharing a flat in Hulme with DJ Joe Strong at the time (Hucknall seemed to move mysteriously about once every two months, living with Strong at one point, and then Rashman, and then on Burton Road, West Didsbury, and back to Hulme and over to Whalley Range, etc.) had been exposing his ears to unhealthy amounts of Gene Vincent. A surge into rockabilly seemed imminent. With this in mind, he asked Rashman if he knew anyone who played double bass. Rashman naturally thought of Mog, and politely asked the ex-'Brookside' character if he'd like to meet Mick at one of the Black Rhythms evenings at Manchester Poly.

It was – once again, like Eagle, like Rashman – a meeting of minds. As soon as Mog had glimpsed Hucknall's record collection, a bewildering and colourful mass of record spines, spanning the living room in the Hulme flat, then that was it. They talked and worked. The band, Mog noted, was hardly together at all. The Hannett demo was now a memory; to this day it remains unheard by Mog) and the band, Dave Fryman, Eddie Sherwood and a departing bassist called Pete, seemed incapable of sustaining and building upon A & R interest.

Mog's only memory of Hucknall, prior to that time, had been back at Tony Davidson's rehearsal units when he saw the Frantic Elevators comically scampering around and trying to blag a taxi ride to take them to a gig at Eric's. He had little idea, until he wandered into that Hulme flat, just how magnificent that Hucknall voice could be. At first, however, he was reticent. Fryman had openly expressed doubt about Rashman's endless tales of A & R interest and frankly even the stories of Seymour Stein seemed dubious to say the least. Furthermore, Rashman – who was pleading with Mog at one point – could offer little in the way of financial recompense. It was all just the usual hot air. Even for a natural musician who was not only quite stunned by Hucknall's voice but also seemed to be sinking into a deep friendship with the fiery singer, the prospect of giving up his acting aspirations, his stab at further fame, and falling back on to the dole queue hardly seemed compelling.

Nevertheless, as rehearsals progressed, Mog became more and more the band's linchpin – though Fryman would dispute this point – and it soon became apparent that this band might just have some kind of future. Mog admired above all else Hucknall's vision. He knew other great singers – the downbeat rock and jazz venues of Manchester were teeming with them – but he had never before worked with someone who seemed to know exactly what he wanted, and all the time.

'I soon realised that Hucknall was an arrogant bastard,' stated Mog, 'but in a strange way, I even respected him for that. His arrogance seemed to be justified. It was obvious that he was too good to be in such a lowly situation.'

Rehearsals began in the Hulme flat and then in Burton Road and finally, more sensibly, at the Poly. After his first rehearsal Mog brought Ojo into the band. Ojo was an unusual character with whom Mog had played in an equally unusual band, Kid Kharki and the Kallamojos down at the Lamplight in Chorlton. Mog's influence on the band was blossoming magnificently, and he even brought in Neil from the Smirks, if only for a short while. Curiously, Tony Bowers, the old bassist from the Albertos and a close friend of Rashman's, joined the band on sax before being swiftly sacked. Unknown to the record companies, this band was obviously in a serious state of flux.

The band's first gig took place at the Poly. Using the name World Service, they supported a frankly unimpressed Alexei Sayle who would later remark, 'That band aren't going anywhere. The singer has a terrible voice . . . and his hair's all funny.'

It was about this time that Mick starting calling himself Red – in a fit of pure affectation according to one ex-band member – and the band name, which seemed to change daily, settled for a while on Red and the Dancing Dead. Under this ungainly monicker they supported Billy Bragg, also at the Poly. At the Band On The Wall, a nostalgic gig for Hucknall, they used the name Just Red, which set more than one alarm bell ringing in the justifiably suspicious minds of the band members. Finally, at the Manhattan Sound – a Manchester city-centre gay venue which had been used most effectively for mid-week local band events, and by Sade, who performed around the same time – they settled on the name Simply Red. It was a name that nobody, Hucknall and Rashman included, really expected to stick. After all, could anything sound more 'wimpy'? Mog, in particular, was nervous about the name. The vision he had for the band, which seemed to concur with Hucknall's, was for a hard-edged funk unit, a groove band capable of storming sweatily through no-holds-barred sets in hot, smoky venues. Somehow, the name Simply Red just didn't seem to fit.

By this time, Mog and Hucknall had become extremely close friends more than willing to head off on hedonistic jaunts into town. After rehearsing on Mondays, for instance, they would hang out together down at the Venue on Whitworth Street where DJ Hewan Clarke would run a jazz disco. Although sparsely attended, it was a perfect place to sink slowly into intoxication, listen to great jazz and plan their future until

2a.m. when they would stagger back to Hulme, or catch a taxi to Mog's flat in Chorlton.

Strumming acoustic guitars, mostly absurdly, the pair would work on songs in Mog's digs. Fryman would contribute equal input, though in different rehearsals. This was obviously a curiously disparate band. The songs would then be put through rigorous full band rehearsals before emerging in a reasonably polished form. At the heart of the set would lie *Every Bit Of Me*, *Red Box*, *No Direction*, *So Green*, and later, *Holding Back The Years* and *Money's Too Tight To Mention*. To loosen up, they would launch into Prince's *1999* during which the band would fall into a shouting break, later to resurface in *Come To My Aid*. For encores they loved to play the Undertones' *Teenage Kicks*. This latter song perhaps clearly stated the fact that the Simply Red of 1984 were a far harder, gutsier proposition than what was to come.

This can be proven by a swift listen to a tape of one of the band's rehearsals at that time. It is fascinating to note the staggering improvement in the quality of both musicianship and songwriting since the Hannett demo. In short, the tape now stands as a harder, gutsier version of *Picture Book*, complete with a superb Joe Gibbs-style dub break on that particular track. Another song, *Sad Old Red*, sounds like the kind of jazz one would expect to hear busked heartily on a Parisian night. *No Direction* is solid funk, complete with the distinctive Hucknall growl that survived until the first album. In short, the practice session tape is proof that the Simply Red of the *Picture Book* era had been working in a harder format a good eighteen months before the album's release, and before any changes in personnel. On another level, I must add that I find the tape infinitely preferable to *Picture Book*, but that's only because I love to hear Hucknall screaming, 'Any chance of lager?' in between songs.

'The fact is that both Mick and me were Manchester punks,' stated Mog. 'And we wanted to reflect this in the band.' The rockabilly leanings had long since been forgotten and the search was on to find an acceptable brass section. As it happened this wasn't such a tall order. The brass trio led by Royal Northern College of Music student, Tim Kellet, had attached themselves to a number of bands around town, from notables like Durutti Column (Kellet is heavily featured on Durutti Column's finest album, the extra-long live in Japan platter, *Domo Arigato*) to little-known temporary outfits like Blast of Defiance (see Chapter 14 Life With The Reds).

Fritz McIntyre, also from the esteemed Royal Northern College of Music, came in on keyboards, promptly sat down and communicated little with the band. This procuring of talent from academia was obviously a result of Hucknall's new-found thirst for quality. That said, McIntyre was actually recommended, not by any high-ranking lecturer, but by a Polytechnic bouncer. An enormous and precious talent, McIntyre preferred, and still does, to allow his musicianship to speak for him. Even though he kept his head down, avoiding the often thunderous ego clashes, McIntyre's addition seems to have been welcomed from all quarters. His inclusion would ultimately become Hucknall's finest and most rewarding decision.

Finally, in September 1984, Rashman and Hucknall proclaimed most emphatically that Simply Red was, and would always be 'a band'.

Cover versions would pin down the set and the oddest of all these would be a stunningly poignant and soulful version of the beautiful Talking Heads song, *Heaven*. Hucknall had initially fallen in love with the song back in 1979 after buying Talking Heads' seminal bedsit album, *Fear of Music* (the kind of album that Factory Records always wanted to release and never quite found the talent, despite A Certain Ratio). Hucknall would take the album around to Mog's flat, more for inspiration than emulation. When the pair began slicing through *Heaven*, and the band later added a soft groove, Hucknall expressed grave doubts.

'We'll just never get away with doing that,' he announced. 'It would be bad for our image and everything.' Mog and Fryman convinced him otherwise, and even the eternally paranoid Rashman could soon see no reason why a Simply Red set should not be enhanced by what was turning into a great working of a great song (which should have eventually become a single, but never did).

Although the Simply Red of late 1984, who had begun to attract serious A & R attention, seemed to be very much a band in total control, there was still much confusion and a certain amount of acrimony within their ranks.

'Elliot,' stated Mog, 'had this knack of instilling bitchiness and paranoia within the band. He would deliberately wind musicians up, play on their egos. Or he would simply ignore them. He would also have favourites . . . that is, apart from Mick who he clearly adored. Mick was like the son he didn't have . . . But he also seemed to make you a favourite when you first joined. I'll never forget my first few months. It was all, "Oh did you see Mog last night . . . he was wonderful." And then the next thing he would be moving your mike stand to the back of the stage and asking you not to move around too much, not to steal the show from Mick, basically.'

The band had huge problems with image. Being musicians and, more importantly, being on the dole – apart from David Fryman, who was a teacher – they simply could not afford to dress to the standard demanded by Rashman.

'Look Elliot,' came the constant jibe, 'give us a grand and we'll definitely look the part.' It was a constant worry. Fryman and Mog in particular found themselves regularly incensed by Rashman's meticulous views on image.

'We'd have terrible arguments about things that simply didn't matter,' stated Mog. 'Elliot was always doing that . . . sometimes we thought he was just doing it to wind us up. He'd pick on something we would be wearing and turn it into a huge issue. In some ways he certainly had a point, but he had absolutely no idea about tact . . . he didn't know how to handle people.'

Such arguments were not confined to image. The huge spectre of publishing, which darkens the friendships of every band, successful or hopeful, descended with force. It settled, of course, on the method of songwriting. Hucknall would almost always be the one to approach the band with the germ of an idea. Fryman and Mog would then kick it around and slowly the rest of the band would be introduced. It was a good system, but the two secondary members soon began to think that they were not getting their fair share of credit for songwriting.

Mog in particular had always been associated with bands who used a Utopian approach to songwriting. In the Smirks, the two main songwriters received a third each, while Mog and the drummer received a third between them. In the Albertos it had been a simple six-way split.

But there was more, they agreed, to songwriting than simply coming up with the idea. For a start, just being there was to make a valuable contribution. As Mog later stated, 'If you put in a year's rehearsal, on no money at all, and you polish the songs that would one day fill a huge-selling album, then once that money was split up, you would surely deserve something?'

Mog and Fryman went to see Elliot who had been stating that the songwriter would be Hucknall and only Hucknall. It was a simplistic approach to an incredibly complex argument, and an argument that is destined to forever ruin friendships between musicians. They demanded a cut in the royalties. The argument was a hefty one, verging on screaming. What's more, it was left to simmer rather than to be resolved. By the time the autumn of 1984 had arrived, and with the country's A & R men honing in with intent, Simply Red were falling apart at the seams. The practice room bonhomie would be shallow. Below the surface lay a swell of bitterness.

Hucknall and Rashman had decided to form a production company, sign the band to this company and then sign to a record company. It was, as they would often inform the bemused musicians, a logical arrangement.

'All the time,' stated Mog, 'Elliot would assure us that this was just standard practice . . . that Simply Red were very much a band. I don't really harbour any bitterness . . . none at all, but I can quite categorically state that Elliot and Mick never had any intention of allowing Simply Red, in all but appearance, to be anything like a band.'

Simply Red were in a strange position. Elliot had started to play the A & R game quite brilliantly, but the more that record company interest grew and bigger and bigger figures were being bandied about, the more the pettiness and arguments would rise to the surface. At one stage it seemed that the whole thing would just explode, leaving nothing but a totally confused band watching the record company A & R men scurrying away to seek out the next set of suckers. Mog, for instance, was banned from displaying his CND sticker on his bass. When he challenged this decision he was told that it might harm the band's attempts to get into the USA. Mog thought this indicated a terrible streak of paranoia if not downright hypocrisy. Rashman thought it to be simple common sense.

The gigs, however, were ecstatically successful. Legend has it that at University of London Union the vulturous A & R men were scrambling in through the toilet windows and, more importantly, at the Tropicana disco in Manchester – dealt with elsewhere in this book – Rashman had to lock the band in the dressing room while a signature-seeking scout hammered on the door. This is the stuff of mythology and it can be clearly stated that every rock manager in the country with an unsigned act on his hands was, at that point, insanely jealous of the Elliot Rashman set up.

Absurdly, and probably in an affectionate nod back to Rashman's hippy idyll, Simply Red played at Hebden Bridge Trade and Labour Club – not a gig normally associated with a band striving for an image of elegance and taste.

At Sheffield Leadmill things really came to a head. The basic argument hinged around Mog's waistcoat. 'You must *not* wear *that* thing onstage,' screamed Rashman, and as the ensuing row became louder, Mog's mike stand was again placed at the rear of the stage. This actually contradicted the band's basic notion of its onstage image. Hucknall, Fryman and Mog had all been in agreement; Simply Red would assume the dynamic three-man front line, as perfected by their punk heroes, the Clash. But suddenly, things seemed to be changing.

Despite the arguments, Rashman and Hucknall assured Mog that he would remain in the band, whatever happened next. David Fryman, however, did not have cause to feel so secure. Rashman and Hucknall had already attempted to sack him, on the grounds that they thought he should no longer be pursuing his teaching career. Fryman couldn't offer the degree of commitment that Rashman demanded, a fact that would continually incense Rashman and Hucknall. Their intolerance of Fryman's double life was, perhaps understandable if not wholly realistic. At this point, neither Rashman nor Hucknall had any doubts whatsoever about what was about to happen. They were, quite simply, 100 per cent dedicated and couldn't understand how anyone else who was involved could approach it in a different manner.

Once again, it was Mog who convinced them that Fryman had to live in the real world and that there was nothing wrong with him hedging his bets. Fryman, for a while, remained in the band. Drummer Eddie Sherwood, however, was jettisoned with haste. Strangely, it was Mog who instigated Sherwood's departure. 'I suppose I'm the man who invented sacking within Simply Red,' he stated, 'which isn't something I'm proud of, but I just couldn't cope with Sherwood's time-keeping anymore.'

Ironically enough, it was at the Sheffield Leadmill gig that Mog asked Hucknall to sack Sherwood. Following this, Simply Red tried different drummers. At a meeting attended by Rashman, Hucknall and Mog, Chris Joyce – who, of course had been the sticksman in Dave Rowbotham's version of the band – was suggested by Rashman. Hucknall wasn't keen and Mog uttered a defiant, 'There's no way I'll play in the same band as Chris Joyce.'

Mog later came to believe, although it would be impossible to prove, that this was the point when a plot was hatched to bring not only Chris Joyce into the band on drums, but also Tony Bowers on bass, effectively to replace Mog. As Christmas 1984 dawned, something strange began to happen within the cramped confines of Mog's flat. The telephone, which had for so long been alive, in cartoon fashion, with endless frantic calls from Rashman, fell into eerie silence. Mog knew what was about to happen. Three weeks later, Hucknall and Rashman arrived at the flat to tell Mog that his services were no longer required. A pay off – quite generous if one was to look at the state of the Simply Red bank account at that point – of £1,000 was agreed. But as Mog later stated, '£1,000 for a full year's intensive work, with no chance of any publishing claim . . . is that not an insult?'

There are of course two ways of looking at it. There is no doubt that Rashman and Hucknall, having reached their decision, did try to do the right thing, even incurring the wrath of their bank manager in the process. On the other hand, the first Simply Red album did evolve into one of the classic records of the eighties, and as Mog states, 'that record is littered with my bass lines . . . but it's more than that, it's the work that me and Dave in particular put in during the course of that year . . . that's what still rankles. But I'm not bitter, I'm really not. To tell the truth, I think that Mick and Elliot were correct to sack me, simply because the vision they had for the band no longer squared with my ideas. That is fair enough . . . but it was done in what I consider to be an underhand manner. I actually rang Andy Dodd [the Jazz North West promoter who would soon team together with Rashman to form the Simply Red management company, So What Arts] who was living in the same house as Tony Bowers at the time, to tell him that I had been sacked . . . and the truth is, they both seemed to know about it already.'

Later, Mog would be understandably incensed reading in an article in *Q* magazine that he had been jettisoned because of incompetence. Storming into the Whitworth Street office of So What Arts and threatening to smash the furniture, he was appeased by Rashman who explained that Hucknall's statement had been out of context.

It was a messy period, but practically over. The band was almost ready to sign, their personnel: Hucknall, Fryman, Bowers, Joyce, McIntyre and Kellet. Soon after signing Dave Fryman would be predictably ousted, cruelly perhaps, with one foot over the winning line.

Elliot Rashman and Andy Dodd, despite their high profiles in the Manchester music scene, could not be reasonably expected to finance the gelling and honing of a killer soul band. They took tapes of Hucknall to their bank manager, Colin Cook, and nervously played them to him, while Cook tapped his feet appreciatively and attempted to look impressed. The truth is, although knowing little about the music business, Cook *was* impressed. Unlike much of the radio noise which so irritated him every time he accidentally flicked on to Radio One, this stuff sounded well, like real music, real songs sung by a real singer. Cook reasoned that, if a self-confessed musical Philistine like himself could appreciate it, then so could thousands of others. Cook, based at Salford's Chapel Street branch of the Royal Bank of Scotland, would use his experience with Simply Red to handle the accounts of Manchester band James and curiously enough Roger Eagle. But the music on Rashman's tape at that first, crucial meeting proved ironic, to say the least. It was the first, rough mix of *Money's Too Tight To Mention*. Adoring the irony, Cook agreed to help the band.

Chapter 13
Picture Book

Simon Potts, head of Elektra UK in 1985, had taken the 'difficult' route to his precarious position of prominence in the record industry. His tenuous links with Manchester had begun in the mid-seventies when, like most on-the-road record company reps, he would spend time sitting on the counter chatting to fellow reps at the city's hilariously anarchic Virgin Records store on Lever Street. Most of Manchester's popstars and peripheral luminaries of the seventies and eighties, including Hucknall, spent many an hour within the tiny but congenial confines of that shop. It was more of a club than record shop, complete with community notice board and sofas intended for listening, smoking and swapping bitchy underground gossip. It was a shop in which things happened and scenes formed though rarely, one would suspect, would it be to the benefit of Virgin Records.

Potts moved on and became the car sales rep for Anchor Records. Later, while working for Arista, his eccentric purchase of an old shack just outside Marple, Cheshire, became semi-legendary when he sold the same shack to Aztec Camera's Roddy Frame who used it as an inspirational retreat from life in general and the music business in particular. Whatever glamour there was to be had from working in the music business seemed nothing more than a well-deserved perk to a man who worked on the 'front line', plugging the likes of the Beat and the Thompson Twins to bored Radio One DJs. Potts graduated into A & R, and most successfully too. One can even forgive him for inflicting the Stray Cats on an unsuspecting and undeserving world.

He left Arista to kickstart Elektra UK, a new label funded by money from the American WEA corporation. His brief was simple – to sign UK acts to a UK base. As far as the nature of the signings was concerned, Simon Potts had a carte blanche. His most important signing, naturally, would be his first. The first act on any label helps define the nature and scope of the label. More importantly, perhaps, it displays its commercial possibilities and begins to establish a reputation.

Potts had a tiny staff. His main A & R man was Saul Galpern. The arrangement was simple. Galpern would spend his days in classic A & R style, travelling the country dressed in black Levis and staying in four-star hotels, attending gigs and accepting drinks from overtly hopeful band managers who still believed the myth that A & R men were benevolent godsends who were employed solely to shower unoriginal no-hope rock saps with copious amounts of money.

Galpern was bright and, although eventually dismissing the songs on Simply Red's Strawberry demo and quite rightly regarding the musicianship as naive, he could not dismiss the possibilities of *that* voice. Seymour Stein, the first powerful music industry man to latch on to Hucknall, was not stupid. This lad Red could go far, with the right backing.

The A & R department at Elektra UK, although not yet a label as such, was typically awash with what the record industry cynically refers to as 'the idiot tapes'. They were a ballast of mediocrity. Even the odd gem would be dismissed by Potts who knew too well the enormity of his task – to seek out an act worthy of launching Elektra UK. It would have to be a very special act indeed. Also, if he was to really make his mark, it would need to be an act that already had most of the other major labels sniffing around. He had sensed the possibilities of the Hucknall voice and was even reservedly impressed with Rashman, even though that wouldn't particularly matter. If need be, Rashman could be dealt with later on.

Rashman's operation had shifted from the Poly office to a house in Didsbury that duplicated the Hebden Bridge abode. Far from being neat, ordered, hi-tech, elegant and new age, as would soon suit the Rashman image, it was a house simply swimming in the discarded scatterings of a burgeoning rock-biz lifestyle (as John Barratt exclaimed, the Didsbury house was in complete chaos, with record sleeves and half-opened letters lying everywhere, ashtrays overflowing with fag ends, grubby tea mugs, half-read copies of the music press. It was like the flat in 'The Young Ones', a studentish nightmare).

Standing in the canteen of the Mandela Building, Elliot Rashman, resplendent in black, failed to suppress a smile of satisfaction. Creating an A & R buzz and exaggerating it beyond belief had been almost too easy for him. It was based on the interest of Seymour Stein from Sire – a fact which had alerted just about everybody. A deal with Warners had, upon falling through, merely increased the buzz. All Rashman had to do was sit back and wait for the telephone to begin ringing, and so it had. The one thing needed to intensify this interest was, naturally, a showcase evening. It would have to be carefully organised, though.

The buzz in Manchester was such that, with a little prodding of the local media and the bribing of a good few friends, a sizeable audience could at least be relied upon to attend. Rashman arranged to promote a gig in association with Manchester's esteemed listings magazine, *City Life*. This would not only ensure exposure by way of posters and advertisements in the magazine, but also cement the band's image with the magazine's trendy, largely twentysomething readership. It was a clever move for both band and magazine because at the time they seemed quite effortlessly suited to each other.

The gig wasn't to take place at a traditional band venue at all. It would happen in an historic plastic palmtree nightclub which had been an integral part of the city's stag and hen party scene throughout the sixties. (DJs Dave Lee Travis and Jimmy Savile both had extremely strong connections with the club.) It could be argued that in its heyday the club, called the Tropicana, had been the city's centre for Tamla and Philly. The image that most readily springs to mind is of a white-trousered, spearpoint-collared soul poser arriving in a white Ford Capri and dancing the night away to the sounds of Barry White. It was that sort of club.

'Are you coming to the gig tonight?' Rashman asked band manager John Barratt who had been, as always, pestering Rashman for a gig. Rashman continued, 'Half the British record industry will be there . . . I'm telling you . . . the buzz is deafening . . . I think I know where we are going to sign, though.'

On the night of the Tropicana date, Simon Potts rang record promoter and Piccadilly Records disc jockey, Tony Michaelides, at his house in Cheadle Hulme. The pair had been friends, colleagues and rivals since the days spent in the Virgin Records store. They had worked together at Anchor, parting company when Potts opted for a stint at Arista and Michaelides worked for Island. They had a simple, agreeable arrangement. Whenever Michaelides wanted to stop over in London, he would stay at Potts' place and when Potts came to Manchester to see a band, Tony Michaelides' house (called The Edge after the U2 guitarist) would be his natural port of call. More often than not, the two of them would travel together to the gigs. Needless to say, as A & R men from all companies tend to flock together to catch some new hotly tipped act, Potts and Michaelides had seen most of Britain's major pop artists in various stages of infancy in smoke-blackened venues.

On this particular occasion, Michaelides was reluctant to venture out. He had just returned from London and, feeling shattered, did not relish the prospect of seeing yet another dodgy group in yet another dodgy venue.

'Look, you go,' he told Potts. 'I'll just stay in, watch television and maybe we'll have a chat when you return.' But something in Potts' voice convinced him otherwise. It wasn't often that Potts would seem so hysterical about a new unsigned act. Michaelides, although he had heard about Simply Red, hadn't paid too much attention to the local hype. He presented his own show on Piccadilly Radio which specialised in alternative and local bands, but his programme was predominantly rock oriented, and he was unsure about how some upstart young soul band would fit in. He knew Elliot Rashman, though, from the time that U2 had sold out at the Poly and Michaelides, who worked closely with the then precocious Irish rockers, had attempted to persuade the social sec to add a further 200 names to the guest list.

Dubious and cursing his inability to resist the enthusiasm of his friend, Michaelides set off with Potts for the date at the Tropicana. *City Life* editor Andy Spinoza manned the door and inside the scene was nothing short of surreal. Surely, thought Michaelides, every A & R man in London was there and most of them spent the night paying lip service to Potts.

'I had never seen so many A & R men in one place,' he later said. Needless to say Rashman, safe in the knowledge that his lunchtime prediction had come true, remained locked away in the dressing room – as did the band. The set was arguably Hucknall's finest performance to date. The band had started to gel. In particular, *Open Up The Red Box* and *No Direction* glistened like funky jewellery from a set full of intriguing hooklines. Strangely enough the plastic palmtree ambience, which had made the venue so impossible as a rock gig, seemed perfectly suited to the band's soul pretensions.

Nobody had any doubt that night that Simply Red would sign. The only question which remained was to whom? The dressing room door remained firmly, enigmatically shut. As a thousand aspiring rock band managers will tell you, it is not easy to attract the A & R hordes and court them until the desire reaches fever pitch. Mostly they all come, sulk at the bar, go away and refuse to answer your phone calls. But Rashman had played the system superbly. He could have walked out and spoken very seriously to at least five companies that night. The representatives from a couple of them had to be physically restrained from banging down the dressing room door. Rashman could have waited a week, played one off against another and secured a deal with a simply staggering advance. That was what everyone expected would happen. Everyone, that is, except Simon Potts and Saul Galpern.

Rashman had met Potts and had liked him. He had, by this time, met most of the other top A & R men as well and had liked most of them, too. However, they had tended to talk in terms of big money advances and Potts didn't seem to be like that at all. He was level-headed. He had spoken openly, honestly, about his plans for Elektra UK. He had also admitted that a huge advance would be out of the question.

However, having commanded the full attention of Rashman he spoke of strange concepts like 'artist development'. He introduced Rashman to Neil Ferris at Ferret and Spanner promotions who would, if an agreement were to be made, plug the band. He mapped out the entire role the label would play even to the extent of suggesting a possible producer. He had gone easy on the bullshit and hard on fact. Hucknall liked him, too. Elektra UK was exactly the label that Simply Red needed. What's more – and Rashman knew this – as first signing the band would not have to compete with half a dozen other signed but unproven acts, all screaming for the attention of their own record company.

The vast majority of record deals end in bitter disappointment on the bands' part as they find themselves dropped in a state of part development and powerless to attract the attentions of another company. Elektra, surely, would have to give the band a fair crack of the whip. Why then should Simply Red go to CBS or EMI?

The signing, when it finally happened, triggered a surfable wave of rumour in and around Manchester. 'Did you know,' I remember one person earnestly telling me, 'that Elektra have signed that Red bloke for one million pounds?'

They hadn't. The actual figure, though of course broken into portions and guarded by record company options, was £60,000. Not a huge amount as it happens, but the Elektra set up did seem like the perfect vehicle for the band – as long as it didn't implode, as it soon did. What's more, they were the first real company to treat Simply Red as a full band, which was exactly what Hucknall and Rashman now desired. Other companies had dithered about, treating the band, as Chris Joyce would later describe, 'Like a load of kids. The A & R men seemed to think that we didn't know what we were doing. They would constantly say that the voice was strong but the material was weak. We, the band, found that pretty insulting. Elektra seemed to have a different attitude.'

The band were sent to Holland to start recording their first album within two weeks of signing. Once again the bitching started. Who, after all, did Simply Red think they were? Off to record in Holland? What was wrong with Manchester studios, or London even? The answer was quite dull. The assigned producer, American Stuart Levine, couldn't get a work permit for Britain. The only strange element in the initial deal was the mutual agreement that Simply Red wouldn't record any demos. The only time any song surfaced on tape, prior to the actual full-scale recording, was on a Walkman placed in the corner of the rehearsal room.

Stuart Levine had first seen the band live in London and again in Leicester while taking a refresher trip to England, and became suitably entranced by the possibilities of the sound and the undeniable magic of the singer.

Levine's credentials were impressive to anyone with the remotest interest in soul music. Hucknall and the chaps afforded him almost god-like status. After all, this man had worked extensively with the Crusaders, B.B. King and Womack and Womack. But Levine had tired of working in America where, ironically, his legacy tended to drag him down. Most companies, terrified by the possibility of unlucrative innovation, simply wanted him to regurgitate old American acts. He wanted to work if not in Britain then with British acts. He was seeking freshness, vivacity, a youthful, perhaps more naive approach. In short he wanted something which he could take, almost from a raw state and mould it into something special. The clinch came when he told Hucknall that he had worked on Sly Stone's *Ain't But The One Way*. That did it. Hucknall flipped. It was for him, and therefore the rest of the band, the ultimate name drop. Sly Stone was regarded with almost unparalleled reverence within the ranks of Simply Red. Hucknall sensed that a classic artist/producer relationship was in the process of forming.

Hucknall, as ever, carried his present influence around with him inside his ever-present Sony Walkman. Levine was impressed by the singer's absolute immersion in music. This wasn't, he noted, just another spotty kid making a play for stardom. This was a real musician. And let's be honest, the contents of Hucknall's constantly revolving cassette tape at that moment would have impressed anyone interested in black music. It is interesting to note the cocktail of music contained on that tape. A particularly sweet blend of black influences, all of which could soon be tasted in the Levine/ Simply Red album recordings. In many respects, this blend typified the band's basic sound and stance:

Bunny Wailer, *Love Fire* (dub disco twelve-inch)
Otis Redding, *Cigarettes And Coffee*
Lee Perry, *Black Art In Dub*
Augustus Pablo, *King Tubby Meets The Rockers Uptown*
Miles Davis, *Love For Sale*
Charles Mingus, *Ah Um*
Dennis Brown, *Ghetto Girl*
Sylvester, *We Can Do It*
Sly and the Family Stone, *Ain't But The One Way*

But Levine's approach was less than fawning. He disliked Hucknall's idea of a straight soul band complete with obligatory brass section. That, he thought, was for pubby R'n'B outfits. It had begun way back in the days of the Frantic Elevators when the band had struggled to take on board a plethora of R'n'B clichés that were, in any case, way beyond their means. Before going to Holland, the idea was to take the horn section over later but, as Hucknall explained, 'Levine encouraged us all to kick the shit out of it. All the clichés went out the window, and we started to work on something original. When we came out of the studio we were a different band.'

Even Levine was fooled. At the Holland recording he stressed that he thought *Money's Too Tight* especially was a very American sounding record. But once back and resting Stateside, he played the tape to friends and couldn't believe how utterly 'English' it sounded.

Although Hucknall had yet to discover that he was born of Irish descent – he found this out, much to his absolute delight, at Christmas 1985 – he was feeling more and more at home in the Irish pubs which peppered Manchester's All Saints district, sipping Guinness and playing pool. These simple pleasures offered him a retreat, of sorts, from the risks and callousness he was beginning to encounter on a daily basis within the music business. Whatever happened, there would always be the pub – and the foaming Guinness. It was this, he believed, which had given him the strength to ward off Seymour Stein a year earlier. And it continued – the pub, the Guinness, the pool table – throughout Simply Red's volatile formation period. Hucknall also knew that the plug could be pulled out at any time, as happened with so many bands.

The pub would be the bottom line. He would never do anything that he didn't want to. He could always go back to the pub and back on the dole. He could always, as he would endlessly state, 'Get pissed and have a good time. You don't need to be a popstar to do that.' In fact, he was soon to find out that becoming a popstar is one of the few careers capable of taking away the pub, the pool table and even the Guinness (it's just not the same when supped in the privacy of your own home).

The decision to opt for a cover version as the first single caused considerable controversy and vehement debate within the ranks of Simply Red, especially as the song wasn't exactly brimming with soul mythology. The Valentine Brothers, being rather late arrivals to the soul hall of fame, hardly conjured up visions of wild youth spent in soul dance halls. It was surely too recent. In simple terms it would be scoffed at by the serious (snobbish) soul collector. It just wasn't hip enough. But *Money's Too Tight To Mention* was also a classic double-edged song which was glorious to dance to and simply brimming with obvious message. And it was French polished to a mighty sheen by the skilled hand of Stuart Levine.

Hucknall subconsciously knew – from back at the Sandpipers disco, hassling Richard Searling – that the Valentine Brothers' song would play an important role in laying down the foundations of Simply Red's image. In 1985 the song, which should have been such a massive hit the first time around, was fantastically relevant. This was what it was like living on the dole in Thatcher's Britain: dreaming up big ideas while walking alongside canals, living in a musical fantasy world, while the landlord screamed for the rent. That very first line – Hucknall's introduction to the pop charts – seemed so powerful, so irresistible. Who could not be impressed by a song which began, 'I've been laid off from work my rent is due'? Surely, even working-class kids back in Haughton Green would relate to that? The fact that the song and the image tended to glamorise the life of a pauper, Tom Waits fashion, surely paralleled the spirit and fire behind the old Northern Soul craze.

Hucknall, who always stated that he would oversee any of the band's graphics found that task to be quite impossible – which was a shame because he soon realised that he loathed the sleeve to the single. 'I am disappointed with the sleeve,' he calmly noted. 'That's not what we are about or what we look like. We are not the Thompson Twins.'

But it was perfect – well, almost. Hucknall, although hugely impressed by the sheer professionalism displayed by Levine and feeling, like most new signings, somewhat inadequate in the producer's company, wasn't completely happy with the amount of gloss which had been laid over the song. In one tantrum, his words ricocheted around his Whalley Range flat like a pinball. 'It's too bloody smooth . . . it's too bloody soft . . . we'll be seen as just another bloody bland pop group . . . it's not what I want . . . *it's not!*'

As this argument raged, the entire framework of Simply Red began to shake. They had reached the first fundamental barrier. Were Simply Red going to play this pop game for real (which is what the record company and Stuart Levine wanted), or were they going to head off on a wave of indignant obscurity? Simply Red had reached that watershed. Hucknall's tantrums, and there were a few, were his way of dealing with it.

When Hucknall had first heard that they were to use Levine, the alarm bells had rung. 'Christ,' he told *Melody Maker*, 'they are going to clean us up.' He was right, too. The first item on the record company agenda, whether it is hidden or not, is to sweep away any naive notions about changing the world that the singer might be harbouring. At first, it didn't look like they would succeed. Their record company's attitude scared Hucknall. He couldn't understand all the paranoia surrounding the first release. He wanted it to be a bit rough, he wanted to make mistakes even. The company wanted everything to be absolutely perfect, from the word go. Hucknall wasn't sure whether he could come to terms with that or, indeed, whether he could match up to such expectations.

'They should take a few risks,' he said. 'They should learn to let go a bit, y'know. They should get that fucking record out and start having a good time.'

One thing, above all others, was worrying Hucknall. He had long despised practically all the other white popstars who pursued the mantle of 'soul artist'. He loathed, for instance, Paul Weller's Style Council who he thought sounded, 'Whiter than Omo'. Even worse in his opinion were the cleaned-up versions of soul classics performed by the likes of the Kane Gang. It suddenly dawned on Hucknall that the end product might not have been the fault of the artists. What if, for instance, Paul Weller had entered into an agreement intent on producing hard-core soul, complete with rough edges, and had been poked and cajoled by a record company who slowly, surely, successfully had transformed him into one more wimpy popstar? Would the same thing happen to him? Was it already happening? Who could he trust in all this? Was he alone?

These were far from paranoid thoughts. Most artists go through exactly the same process and the record companies, no matter how concerned they might seem, always use this state of high anxiety to push home their points, to get their own way. It had been easy for Hucknall when he had been top dog, jettisoning musicians left, right and centre in the search for perfection – a search which, much to the consternation of every Simply Red musician, continues to this day. But who was top dog now? Himself? Elliot? Andy? Or someone who he hadn't even met? Who knows what strange unseen forces push and pull the political strings of a record company and even beyond. As a hit single was edging into view, Hucknall was becoming increasingly terrified. But the ball was rolling. It wouldn't stop now.

Tony Michaelides, resplendent in floppy hat and noisy Hawaiian shirt, parked his car in the usual spot on the rooftop car park of Manchester's Piccadilly Hotel. His car bore all the trappings of a record plugger-cum-alternative local radio disc jockey. Inside was a scattering of cassette tapes, two neat piles of LPs and a large canvas bag, coated with overlapping 'Access all area' passes.

Tony had been successful and it was difficult to believe that his lengthy and esteemed career at the sharp end of the music business began with a small scruffy job advertisement in the *Manchester Evening News*. By 1985, he had worked closely with the likes of U2 and Frankie Goes To Hollywood, principally with Island Records. When finally offered his own show on Manchester's Piccadilly Radio, he simply opened his Filofax and called in the stars for jingles, interviews and sessions. His show, 'The Last Radio Programme', became an integral groundbreaking aspect of the Manchester scene. It mixed the sounds of visiting bands such as Green on Red, the Rain Parade and REM with examples of Manchester's musical contribution, past, present and, in the form of local band demos, the future. Scheduled late on Sunday night, hence the 'last' radio programme, it was a format which sat encouragingly well with the traditional safer shows of a radio station not noted for its policy of innovation.

Under the expert guidance of Head of Promotional Development, Brian Beech, Piccadilly had been involved in a series of low-cost, high-profit music promotions: the Magic of Motown; the Magic of the Sixties; Nostalgia Nights. They had also linked up with various promoters for fairly safe coproductions usually at Manchester's most obvious large venue, the Apollo. Although expertly orchestrated and certainly fun for the mainstay Piccadilly Radio audience (more Johnny Mathis than Johnny Rotten), the events contributed little to the simmering local music scene.

Tony Michaelides (or, as he sometimes preferred, Tony the Greek) was forever trying to change this policy and persuade Piccadilly to support up-and-coming local acts. In the days when playing U2 in the afternoon seemed positively anarchic, it was an uphill battle. Brian Beech knew his job well. Much as he would personally have liked to patronise a more left-field area of talent, he could not risk alienating the staid mainstay of Piccadilly listeners.

Tony Michaelides constantly pushed Beech. The question,

'Why not put this band on?' was more often than not followed
by some strange name and cacophonous demo tape. 'They may
not be much of an attraction now,' Michaelides would say
before concluding with the inevitable, 'but soon they will be
massive.'

One day he burst into Beech's office, screaming superlatives
about Manchester's newest big act which was still strangely
ignored by Piccadilly. 'The singer,' exclaimed Tony, always a
master of understatement, 'has the best voice of anyone I have
ever heard in the world.'

Beech was singularly unimpressed. Nevertheless, he saw no
reason why he shouldn't take up Michaelides' offer to listen to
this new band in a vacant studio. 'Just close your eyes and
you'll be convinced this guy is black,' instructed Michaelides.
Money's Too Tight To Mention blared out from the speakers.

'Hearing it,' exclaimed Beech later, 'I thought Tony had
undersold the singer. It was incredible.'

Beech agreed that Piccadilly Radio should most certainly be
seen to be promoting this new band. It was, after all, a band
which had its roots firmly in the soft soul tradition of the
station.

Michaelides arranged a meeting between Beech and Rashman in the coffee shop of the Piccadilly Hotel, where it was
agreed that Piccadilly Radio would promote a gig for the band
at a suitable venue in Manchester. Initially, it was going to be
at the Ritz but this was soon switched for no apparent reason
to the International – coincidentally under the expert booking
guidance of Roger Eagle. The deal was simple. Piccadilly
would promote the concert on daytime and night-time radio
and, in return, would have the right to record the gig, which
they did under the supervision of Peter Johnson.

Unfortunately, it was never broadcast. Rashman in particular was far from happy with the results. Not that it mattered.
The fact was the Piccadilly Radio van was parked outside the
teeming venue. They were seen to be there at the very
beginning of the career of an important band. Michaelides'
sharp promotional instincts had been vindicated. He had quite
rightly goaded Beech and station manager, Simon Cole, about
Piccadilly's lack of interest in the 'happening' bands of the city

(Joy Division, the Fall, the Smiths, New Order had all been conspicuous by their absence from Piccadilly play lists). Michaelides' late-night radio show was simply a token gesture to what was irritatingly referred to as 'alternative'.

Simply Red, thought Michaelides, had the potential to grow into the largest commercial band Manchester had ever produced. An early liaison between Piccadilly Radio and Simply Red, if only superficial, would do the radio station no harm at all.

Hucknall, at this point, was eagerly lapping up any media attention which came his way and agreed to be interviewed on Tony Michaelides' 'Last Radio Programme'. It was a strangely frosty exchange with little of note being said. Michaelides, no stranger to rock'n'roll hedonism, was particularly offended by Hucknall's mild state of intoxication and absolute refusal to answer questions in a reasonable, coherent manner. Not that it mattered. It made great radio. The broadcast, although low key, was hugely significant. After just one hit single, Hucknall had attained the status of a veteran within the confines of the Manchester scene.

Hucknall's unease about the gloss of Levine's recordings had been tempered considerably by his liking of the producer. Levine came into the group in Holland, and ate and lived with them, essentially becoming an integral part of the band. He wasn't the kind of producer who leered at the band from behind a mixing desk; he got right into the band. He had become the conductor, the man in control – for the duration of the Holland recordings at least. Stuart Levine, though he would never admit it, was top dog. The first single was going to be *Money's Too Tight To Mention*, and Hucknall's reservations would just have to take a back seat. Simple as that.

Thankfully, the single's overt blue-collar stance was sufficient to provide the band with the required image and even allowed Hucknall to vent his political feelings openly within the pages of *Melody Maker*.

'When the Tories get in,' he lambasted, 'the rich get richer, and the poor get poorer. It's always the same. I'll never vote for them. *Never*. They stink. I hate them.'

One might have been forgiven for regarding this new band, Simply Red, as another gang of poseurs spouting Mickey Mouse polemic.

'The working class are betraying themselves,' screamed Hucknall. 'They don't see what they should be fighting. They only realise when, at forty, they are suddenly made redundant and thrown on the scrap-heap. When they have got jobs they'll probably vote Tory – it's madness. There's too many people blaming Scargill instead of Thatcher. But she's starting to get arrogant now. I think she's in for a fall. I just hope she gets her arse busted at the next election. But I'll not spout about it. I'll vote, but that's it. I don't want to have my picture taken with Neil Kinnock. I mean, I don't even think Kinnock is going to make all that much difference. Even if he gets in he's not going to make a radical change and share out the wealth is he? Still, you have got to vote. What else is there?'

As it turned out, Simply Red transformed the Valentine Brothers' song into a veritable classic. It was even a bedsit anthem and would emerge on so many evenings on record decks normally reserved for the likes of Morrissey and the Cocteau Twins. Hucknall would surely become over-excited if informed, at this juncture, that this would be the very last time that Simply Red would be seen in such company. For Simply Red were destined for higher things, commercially at least.

Nevertheless, for students wondering how on earth they were going to make their grants stretch to the next year, or even how they were going to afford tickets to see the Fall at next week's Students' Union bash, *Money's Too Tight* had an all too familiar ring about it. The song could and would soundtrack a million lives dominated by financial pressures. It was true ragamuffin and sounded mighty fine when taken with a drink, a smoke and youthful bonhomie.

It was also good to dance to. Dancing was not something that students, be they at Manchester Poly or Warwick University, were thought to be terribly good at. It was still generally regarded as the chief occupation of the pastel-coloured trouser sector, even though in Manchester gatherings known as warehouse parties were beginning to become commonplace. One day they would be known as raves and dancing would be hip. Mick Hucknall, to his credit, had never had time to entertain any notions of hipness in regard to dancing. He saw absolutely nothing wrong in spinning across a floor to the sound of James Brown's *There Was A Time*. It is perhaps no coincidence that Simply Red's first single would transcend such barriers with consummate ease. It is, even in retrospect, quite impossible to think of a song more apt. It was blue collar, had enough melody to tame a confused pop market and enough raw rhythm to pull people on to dance floors, be they at weddings in Accrington or Freshers' Balls in Merseyside.

The single climbed to number thirteen in the UK, neatly placing the band alongside 1985's other main newcomers, the Fine Young Cannibals. Naturally, it was accompanied by a marvellously downbeat video. Hucknall, if not the other band members, relished the opportunity to stage the work in a visual format. It had been mooted that the video might be set in Hulme or Moss Side or Whalley Range, and feature a bedraggled dole queue with Hucknall sauntering along, occasionally chatting to some of the genuine characters of the area. Fortunately, the idea was dismissed – for it would surely have been as patronising as hell – in favour of an interior shoot in a seedy poolhall. It was deliberately set in cliché, just one step away from sepiatone with swirling smoke, fights and bets, drunken hollering and pool sharps. The band were seen to set up at the rear of the club, scruffily garbed to suit the ragamuffin look, before launching into *Money's Too Tight*. The video has remained interesting mainly because it offered the only available glimpse of guitarist David Fryman looking ungainly in a leather jacket and striking dubious rock poses. Looking at the video, while not doubting the guitarist's ability it is easy to see why, within weeks, Hucknall and Rashman would be asking him to leave the band. It just wasn't working, and as the band progressed away from ragamuffin towards sartorial elegance and from rough-cut white funk to flowing musical sophistication, Fryman's rocky edges would have seemed more and more out of place.

A short British tour followed, partly to capitalise on the

success of *Money's Too Tight*. The tour, pulled together by Rashman's extensive knowledge of the college circuit, was very much a Transit van down the motorway affair, possibly the first and last time that Simply Red would contend with the oily realities of being in a hard-working but struggling pop band. During this period, Rashman had cleverly decided to wrap the band in aloofness and keep them away from the prying questions of stray journalists or even odd passing well-wishers. It was the beginning of a period which gained Hucknall, the band and Rashman a reputation for arrogance, a reputation that still exists to this day. After all, with just one hit single and a cover version at that, who the hell did Elliot Rashman think he was? In Manchester, at least, that was a most frequently heard comment.

The situation is probably best summed up by Rashman's treatment of up-and-coming Mancunian journalist, Ro Newton (later to co-present 'Whistle Test' and produce Pete Waterman's 'Hit Man and Her' clubland television programme). Commissioned to write a short piece for *Jamming* magazine, Newton approached Rashman with a view to interviewing the band. This shouldn't have posed any problem. Simply Red were being pushed hard by a record company greedy for as much media space as possible. Surely a meeting with the band over a swift half in a Manchester hostelry would suffice? Not so. 'You'll have to come and interview the band in Leicester,' said Rashman. 'If you can get down there, you can have the interview.'

Ro agreed. A young eighteen-year-old journalist making her first tentative connections with rock stars would agree to anything. Unfortunately, and for reasons he kept to himself, Rashman resolutely refused to allow Newton to travel down to the gig in the van with the band. Needless to say, this made the prospect of the interview, all for a fee of around £20, rather difficult. The somewhat embarrassed Newton cadged a lift off her father, who found himself in Leicester surrounded by the full force of a Freshers' Ball. 'Hey,' greeted a cheery Hucknall, post gig, 'why didn't you come down in the van with the band?' Just as Newton was about to reply an extremely 'gothic'-looking Rashman leapt over the back of a thankfully vacant settee and sat there, arms folded menacingly, throughout the interview.

The biggest anti-climax of 1985 was Simply Red's highly publicised support spots to the James Brown band, including a night at Ronnie Scott's Jazz Club in Soho. Although much was made of the gig beforehand, Rashman and Dodd must have thought it an incredible wheeze. The two bands hardly met and even Hucknall was left feeling a little indignant at the lack of interest shown by his great hero.

Simply Red were often to be seen at the gigs and clubs of Manchester during mid-1985. A favourite haunt, quite naturally, was the International, complete with Roger Eagle forever attired in Hawaiian shirt and jeans. It was during these pleasure-seeking forays that the cynical element of Manchester started to pin the tag of 'poser' on to Hucknall's weary shoulders. This was, perhaps, largely due to Hucknall's love of dance and his tendency to unselfconsciously leap into action on the dance floor (once he had convinced the DJ, usually Joe Strong or Eagle, to take the Aztec Camera record off and replace it with James Brown). On one occasion, dancing on an empty floor prior to a sparsely attended gig by local band First Circle, Hucknall attracted a larger and more enthusiastic audience than the hapless band could muster.

It was, perhaps, mostly out of respect for Stuart Levine that Hucknall and sidekicks attended the International gig of Womack and Womack. The Womacks had encamped, complete with plethora of children, in the nearby Britannia Ringway Hotel. Hucknall didn't turn up as requested to meet them. Instead he chose to melt into the audience only emerging, sullen faced, after the ecstatic finale of *Love Wars*.

'I didn't enjoy that at all,' he said. 'It was really old fashioned . . . too slushy, too cabaret. I can't stand all that "Now all the people in the audience who are in love hold up your hands" crap. That's what killed soul music. I'm not saying the band weren't good; they were excellent, and the songs were pretty good too . . . but I can't stand drippy soul . . . drives me nuts . . . give me a bit of funk any day . . . this would have been a good gig for newlywed twenty-five-year-olds.'

* * *

As Social Secretary at Manchester Polytechnic, and with the help of events manager Rashman and ex-DJ Hucknall, Brian Turner was perfectly placed to conceive, organise and promote a free music festival in Manchester to be held on Platt Fields Park, Moss Side and adjoining the ever-bustling Manchester Festival. It had been some time since anything of the kind had been held in the city but the timing seemed perfect given the scene's new-found impetus – granted by Eagle's superb booking policy at the International and the new, 'aware' local radio station (Tony Michaelides at Piccadilly).

A strong bill could easily be arranged, featuring a neat cross-section of the new bands operating in the city. As it turned out, the festival would prove to be one of those once-in-a-decade gigs. An inspiring, positively magical occasion which would later be seen as the base from which a new age of Manchester music would grow. It was no less than the first, faint stirrings of the 'Madchester' explosion which would seize the worldwide spotlight four years later.

Initially Turner had intended no particular connotations to be attached to the festival. Under the influence of Manchester City Council, however, it would proudly sport the banner International Youth Year Festival or, as everyone would grow to call it, the 'IYY'. The gig would run from 2p.m. onwards until the last few visitors to the Manchester Festival, taking place in the next field, drained away. If nothing else, thought Turner, it would give a collection of local bands from Manchester a chance to play in front of a sizeable audience, even if most of them would be either attracted by the absence of an admission fee or curious stragglers from the main event.

Arranging a bill would prove simple, even if getting the same bands to perform patiently, one after another without complaining too much about 'monitor levels' or falling into the inevitable clashing of egos, would give Turner the obligatory promoter's headaches by the score. It was during the planning of the IYY that Simply Red's *Money's Too Tight* charted, effortlessy propelling the band managed by Turner's Polytechnic partner to the top of the bill. Post New Order and post the Smiths, the Manchester music scene, although definitely in

151

love with itself, boasted no names of serious national repute. There were, however, hundreds of serious contenders and, more importantly, an interested, growing audience base. Even the Hacienda, cold and cavernous for four empty years save the odd Simple Minds gig, was showing the beginnings of a 'scene' of sorts.

The bill was disparate although mostly pulled out of Colin Sinclair's practice room complex at the Boardwalk. It was to start with the cool, haunting rhythm of the greatest band never to make it out of Whalley Range, Yargo – a simply fabulous rhythm section fronted by the enigmatic Basil, though not, it seemed, a band ever capable of commercial success. The Jazz Defektors followed, their slick, be-bop dancing, sharp suit image clashing noticeably with the bedenimed, cider-quaffing hordes who slumped, freak like, in the mud à la Woodstock. Next was Kalima's latin jazz, seeming equally out of sorts out there in the open air while their music yearned for smoky tequila dens and pencil moustaches. Marc Riley and the Creepers were an indie band yawn, a bad, uncomfortable, unmelodic, witless slog.

Some people danced – the weather, perhaps, dictated the mood which was good if not magical. How strange that the music failed to live up to the promise, but not that it mattered. The International's Lesley Lee, herself quite the embodiment of the new, fun-loving Manchester scene, flitted about the crowd and handed out leaflets inviting inebriated, mud-covered students to the evening's gig which featured Rhonda, Terry and Jerry, and John Cooper Clarke.

Easterhouse came onstage. Poor fools. Blessed with the talent of a U2 no less they would duly squander their true chance to break big with their insistence on preaching out-moded ultra-left clap-trap. Easterhouse, this bill's 'band most likely to' at least after Simply Red, were just too earnest and dour to be allowed to represent a new Manchester scene that wanted to thrive on vivacity, on bodily fun and unpretentious glee not glum introversion. Things were changing all right.

Of all the support acts, only James displayed any true originality, any true passion with Tim Booth's manic jerking, hilariously egged on by the band's folksy power. More people danced. It would take James another four years, another three record labels and a brief flirtation with the management prowess of Elliot Rashman – more of which later – before they would connect with a mass audience and transform from being invigorating but unsuccessful heroes to dull popstars.

Backstage, following James's blistering set, things were rapidly changing. Everyone was pushed into one corner as a huge van – comparatively huge, next to the row of grubby Transits – backed menacingly into position. Burly roadies pushed the crowds back as the van doors burst open and huge speakers were unloaded. Simply Red had arrived, creating a scene heavily reminiscent of PIL at Futurama. Suddenly, a bullishness fired the atmosphere. The Easterhouse entourage, led by the flamboyantly intoxicated John Barratt, were unceremoniously shunted to one side. Suddenly, the James vegetarian spread disappeared, to be replaced by lush baskets of fresh fruit and a hundred varieties of cheese. Elliot Rashman shrugged when a disgruntled Barratt challenged this show of prestige. Simply Red were delivering a message to the Manchester inner circle. Simply Red were popstars. As the crowd's impatience began to rise, Mick Hucknall, scruffily clad in the ragamuffin chic that would soon grace the cover of the debut album, stood chatting to trumpeter Tim Kellet. Two young boys, all acne and trainers, burst into the VIP ranks and stood tugging at Hucknall's sleeves.

'Hey Red,' they said. 'Hey Red, we think you are great. Hey Red!'

Hucknall, or rather Red, (I swear) blushed a little. 'Thanks a lot lads . . . appreciate it,' he stammered, perhaps rather nervous at the thought of the onstage ordeal ahead. Before another bland, nervous word was said the two lads were hastily ushered away by the burly roadies. Hucknall shrugged, 'Er . . . sorry lads.'

It was the beginning of the great barrier for Hucknall. Although he could still catch a bus from Piccadilly to his Whalley Range flat without attracting hassle, it wouldn't last. He knew that he now stood right on the edge of popstardom and there would be no turning back. No scurrying back to the safety of the little world of the Frantic Elevators, all laughing together in their garage. To Hucknall, standing backstage at the IYY, thoughts of the Elevators might warm him. But that was then, and this –! A cheer and a surge and Simply Red were on the rickety stage, the trumpet fanfare heralding the opening of *Come To My Aid* and the set.

Out in the crowd, ex-Distraction Mike Finney wandered by, smiling sweetly at the scene. 'Aren't this lot bloody awful?' he said, before drifting away into the still teeming Manchester Festival, complete with gerbils and prize fruit cakes. Three-quarters of an hour later, as Simply Red went into the beautiful Talking Heads song, *Heaven*, and with the sun finally setting, the fireworks of the Manchester Festival began to explode in the sky. It was a moment of sheer bliss. A time to dream. Even Hucknall gasped mid-song at the beauty of it all. Outside in the mud, the crowd sat back savouring the moment. Ten minutes later, they were trudging wearily off and down Dickinson Road in search of the International, complete with Roger Eagle resplendent in a blue Hawaiian shirt and eating Lancashire cheese and drinking whisky. Later Eagle would have another drink with his old pal, an exhausted Mick Hucknall.

I met three members of Simply Red – Mick Hucknall, Tim Kellet and Chris Joyce – in September 1985 when I interviewed them for the now defunct *Jamming* magazine. I met them in the part of Manchester city centre where six Piccadilly Radio DJs look down inanely from six giant posters suspended thirty feet above the bustling street. The commuters cast curious glances of part-recognition at the one with the red hair and the walking cane as they went by. Was this the same person they saw performing on the Wogan show? That night they would make discreet enquiries of their children. Maybe they would come to regret not asking for his autograph.

Across the road stood a news kiosk bearing a rock press, proudly slaying their second single *Come To My Aid*.

'Who are you then?' snapped the red-haired one addressing me as he crossed the road, holding his cane before him. He had approached me before, on the phone, in person and in letter form – but things seemed different now.

'Oh it's you is it . . . we meet at last . . . ha ha . . . I knew
you would come round to my way of thinking in the end.
I knew you would want to talk to me . . . to interview
me . . . you never wanted to know in the days of the Frantic
Elevators, did you? Ha ha . . . it's different now, isn't it? . . .
ha ha!'

Yes, of course it was. But the band was different, radically
so, the music was different and the times, thank goodness,
were very different indeed. Meeting Mick Hucknall in the
Angel perhaps, or the Whitegates was not an experience
that most people would dream about in the past. The shar-
per, happier, 'happening' Hucknall of 1985 was, of course,
a different proposition altogether. For a start, it wouldn't be
a case of scoffing the old smoky bacon crisps and downing
swift pints of sediment-sodden beer. Yes, it would be different
all right.

'I'm into food in a big way,' he announced, as if to dispense
with his somewhat Philistine roots of yesteryear immediately.
This quite obviously was the new, cosmopolitan Mick Hucknall, man of Europe, talking. Actually, I mean not to mock,
but a transformation had occurred. It was as stunning mentally as sartorially. As Mick Hucknall wandered across Chorlton Street, even those whose idea of a popstar was still Frank
Ifield would surely believe that this redhead was, at least,
something big in showbiz.

'We'll go and eat at my fave Indian,' he quipped, eagerly
acknowledging the encouraging nods from Kellet and Joyce
who, it must be said, filed neatly and obediently in line. They
led the way to the Assam Gourmet, a now defunct upmarket
Indian eatery boasting a clientele culled from, if not the music
business, then certainly the media. Hucknall's face was
obviously already recognised as a regular. There was much
bowing and scraping and the head waiter, convinced he was
attending to a star of quite magnificent proportions, offered a
look of utter and absolute heartfelt concern as Hucknall
twitched his nose in distaste at the Asian classical muzak
emanating from well-hidden speakers. 'Listen mate,' offered
Hucknall (who for a moment resembled the archetypal
vindaloo-eating British yob) pulling out from his pocket a

cassette tape, 'can you take that crap off . . . and play this instead? Please?'

The tape was duly replaced and, perhaps for the first time ever, the sound of Gregory Isaaks flowed sweetly through the restaurant's plush, white interior.

'That's better,' he laughed. 'I tell you what . . . I consider myself a man of the world. I love all kinds of music but I'm not sure about all that Asian stuff . . . not when I'm eating me dinner, anyway.'

It wasn't an untypical meeting between an aspiring star and a nervous journalist. The banter was tennis like, with exceptionally polite, carefully expressed interjections from Joyce and Kellet.

'My manager,' exclaimed Hucknall, 'thinks that this is going to be a set up. He thinks you will be incredibly polite but poised with a hatchet. He thinks this article is going to be the first part of a Manchester backlash. Is this true?'

Of course it wasn't true at all. But it was evidence of a certain paranoia that had been creeping into the Simply Red camp ever since the IYY festival. After all, they were a Manchester band making an obvious beeline for popstardom which was unheard of since the days of Herman's Hermits. The raincoated hordes, the serious brows who had unfortunately become synonymous with the Manchester attitude since the rise of Joy Division, surely resented such brash commercialism with a vengeance. And as for Factory – what could be further away from the dour funk and downright unlistenable art crap that typified their roster than a band who just loved to play the pop game?

Worse, how could the rest of the Manchester pop fraternity possibly love a band who, at least since that inspirational evening at the Tropicana, had success stamped all over them? In truth, they couldn't. From that gig onwards the rest of Manchester rather pathetically embarked on the most intense and shallow of hate campaigns. It was mainly pure, unadulterated jealousy of course, but the jealousy was certainly fuelled by endless tales of Hucknall's arrogance. And so the spiral continued acrimoniously downwards.

'To be honest,' spat Hucknall, 'I am pretty disgusted by the way the rest of the Manchester bands have treated us. I hear such incredible rumours about us. Hurtful stories which are totally pointless. We have never harmed any of these people, we are nothing to do with them. Why do they attack us? I heard one story that we sacked our guitarist because he was too ugly. That is totally untrue. We sacked him because he wasn't good enough. It's as simple as that but he goes around with a big chip on his shoulder.'

I asked Mick if he regretted the isolated, albeit elevated position he had adopted by this time. Didn't he miss the local pub? The Whitegates?

'To be honest, I used to despise the local people in a way. Simply because I used to get terrible flak for being an idiot with a punk haircut. I completely hated their narrow-mindedness. They couldn't understand anything outside their own little circle. It sickened me. I don't feel that I have to go into pubs to be with real people, anyway. I still have my friends. Although I know that I haven't changed, I realise they have changed towards me. That worries me. I got a letter from an old friend this morning and he seemed totally paranoid. I'm not, but he is. I find that disturbing. Also, I hate the way people are suddenly turning from being complete cynics to being complete supporters. That's really sick, don't you think?'

I didn't really. Surely the prospect of changing people's minds, drawing them closer is a measure of success. But if that is what was happening elsewhere it wasn't happening in the Manchester inner circle.

'I don't care,' laughed Hucknall. 'I couldn't care less. I'm delighted that our music is being released all over the world. To me, that justifies the way I have been with certain musicians. Here I am doing it, doing the one thing that I was brought on to this planet to do. It's as simple as that. I had years of getting no success at all with the Frantic Elevators. What do people want from me? Do they want me to be a good-hearted failure? Because, if they do, if that is really true, then they are going to be mightily disappointed. But our situation, right now, is a little stupid. We are massive in Italy, for instance, but we haven't as yet even played a note outside this country. All we have done is go over there and mime on pop shows.'

'What,' I asked, 'you mean really crass, Europop shows? How could you?'

'They are no worse than "Top of the Pops". How dare you slag off Italy? You know nothing about it. I'm telling you, the Italians know a good band when they see one . . . which is more than you can say for a lot of these bloody Mancunians. Oh, the real Manchester people when they become fans of ours, and they will . . . they are all right. It's just the left-field music types. Those who still sit in bedsits listening to old Joy Division records . . . or chat about politics with Easterhouse playing in the background. They make me sick. I'm as political as the next guy but, unlike them, I understand market forces. I live in the real world. I'll tell you something . . . this band is going to become massive . . . massive on a worldwide scale. I know this and, when it happens, I'll be mightily proud. But it ain't going to stop me supporting the Labour Party . . . but I'll do it privately and not in a really patronising, publicity seeking way. Are you [Hucknall's face closed in on mine] listening to me? Are you? Do you realise how big we are going to be? Do you care? Oh maybe I'm being arrogant now. Maybe they are right to slag me off. Is my ego exploding? I don't know . . . but I know I'm lucky to have found my true niche. To be able to sing at this level . . . and improve, as I will. I still have those albums, you know. Those Otis Redding albums – that's the level I'm aiming at. That's how far I believe I can go. Do you think that's funny?'

I didn't. Not being a musician I had no idea just how good that Hucknall voice could get. I did know one thing, though. As good as Hucknall was, he couldn't, at that moment, make my heart skip a beat like Nat King Cole, like Ella Fitzgerald, like Billie Holliday, like Garland or Minnelli, like Redding or Robinson. At the IYY I had stood ten feet away from Hucknall during *Holding Back The Years*. It didn't make me weak. It didn't make me swell with emotion. In the future, Mick Hucknall would truly reach such standards, but in 1985 it wasn't even on the horizon.

'You are not that good,' I told him.

'Just you watch,' he replied. 'Just you listen. I will be . . . I will be . . . won't I Tim? Won't I Chris?'

The man on the next table, unlike me, was a musician. He was a good and successful one, even if his considerable musicianship would always be deliberately underplayed. It was Mike Harding and he was laughing into his korma.

'You know something?' interjected Tim Kellet. 'Mick is that good . . . and so are Simply Red. But we do have to do those miming sessions. It's the professional thing to do and, while we are doing them, people will just class us as another pop group. We hate doing "Top of the Pops". They treat people like shit on that show. The crowd, I mean, not the artists. That's why it is so soulless. One day we'll be beyond that.'

There were, I tentatively reminded them, a few people around who thought that Simply Red were just too clinical to be true. Too false. Too soulless.

'We are not anything,' replied Hucknall. 'What we do, I believe, is soulful. When David Hepworth interviewed us for "Whistle Test", he asked for a list of influences which I gave him. He seemed astounded. He couldn't understand why they were all black. So what? There is an inverted racism about white so-called soul bands but I find it insulting to be asked if white boys can sing soul. That's a ridiculous notion. Why not?'

Indeed, as Scott Walker would no doubt testify. But soul fans, I reminded him, did tend to be purists. Could they accept a band from Manchester who drew strongly from black influences? 'I couldn't give a shit really', came Hucknall's bored, dismissive answer.

Of course, the real question and one which, to date, remains unanswered is would Mick Hucknall, given his vast collection and knowledge of black music, accept Simply Red if he were not involved? The question became lost in the scramble to leave the Assam Gourmet, much to the relief of the increasingly exasperated Mike Harding.

That night we went back to the flat Hucknall shared with his girlfriend in Whalley Range. It was typical low-rent bedsit Bohemia. An uncomfortable futon rested against the hallway wall, and there were ragged carpets partly covered with rag rugs, assorted pine and wickerwork furniture. Most note-

159

worthy were the stacks of LPs and one enormous, wholly dominating hi-fi from which poured four songs that night. *Jericho, No Direction, Holding Back The Years* and *Picture Book*.

'That's all I'm letting you hear,' Hucknall said. 'And that last song, the reggae one, is called *Picture Book*. That will be the title of the album. Do you think it will become big?'

Before I could utter my embarrassed answer, Hucknall's girlfriend entered the room. 'Elliot's on the phone,' she said. 'He wants a chat . . . he was hoping you would have finished the interview by now . . . I think he wants you to fly off somewhere . . . again.'

The second Simply Red single, *Come To My Aid*, made a perfect opener for side two of an album. As an all-important follow up single, however, it was too similar in feel and in pace to *Money's Too Tight*. Hucknall would rigorously defend the song in the face of overwhelming criticism. 'I genuinely believe that it is a better song than *Money's Too Tight*,' he would offer, though few would agree. The single release was the first real miscalculation in the nurturing of the band's career. Had the follow up been the band's reworking of the Frantic Elevators' song, *Holding Back The Years*, as expected, then the initial rise might well have been more meteoric. As it was, *Come To My Aid* peaked in the charts at a mere sixty-six. This was not good enough to provide the band with a feeling of stability or to prove to those who had bought *Money's Too Tight* that Simply Red would be anything more than yet another crew of white funksters, worthy of a couple of hits and a few sharp haircuts.

However, of one thing Hucknall, Rashman, the band, the record company and the few people like me who were treated to tantalising tasters could be certain, the nine songs which gelled together to form *Picture Book* would represent something which could never be repeated, come success or failure – and there would be nothing in between. In many respects, and like any decent first album, these nine songs would be the proud culmination of many years of unpaid toil.

Mick Hucknall certainly hoped that he would never again

be in the kind of position necessary to write such songs. The album's strength would lie in the undertone of desperation, the whiff of youthful poverty, which nestled in each and every song – apart from *Heaven* but certainly including *Money's Too Tight To Mention*. The Valentine Brothers' song had provided the foundation. The rest of the album proved to be a palatable cocktail of images and emotions from Hucknall's youth. It was all there from drifting through Hulme at night, on foot, on his way to see a gig at the Russell Club to DJing to a capacity crowd at his Black Rhythms night at Manchester Poly. From falling in love with girls in Longsight, to falling over at parties in Whalley Range. From dressing cheaply and garishly, to living to Bohemian excess and smoking dope in other people's bathrooms. The songs relived experiences like cycling frantically down the middle of Burton Road, West Didsbury, chased by an angry, failed songwriter after honing in, just a little too expertly, on his girlfriend. They brought back memories of quaffing Guinness in the Cyprus Tavern; devouring kormas in Rusholme; drinking Earl Grey tea from heavily soiled mugs in Whalley Range flats and plucking magic mushrooms from unlikely fields in Altrincham. They were about living in Manchester, too skint to go to the football; venting fury at enemy Thatcher; talking left-wing politics with Socialist Workers in Salford tap rooms, and always dreaming of a future success – a success that would swoop down and take him away from all of this.

The songs on *Picture Book* represent a Hucknall still in the grasp of failure. A Hucknall who, if the truth be told, was screaming in the face of quite impossible odds, despite his talent. It was a Hucknall who had to be either incredibly naive or unbelievably confident in his own talent, or both. It was a left-wing Hucknall who still looked like a loser. A Hucknall who believed in magic.

Perhaps the most poignant three minutes on the album were taken up by the song *Sad Old Red*. One could hang a lengthy novel on the title alone. And when a dipping jazz bass supports the lyrics, 'I'm Sad Old Red, sat at home, Sad Old Red, living on his own,' one is faced with visions of bedsit hell. It conjures images of freezing rooms and lonely treks to the

DSS and waiting endlessly in soulless rooms smelling of stale tobacco and poverty, and vacant officious counter staff exchanging knowing glances before patronising the hell out of the claimants. Of late night sessions spiced by the possibility of violent intrusions. Of the Hulme Crescents curving endlessly, housing people with tremendous strength of spirit holding wonderful parties in the face of abject poverty. *Sad Old Red* was pure autobiography. It told the story of the dreamer student drifting through Manchester's downbeat inner city from party to party, pub to pub, girl to girl, and watching French films in the Arben Cinema, while rioting was going on outside.

From the moment the first fan placed the first stylus on the first bought copy of *Picture Book*, *Sad Old Red* became a Simply Red favourite. Strangely it was never seriously considered as a single, although Simon Potts and Elliot Rashman did have a meeting about the possibility. At gigs it would tease audiences with its simple imagery and tendency towards the jazz end of the wide Simply Red musical spectrum. *Sad Old Red* was surely written on a deadening Sunday afternoon in winter, the writer not even having enough money to take him to the warmth of the local pub.

But the song did have one fault. If played too often it tended to sound faintly pathetic, most definitely submissive. It was the sound of a young man wallowing in the drama of his own misery. When written, the writer had hardly two pennies to rub together. There's an interesting time warp we can explore here. Mick Hucknall, when writing *Sad Old Red*, was suffering considerable hardships. Hardships that would scarcely exist in the lifestyles of the bulk of his vast future audience. Just for a change, and admittedly with the advantage of this time warp, here is a popstar who is considerably poorer than his audience. That one point increases the magic of *Picture Book*. Mick Hucknall would never again be able to write a song like *Sad Old Red*. In the future he would be able to sing it, but it would be a performance, an act, a piece of entertaining nostalgia.

Musically, the album was to swing across a number of barriers. Perhaps too many to be able to create an instantly

reliable fan base. In fact *Picture Book*, soon to become one of
the classic albums of the eighties, fared rather badly when
first released. Rashman, Hucknall, band and label were dis-
mayed to see the impetus begin to slow and the album peak at
a mere thirty-four in the charts.

The sudden demise of Elektra UK shortly after the release of
Picture Book caught Simply Red completely unawares. It is
doubtful, however, that it surprised Simon Potts. He knew
from the outset that the powers that be in America were often
prone to 'blowing hot and cold'. It didn't seem to matter that he
had not only set up the British side to the label but had also
managed to sign the most sought-after band in the country
and had nurtured them skilfully – turning them into a hit
band after just one single and releasing what was to become
one of the classic pop debut albums of all time. The plug was
cruelly pulled for reasons beyond Potts' comprehension. Elektra UK was defunct. Simply Red were the lucky ones. They
had already established themselves as a band with quite
fantastic potential and Elliot Rashman could simply hop from
record company to record company, accepting only the most
incredible offers. But no one was going to let go of Simply Red
and as Potts' little subsidised operation vanished they were
taken under the mighty corporate umbrella of WEA, Elektra's
American parent company. Suddenly Simply Red found themselves having to slot into the tremendously complex schedul-
ing of a major record label. This would be a problem. Rashman
and Dodd felt safe with the Elektra UK set up. They had also
begun to enjoy the feel of being the 'big fish in a small pond',
even if the smallness of Elektra UK was only an illusion.

Rashman was no fool. He was fully prepared for the inevitable challenge. WEA quite openly wanted him out. This wasn't
anything personal, merely standard practice. The very first
thing a large record company attempts to do with a new signing
is to try to oust the manager. This might seem cruel as, more
often than not, the hapless manager would have spent a
considerable amount of time, money and effort in building a
signable artist or band to sell to the record company. In all
probability, he/she would have wet-nursed the various musi-

cians, taken the full force of the blame when things went
wrong, soothed a mess of conflicting egos, driven Transit vans
up and down endless motorways *and* humped too many large
speakers into and out of seedy rock venues. However, as
expert as one might be at getting paid top wack for the odd
Freshers appearance or even building up an A & R bidding
pool, taking control of a huge international rock act is a very
specialised business.

Record companies strongly prefer to 'present' a suitably
experienced manager to an artist, rather than constantly
battle with some upstart who is little more than the friend of
the bass player. The line they take seldom varies. After a
series of 'secret meetings' (there are secret meetings lurking in
the background of practically every rock act on the planet.
Many of them, if eventually disclosed, would surprise even the
artists themselves) the artist is approached in a casual manner. It is then tentatively suggested that he/she/they might be
moving into a bigger league now and their progress would
surely be hindered by keeping the services of an out-of-depth
manager. It's a simple tactic and one that often succeeds.
However, if an aspiring manager really does have the mettle
required to guide a band and himself to the very top, then
he/she will be well equipped to deal with this expected broad-
side.

Brian Turner spent a good deal of time in Elliot's office
during the early months of Simply Red's drift into WEA.
'Some of those phone calls,' he later said, 'would be terrifying.
You have no idea just how intense it all was. Elliot went
through hell . . . it was probably worse than the period when
they were sacking musicians and putting the band together. It
was obvious that the relationship between Elliot and WEA
would always be bitter.' Photographer Steve Wright also
noted this period of tension. 'They wanted rid of Elliot, it was
as simple as that. But there was no way Elliot was going. It
would have been impossible to shift him. The core of Simply
Red was always Hucknall and Rashman. That agreement
went back to the early eighties. Elliot knew he would have to
face all this aggro sooner or later. But, just as he had taken on
and beaten Seymour Stein he would take on and beat WEA.'

Chapter 14
Life with the Reds

Sylvan Richardson's family moved to Manchester from London when the future guitarist and jazz bassist was just three years old. Living in the Stretford/Chorlton area and attending Oswald Road Primary School, his late-sixties childhood was typically Mancunian and seemingly lacking in any noticeable musicality.

This situation changed when the intelligent and shy young Sylvan progressed on to Manchester's notable Birley High School. It was, and to all intents and purposes still is, an extremely creative establishment. Sylvan couldn't believe the sheer enthusiasm of the teachers whenever an ounce of prowess or creativity revealed itself in his schoolwork. Always a popular if shy lad, he perhaps surprised a few of his fellow pupils by excelling in art and music. His academic results were good too, but his heart was firmly set on every aspect of art or performance, much to the undisguised joy of his teachers.

'All the resources were there . . . on tap,' he would say. 'It was a quite fantastically equipped school. I knew then I was very lucky so I made full use of that school. And as for music . . . music was just a love.'

Indeed, Sylvan's music became so all consuming that even his teachers began to wonder just where this would lead. In truth, he had absolutely no idea. He simply knew that music was what he had to do. A career would just have to present itself along the way. Teaching perhaps, or just possibly professional guitarist? It didn't seem too likely. The careers officer seemed intent on pushing as many people as possible into teacher training college and was less than impressed by Richardson's, 'Well, I just want to play . . . and see what happens,' attitude and, naturally, Sylvan's parents took a similar line.

He moved on to the Abraham Moss Centre where he took psychology, art and music A'levels. Even here, the prospect of professional musicianship was not really treated as a serious option. Sylvan, it was generally thought, was just going through a phase.

As it happened his career had already begun. While still at school he had started to guest in local pub cabaret bands, happily strumming the pop hits of the day or, on odd occasions, rock songs like Lynyrd Skynyrd's *Freebird*. It had gradually begun to dawn on Sylvan, if nobody else, that he was already making a living, of sorts. By the time he was immersed in his college courses, he had progressed on to more serious music, often finding himself in demand to add a touch of polish to studio sessions. At this point, he cofounded a band called Inheritance. They performed funk/rock/jazz fusion around small Manchester clubs, the Band On The Wall in particular and Sylvan, like Tim Kellet, soon found himself embroiled in Manchester's musical network. He had, however, no academic ambitions beyond A'levels and left college intent on nothing other than music.

Richardson took a job at McDonald's on Manchester's Market Street so that he could buy essential amplification equipment. There were people around him who scoffed at such a practical solution. But Sylvan, fired not so much by the work but more by his desperation to get hold of those amps, actually found himself enjoying heating burgers and keeping the fries on the go. 'It was a crazy, frantic atmosphere . . . after you had finished work you felt totally drained, and I did gain considerable satisfaction from knowing that I had done a good day's work.'

He was still living with his parents, enjoying the subsidised lifestyle, and found no reason to stay at McDonald's once he became the proud owner of the desired equipment.

Sylvan's Inheritance secured a prestigious slot at the Bradford Jazz Festival in 1983. This was a thrill as jazz then (as now) was generally regarded as one step above and beyond the scope of pop or rock. To perform at a genuine jazz festival, even if only in front of the somnolent intelligentsia of the jazz fraternity, was a sure sign of artistic prowess. One of the promoters of the festival and guiding light of the Band-On-The-Wall-based Jazz North West organisation was Andy Dodd. Dodd, an intelligent 'musician's' promoter, rather than the standard 'breadhead' variety, respected Richardson's obvious talent as well as taking a shine to the lad. After the festival they kept in loose contact.

In 1984, Richardson fell into a band – yet another project put together by a drummer and heading nowhere. The band failed to progress to named status and never made it past a few disjointed rehearsals, but they included a keyboard player called Fritz McIntyre. After the inevitable implosion of the project, McIntyre told a sceptical Richardson that he had enjoyed working with him and would contact Richardson again should any similar project spring forth.

'Yeah, yeah,' muttered a world-weary Richardson. 'See you again sometime, Fritz.'

But after a lapse of twelve months the phone did ring. 'I knew that Fritz and Andy Dodd had become involved in something that everyone was telling me was really exciting,' said Richardson. 'But I wasn't sure what it was.'

This was in April 1985. Sylvan wasn't sure, however, that life in a pop band, even if this band did fulfil its apparent promise, was quite what he wanted. He was first and foremost a musician. He was deadly serious about his music and had plans to progress in the world of jazz. He had also made quite a name for himself, albeit very much in musicianly circles, and found himself increasingly in demand for studio work. Taking time to mull things over, he failed to return Andy Dodd's call. Finally and amazingly, considering that every freelance musician in Manchester would have donated a lower limb for the gig, Sylvan agreed to audition for Simply Red. This call was on Friday 29 May. The audition would be on the following Monday. Many times during that worrisome weekend Sylvan found himself reaching for the phone to call it off, but come Monday he arrived at a huge empty factory in Rochdale, partially converted into rehearsal rooms. Sylvan was nervous. He knew nobody in the band at all apart from McIntyre who he hadn't seen for twelve months. They were hardly bosom buddies. What's more, how could he be sure that this was what he really wanted?

The first audition passed swiftly and, throughout the next two weeks, Sylvan found himself constantly asked back. He was stunned by their staunch professionalism, especially as the band in question had yet to secure any measure of success. With Hucknall swirling around like a manic conductor in the middle of the room, the band settled into a fifty-minute set.

'It was like a dream,' said Sylvan. 'I couldn't believe how easily I seemed to slot into place. That's what partly convinced me that this was definitely the band to join. Also, after the fairly loose musicianship that I had been used to, this was obviously a very tight ship, in every way. It seemed so fantastically professional. The songs, of course, were fantastic. However, I didn't envisage just how big things would get. None of us did . . . apart from Mick and Elliot.'

Money's Too Tight To Mention was released during Sylvan's audition period. Suddenly it really was a hit band. Sylvan felt the sensation of being slowly picked up and primed for a huge surge – an instant, magical, dramatic change in lifestyle.

Arnold Kellet was, to use his own description, an 'old-fashioned type'. He was an effortlessly conservative dresser, a retired teacher, a Methodist preacher and a former mayor. His love of music was profound. His youthful days were sound-tracked by violas and violins. He did his courting to classical concerts and violin duets. He loved the swirl of melody and shrieked whenever confronted by the savage snarl of modern rhythm. Ever since he saw William Bendex protest to Alan Ladd in *The Blue Dahlia* about his headaches being caused by the 'regular thumping of monkey music', he had adopted that unflattering phrase.

Whenever his son, Tim, or his two daughters sat glued to the obligatory weekly session of 'Top of the Pops', he would complain bitterly. 'This monkey music,' he would screech, 'it's utterly moronic!' This reactionary stance didn't weaken with age and he felt a wave of relief when Tim decided to take up the classical trumpet seriously.

Tim Kellet's obsession with brass instruments began at the age of five. On a family holiday in Morecambe, while watching a passing brass band, Tim became transfixed. Holding up his tiny bucket and spade, he began to imitate the musicians. There was something quite moving about the sheer splendour of the event even to a five-year-old. His eyes became glued to the actions of the trumpeters and trombonists. This unexpected juvenile fascination, his parents were intrigued to note, would not go away. The following Christmas, the most enthusiastically received item in his stocking was a toy trumpet. No doubt there would be times during the next two years when his parents grew tired of its constant squeal. The toy trumpet was never far away from Tim's eager lips. Intrigued by the obvious joy Tim found in the toy trumpet his parents replaced it with a real one. It was second hand, costing just £8. His brief was simple. If he was to continue this trumpet fixation, the cacophonous element must be minimised for the sake of the sanity of the rest of the family. Tim Kellet must learn to play the thing properly. This he did, quite naturally and much to the undisguised glee of his tutors.

Eventually, when he passed his Grade 8, the family relaxed a little. It was, by then, a delight to hear him play. One of his parents' proudest moments came when he performed the whole of the awkward *Hummel Concerto* at a special event in the musical town of Harrogate. Family pride was enhanced when he played Purcell's Trumpet Tune in D at the weddings of his sisters. By this time, Tim Kellet had become a musician, to all intents and purposes. Nobody was surprised when he was accepted for a four-year honours degree course at the Royal Northern College of Music.

His parents relaxed. A career in classical music was assured. But three years later the classical dream was well and truly shattered. Tim, although an exceptional student, had begun to experiment quite deeply in other areas. He had become involved with an insular circle of Manchester musicians, most of whom were endlessly forming bands only to fall out over money from advances that, in truth, were never in the offing anyway. This furious circle would meet in many small venues around the city literally like musical chairs. The Band On The Wall was perhaps the nucleus, especially with its connections with the Jazz North West organisation.

For any half-formed band, with agonisingly disparate musical leanings and no identifiable direction, the prospect of acquiring the services of a gifted trumpet player would seem like a godsend. Trumpets added another dimension. If nothing else they always looked very professional, even if they cut against the general sway of the music. A band with a trumpet player had the look of a proper band – not just a bunch of straggly musos high on dreams and devoid of invention.

So Tim Kellet would find himself asked endlessly to join forces with a band, rarely knowing or caring if playing occasional trumpet granted him full band status. He was bright enough to see what was blatantly obvious to everyone except the musicians involved – most of them were going precisely nowhere.

Tim Kellet looked good though: short, stylish blond hair, more often than not gathered neatly into a jaunty sailor's hat; and sharp clothes, often at odds with the musicians with whom he shared the stage. I remember seeing him one night acting as the pivot of a hastily assembled combo called Blast of Defiance who performed, I think, just the one gig in front of a handful of inebriated friends in the Manhattan Sound. It was a gay disco which was occasionally borrowed by those trying to lure the record company A & R men northwards. This particular evening was a typical event. The A & R men had failed to appear, but the band's leader, the drummer Geoff, remained confident. 'We are almost perfect,' he stated. 'I'm glad they didn't turn up tonight, we are not at our best yet.'

When Mick Hucknall asked Tim Kellet to join Simply Red, and when it appeared that Kellet was treating the offer seriously, his parents naturally felt more than slightly concerned. Tim, after all, had completed just three years of his degree course. To back out at this stage, and especially in pursuit of a career in 'monkey music', would surely be the most tragic waste of talent and tuition. But something was different about this offer. There was an aura of professionalism, even at this early stage, that seemed obvious even to Arnold. Kellet. What's more, Arnold Kellet's anxiety was considerably soothed by the somewhat surprising attitude of Tim's teachers. In particular, the principal trumpet of the Hallé Orchestra, John Dickinson, told Arnold Kellet that this was an opportunity his son shouldn't miss. In the summer of 1985, Tim Kellet joined Simply Red.

Chapter 15
Sex and Sensibility

Mick Hucknall spent the first eleven days of 1986 drifting around the beaches of Jamaica, smoking reefers a mile long and feeling high. It was a fitting reggae holiday, spoilt slightly by his discovery that as far as innovative noise was concerned, the fabulous musical legacy of possibly the entire Caribbean had all but dried up. Rastafarians still drove around with six-foot-high speakers extending upwards from their rear seats, but the music remained stuck in the mid-seventies backwaters of Lee Perry and Marley's golden age. The beat had yet to transform successfully into the more danceable artform of the late eighties. Nevertheless, armed with a sackful of tapes featuring Perry, Black Heart, Burning Spear, King Tubby, Augustus Pablo and regarding himself as a 'dub freak' he allowed himself to soak up a hard-earned 'dreadlock holiday'.

The curious lull, which had begun with the stunning failure of *Holding Back The Years* to dent the British top thirty back in November, was to continue with the somewhat half-hearted release of *Jericho*. In truth, it was an anti-climactic release never designed as a single and barely deserving of its fifty-three chart position. It was more than just an unwise release, the portents it produced were far from good. The band had reached that precarious stage when their front-stacked promotion had dried up, their ace card *Holding Back The Years* had been played and a downward slide into obscurity beckoned.

As the band embarked on their first US tour, they could scarcely envisage the treasures that lay in the immediate future. So many bands, flushed by the success of a couple of quick hit singles and a good album, stumble at this traditionally difficult juncture. Hucknall was furious with just about everyone in sight, repeatedly losing his temper and causing more stress than normally found in a band exploring the USA for the first time. Things improved massively in spring 1986 when the record company, after staggering through endless intense meetings with the incensed Rashman, finally admitted that *Holding Back The Years* had failed because of appalling timing. It had been a promotional nightmare. Everyone who knew and loved the song also knew the truth. It was a massive hit single, the work had been done. There was absolutely no doubt about that. No record company could possibly justify having a song of the standard of *Holding Back The Years* and not being able to turn it into a huge hit. And so the unprecedented decision was taken. *Holding Back The Years* was to be re-issued in May, and would be supported by a considerably more aggressive promotional campaign and sales task force. For goodness sake, even Mick Hucknall's Auntie Nell knew that it should have been a hit the first time around.

The video, suitably reflective after the rumbustious ragamuffin nature of the *Money's Too Tight* images, was set in Whitby, North Yorks. There was a strong hint of a Hucknall searching hippy fashion for his Celtic roots. It contained plenty of morose shots of Hucknall sitting in the kind of bed and breakfast room one might expect to pay £8 a night for, and later drifting past white-washed fishermen's cottages. Occasionally, Hucknall catches a glimpse of a dark-haired, green-eyed beauty before, naturally, entering into the cemetery. Somewhat strangely, Tim Kellet and Chris Joyce had chosen to hold a game of cricket in there, accompanied by the one-man band show of Fritz McIntyre. This comedic line hardly squared with the song's heavy nostalgia, although the steam train at the video's end probably did help in this respect. Tim Kellet would also pop up again, as a ghostly trumpet-playing apparition – and Hucknall gets the girl.

★ ★ ★

As they say, the rest is history. *Holding Back The Years* reached number two in the UK. It effectively lifted the band straight out of their impending doom and put a smile on Hucknall's face, considerably easing the tensions between band and label.

However, as satisfying as that seemed, it was slowly beginning to dawn on the band and on Hucknall in particular that *Holding Back The Years* was really transforming into a genuine classic, a timeless gem. For something fantastic had happened. With astonishing ease, the song had reached number one in America, instantly giving Hucknall, if not the rest of the band, superstar status. It was as if suddenly something had exploded. Life could never be the same. This was the big time and it was unbelievably terrifying.

It was impossible for Hucknall, absolutely swimming with flunkies as he now was, not to cast a profoundly nostalgic nod back to those Friday nights in the Whitegates, listening to *Holding Back The Years* on the jukebox, deflecting the local cynicism and dreaming of future glory. The arrival of *Picture Book* at number sixteen in the USA charts seemed to cement the band neatly in place. Suddenly, they were the band to mention in lunchtime conversations in LA or Chicago. In one sense, it was an unreported English invasion.

One single fact soon came to dominate all record company conversations. *Holding Back The Years*, from being a hopeless English indie flop to an unlikely major label flop had finally sold over a million copies worldwide. Quite clearly it wasn't just the cynics in the Whitegates who had failed to hear the song's class – class that now seemed so embarrassingly obvious. Let's face it, a good version of this classic song by the Elevators had not only failed to attract serious media attention, it had failed to alert the massed ranks of the British A & R men. There it had been, smack bang in their faces. Any A & R man with half a brain should have seen it, should have snapped up the Frantic Elevators, glossed over the rough edges and transformed them into a hit band. But no one had.

It was beginning to dawn on everyone involved that this wasn't just another pop band, it was the stuff of legends. Just a couple of months earlier, Rashman had been standing in Manchester's International club, boasting about the parallels that existed between Simply Red and the Fine Young Cannibals (who had yet to score seriously in the USA). It was a whole different ball game, now.

Mick Hucknall's alleged sexual voraciousness, although somewhat celebrated in Manchester if only in jest, had yet to manifest itself within the pages of a music press for ever searching for telling angles. This situation was to change when Alan Jackson, a very fine journalist from the *NME*, was invited to spend time with the band on their first major attack on America. The article was an important one, if hardly welcomed from the band's point of view, for it successfully shunted the public perception of Mick Hucknall sideways. Suddenly he possessed a sexuality which they truly hadn't been aware of before. (The article started the rumours and the appearance of the single *Do The Right Thing* sometime later did little but fan the flames.) Quite at which point Jackson decided to opt for the 'sexuality' angle remains unclear. However, from fifteen lines in, when Jackson throws in an overtly sexual Hucknall lyric, cruelly plucked out of the previous evening's concert in Minneapolis, the whole affair turned rather seedy: 'If you feel like I feel, Baby come on, oooh come on.'

One sexual anecdote later, Jackson confides that, 'this isn't evidence of some new Get Smutty editorial policy.' But it does, to the untrained eye, seem that way. The story honed in on the kind of sexual encounters which, to be frank, present themselves to every major rock star on every major tour. Nevertheless, it was difficult in parts to remember that you were reading about the on-tour exploits of a red-headed (and blooded, apparently) Mancunian, rather than Ted Nugent or some similar caricature hard-rock legend.

'He gets terribly irritated if he isn't getting it every day,' a member of the road crew voiced, probably more in jest than envy and surely not realising that such laddishness would be used to colour a three-page feature in the *NME*.

The article was, at least according to an amused Sylvan Richardson looking at it with the benefit of hindsight, 'One big joke, really. I remember the whole thing. I don't think that Alan Jackson set out to pin this image of the sexual animal on Mick. I think he intended it as a joke as well, but the image certainly did stick.'

'I'm not really a skirt chaser,' Hucknall offered, in response to the charge of overt laddishness. 'I'm a lover. I make love. The women I know see the distinction and I have great times with them. I have really strong relationships with women and I prefer their company to men's, but I think I was much crazier when I was eighteen than I am now. Every single girl I know, I'm completely honest with, right down the line. I tell them that I see other girls. If they don't like it then they can go home . . . I have got quite a high sex drive and if you are away from home for six months at a time . . . well, let's be perfectly frank, you get women making it perfectly clear what they want to do with you. There's a classic Steve McQueen quote, when his wife found out about his infidelities. He said he just got tired of saying no. Listen, if you've got a beautiful woman standing in front of you, demanding to spend the night with you, you can only say no for so long. In the end you think, I'm lonely, I'm really lonely. I've not seen anybody. I'm not bisexual and I can't get off on men . . . People never see that side of things.'

To be fair, the situation that had been thrust upon Simply Red in America at that precise time (August 1986) smacked of unreality and would never be quite repeated again. *Holding Back The Years* had just slipped from the number one slot and *Money's Too Tight*, although only reaching a disappointing number twenty-eight, did look as though it was going to repeat that success. More importantly, especially in regard to the hordes of women who had fallen for Hucknall's looks, the image of ragamuffin Red had just been implanted into the mind of rock America. No rock star had quite managed to look so different in a land that had never effectively allowed the punk boom to blow away the standard corkscrew look (à la Robert Plant in his heyday). Curiosity abounded from the bars of Des Moines to the Venice Beach, from the sumptuous drives of Beverly Hills to blue-collar New Jersey. Mick Hucknall, be it in pleasure or pain, had to carry this image about with him wherever he went. For him, unlike the rest of the band who could and still can melt into any crowd, the popstar remained. And the girls, especially at that time, flooded to the object of their curiosity. Had this startling development managed to turn the head of Mick Hucknall and transformed him into a blabbering egomaniac with his brains four feet below their natural home, then no one could seriously have blamed him. After all, just a couple of years earlier Mick Hucknall, although sexually active, was a gawky, somewhat unglamorous, ungainly clad hopeful who slouched across the backseats of the late-night 210 bus from Piccadilly, smoking cigarettes and annoying the other passengers. The transformation couldn't have been more extreme and surely it takes a strong, confident mind to be able to deal with it.

America had fallen in love with Simply Red. When Hucknall asked for the bill in a Minneapolis restaurant, the owner just shrugged and said, 'The food is free . . . thanks for the music.' Needless to say, such treatment is not afforded to every group who find themselves stumbling across an American number one record.

Hucknall was well aware of the problems involved with pressure of image. He had voiced his concern to Rashman that record companies are all too often guided by young executives who think too much in terms of image and not enough in terms of music. His concern, though, was far from naive. 'We are living in a marketable age of marketable products,' he said. 'And I understand that it wouldn't be valid or even very interesting if, in interviews, musicians just talked about music. Even I would get bored by that. The trouble is that the image can get out of control. I think I'm pretty sussed about all that, I can deal with it.'

Later, chatting to *Melody Maker*'s Caroline Sullivan, he expanded further alluding furiously to Alan Jackson's infamous 'sex article'. 'The papers try to take a line with me. That article just made me out to be like some sort of carnal fucking beast, going round shagging everything I could get my hands on, like a dog with two dicks. The guy who wrote that was just trying to take a line but I don't play to that theme because I'm not a theme.'

Chapter 16
Running with the Reds

Sylvan Richardson was walking on air. His head was spinning with excitement, tempered only by the solidity of his confidence. During his initial two-week audition, he had been sinking his guitar deep into the heart of the music of Simply Red. This task had seemed to him and to the band utterly natural. Their, by now, rather sophisticated soul had been yearning for a jazz funk tinge which Richardson was quite happy to supply. He knew that the gap he filled had only recently been vacated by David Fryman in a less than amicable manner. Fryman's ghost also continued to haunt much of the music, especially the plodding *Open Up The Red Box* which would carry Fryman's songwriting credit on to *Picture Book* and later on to a less than successful single.

Richardson was a little less than ecstatic, however, about the promotional side of things. He knew that Elliot and Andy Dodd were very serious indeed, and he realised that all the musicians concerned would be pushed very hard. It was not going to be an easy ride.

'I immediately got burnt,' he later offered, 'by doing loads of television promotional photographs. I couldn't cope with all that at all. It sounds simple, but I found it incredibly difficult. We all did.'

As a musician rather than somebody merely making a bid for pop stardom, Richardson felt himself pedalling furiously backwards from a world in which he wasn't sure he'd feel totally comfortable. Hucknall seemed to lap it all up but the rest of the band, all of them, entered into stardom in an extremely anxious manner.

Richardson's first live appearance with Simply Red was at the Piccadilly Radio-promoted affair at the International. In a sense, this would be the final part of his audition. It was also a baptism of fire and it would have been much easier had it been at Loughborough University or somewhere. But to debut at a sold-out home gig, the band's first true home performance as popstars, and in a packed and inebriated International with all his friends looking on – the pressure was intense. Hucknall felt it too, sitting backstage, nervously seeking reassurance from Rashman who was hardly the vision of serenity himself. In fact Rashman, throughout Simply Red's ascendancy, never really conquered the pre-gig nerves he felt for the band and for Mick in particular. Many people who have only encountered him in such situations believe him to be awkward, irrational and irritable. It is a false impression, but one that indicates just how close Rashman and Hucknall were.)

Richardson, although treated kindly by the band, couldn't prise any reassurance from Rashman prior to the gig. So this was the beginning of life as a high-profile pop musician? It was a life that seems so idyllic from the outside. Richardson trooped dutifully on to the International stage to be greeted for the first time by a dotted sea of faces and a roar of approval. He shyly stood to one side, willingly allowing Hucknall to soak up the attention, which of course he did. The following forty-five minutes passed by in surreal dreamtime. Suddenly, sweatily back in the dowdy dressing room, Elliot was saying to him, 'Sylvan ... Sylvan ... you're in!' The pressure immediately flowed out from Richardson who knew that his ego would have struggled to come to terms with anything less than that.

Being part of a hit band was not at all what Richardson had expected. Much to his initial astonishment, he hardly saw or came to know anyone from the record label at all. All transactions happened directly through So What Arts. The band members were paid a wage at least for a year before the publishing started to come through. Far from being mysterious, this made perfect sense to Richardson who had to go no further than Elliot if ever he had a problem. And Elliot, contrary to popular rumour, seemed more than willing to supply any relevant facts and figures.

For Richardson at least, the immediate work was the strangest. Catapulted into popstardom in unlikely Italy, he found himself for ever miming on a seemingly endless series of rather naff Italian pop shows. It wasn't an enjoyable experience but he kept telling himself it was just a necessary part of the fulfilment of his musical aspirations – it just didn't seem like it somehow. Richardson was, naturally, a very intense musician (too serious at the time, he would later admit) and he didn't take too kindly to being wrapped in plastic. He kept asking Hucknall and Rashman, 'When are we going to play?' This was, he reasoned, supposed to be a group of serious musicians working in the pop field.

'Listen Sylvan,' soothed Hucknall. 'You really should just relax and enjoy it a bit more. Treat all this stuff as a free ride . . . after all . . . what's wrong with getting paid to mime? It doesn't come naturally to me, either, but at the end of the day, it all goes to promote the music. Enjoy it.'

This was, of course, rather easier said than done for someone who was intent, as he later stated, 'On becoming the greatest guitarist in the world. I felt insulted, doing all that miming stuff. I could handle it now . . . but then . . . I suppose I was just a bit immature.'

Very slowly, very steadily, tension began to creep in. Journalist after journalist would hone in on Mick who naturally lapped it all up. At first, Hucknall would always select one band member to take to interviews but more often than not this person would sit, in embarrassed silence, while Hucknall and the journalist would fall into deep discussion. After a while, Mick would start going to most interviews alone.

'That's how the media wanted it, anyway,' said Richardson. 'It was natural that such a thing should happen. But it is certainly true that Mick always wanted it that way. Even from the early days I could tell that Mick regarded himself as Simply Red . . . and the rest of us were just supporting him. I didn't mind that, too much . . . although when he went through a stage of making a point to stress that "Simply Red are a band" I felt patronised. I felt a little sorry too for Fritz who I always felt was almost as big a part of the band as Mick. But Fritz didn't seem bothered. But . . . yes . . . it was the Mick Hucknall show . . . I can only say that it felt strange because the band's music was always supposed to be interwoven and it's difficult, especially when you contribute something that you are particularly proud of, to find yourself out in the cold. It's human nature. You find yourself feeling resentful, even though you understand the situation.'

The band's approach towards songwriting was practically organic. The initial idea would invariably come from Hucknall. Sometimes he would just strum a few chords on a guitar and hand it over to Fritz or Sylvan to improvise from that point onwards. Occasionally, Hucknall would actually leave instructions – he would know exactly how he wanted a particular song to develop. For Fritz and Sylvan, these occasions were the most difficult for they had to temper their own sense of expression.

On *Picture Book*, Richardson had been mainly taking up the leads left by the departed Fryman. On the next album, *Men And Women*, however, his influence became profound. His musical competence naturally surging into jazz added complexity to the Simply Red sound – especially on songs like *Shine* and *Infidelity*.

For Richardson, the greatest thing that Simply Red would do would be the coast-to-coast tour of America in 1986. Travelling across America, over hundreds of miles of desert to arrive suddenly in a new city which had a completely different feel about it than the last one, and to perform there and meet the locals was, for the entire band, a profound experience which could never be repeated. (All rock bands inevitably grow painfully weary of too much travel, too many hotels).

The band were lucky because *Holding Back The Years* lifted them above the disheartening problems of bad hotels and rickety transport. They had a supremely comfortable tour bus in which they would lounge about, strum guitars or watch Steve Martin movies or 'The Young Ones'. Everyone felt relaxed. It was the first time that most of the band had really been into the heart of America and, despite the pressure of work, it was like an extremely long and eventful holiday. Richardson, often pairing off with sax player Ian Kirkham, spent half his free time taking in the sights and – bizarrely as far as the rest of the band were concerned – heading off to knock on doors to talk religion. For Sylvan Richardson was a Jehovah's Witness.

Strangely enough, the American journalists seemed to take more of an interest in the other members of the band, and Richardson in particular relished the attention. The barrage of journalists, most of whom simply spent their time asking stock questions, actually seemed to ease the tensions within the band. For a while at least, Simply Red had started to operate as a fully integrated unit.

'We'd dream up different ways of answering the same questions,' said Richardson. 'And it has to be said that Mick was absolutely superb at doing this . . . it was . . . just for a while . . . a wonderful time. It was great to see the same set of songs going down differently at each gig. The differences in the audiences were quite enlightening. As a musician, I found myself fascinated by this. The whole effort of touring became one big experiment. I know that Mick felt the same way at that point. It was probably more profound for him because he was trying his songs out in a totally alien environment. We were adored as well. On the whole, I think we all found that American audiences were warmer than British ones. They often treated us as if they had been listening to Simply Red records all their lives. That really was weird.

'In America, people seem to be aware of just how hard it is to keep a big band on the road . . . and they respect you for it. That doesn't happen in England. But we'd go to towns and musicians would come along and take us out for a meal or something. Not in a sycophantic way . . . it was really very friendly. I found myself going to a lot of gigs and hanging out with lots of musicians . . . making friends with them. A lot of them were players who I had heard on albums and had long since admired if not copied. Then, all of a sudden, I was seen as being on the same level as them. It was really funny, because I found myself suddenly dropped into this huge network of

musicians, from all different areas of music, who all seemed to
know all about me.'

Strangely though, Richardson soon tended to divorce himself from the mother ship of Simply Red. He became immersed
in this musician's network. Apart from his best pal, Ian
Kirkham, he no longer felt able to relax in the company of the
band, and suddenly found himself aloof and when onstage
rather lonely.

'It really was strange . . . when we first began touring
America we were a gang . . . and then the splits would creep
in. All the little personality differences would become high-
lighted. At one point I just wanted to get away from the band
as much as possible. I suppose that is a fairly natural reaction
towards touring.'

Richardson was becoming tired of playing the role of popstar. He was tired, too, of all the frantic clashing of egos that
take place in every band, successful or not. He could no longer
accept the fact that, at the end of the day, this band was only
really about one person. Elliot and to some extent Andy were
still dedicated towards the promotion of Hucknall's career and,
at the same time, he found that he had great difficulty living
with the ego of Hucknall, not that he found it tyrannical more
'all-consuming'.

More importantly, he had grown musically frustrated.
Although he still respected the music of Simply Red, most of
his friends were involved in more intense music forms. His
religion, too, seemed to be telling him to move on. There was
no hint of acrimony when he went to Elliot to deliver the
message that he no longer wished to be involved. Only later,
while he was studying jazz bass in New York, did it dawn on
him just what had happened to him during his time with the
band, how he had found himself becoming a part of a machine
– an expendable part, too.

Sylvan Richardson felt that he had got out in the nick of
time.

The departure of Sylvan Richardson left a void in the ranks of
Simply Red. On the face of it, it was a void that wouldn't be too
difficult to fill. After all, a position in the post-*Men And*

Women band would surely appeal to legions of bedraggled musos. There were many who were quite capable of displaying a technical expertise above and beyond the needs of a light soul band, whatever their reputation of musical accomplishment. But the problem was larger than that. Hucknall demanded not mere musical prowess, but a look, a feel and an attitude. The incoming guitarist, unlike Richardson, would have to show no signs of musical wandering. He, or she, would have to cut and trim any sense of ambition to suit the band. Hucknall was not looking for a great guitarist – he was looking for a great 'Simply Red' guitarist. It was a tall order and one that Andy Dodd, in particular, found difficult to satisfy.

Aziz Ibrahim, of Pakistani extraction, was brought up in lively, cosmopolitan Longsight, Manchester. He was bright, good looking, musical, sporty and endearingly confident. Although an ardent guitarist from the age of eleven, music was and he says still is principally a form of enjoyment. His career ambitions were vague. He took A'levels, attended university and worked, for a short while, as copy runner at the *Manchester Evening News*. More interestingly, perhaps, he became a teenage professional basketball player at the Warrington Club which was later to adopt the grandiose name Manchester United. Although not a particularly well-paid occupation and one which, at least in Britain, did not even offer a spark of possible fame, it did require intense dedication and considerable athleticism.

To relax, Aziz simply played guitar. All kinds of guitar, all kinds of music. He developed a wide-ranging and learned taste from Asian classical music, to jazz, to funk, to fusion, to soul and rock. The very existence of barriers between these categories irritated Aziz. Displaying a maturity not common among young, highly skilled musicians, he decided that music could only be judged by himself, one to one, regardless of hipness, trend or musical snobbery. Aziz, possibly the very antithesis of the insular, jazz-based Richardson, would dedicate his musicality to a spirit of openness.

Throughout his career he has had a number of projects on the go and a number of bands to play in all at once. The notion of being confined to one tightly guarded unit seemed like hell to him. A musical prison, no less. In this respect, it can be argued that from day one Aziz Ibrahim was quite the wrong person to replace Richardson, and the blame for that certainly doesn't lie with the guitarist but with the band, with Hucknall and most certainly with the management.

Aziz, through playing in a bewildering series of reggae and fusion bands in the Manchester area – encountering Fritz McIntyre and Sylvan Richardson along the way – had built up a solid local reputation. Often in demand for session work, he was known as a walking 'guitar supermarket'. He was the kind of musician who could not only adapt at will, but often come up with teasingly complementary solos and ideas. He was also disarmingly elegant in appearance. Without knowing it, he had perfected that clean, sharp, professional, stylish look that had been nurtured and perfected by Simply Red and the management. In this respect, he seemed like the perfect choice. The call came out of the blue. Aziz had not approached Simply Red in any way. In fact, although he knew Richardson very well, he was unaware of any split in the Simply Red ranks. It was an exciting moment, though, and Aziz can still recall the sense of numbness as the disembodied voice of Andy Dodd delivered the message.

'We are back from Europe and just about to go on tour . . . do you fancy the job? We have heard a lot of good things about you.' And that was it. No audition. No trial period. Basically, as Aziz replaced that phone receiver, he realised that he was already a member of one of the world's largest bands. It was quite simply weird. Even stranger was the fact that Aziz had to rush to the shops to swiftly purchase Simply Red's two albums to acquaint himself with the songs, many of which he heard for the very first time.

When the band had all returned from Germany, they booked themselves into the usual rehearsal rooms on Barlow Moor Road in Chorlton-cum-Hardy and invited Aziz down for an intensive two-day session. On the first day, although unsettled by an odd atmosphere of suspicion and the lack of Hucknall, the music gelled perfectly.

'The songs were a cinch to learn, basically,' Aziz said. 'And I think the band understood, from that first day, that I would be fully capable of doing the job.' On the second day, as the band ran through a rendition of *Shine*, Hucknall wandered into the room. Eyeing Aziz intently, he said nothing at first before staring the guitarist full in the face and asking, 'Do you like curry?' It was a bizarre question to put to a Pakistani. Aziz, who didn't know whether to be insulted or complimented by the question decided to opt for diplomacy and replied in the affirmative.

'Good,' said Hucknall. 'I reckon we've got a band again.' It wasn't the initiation that Aziz had expected at all. On top of this, he couldn't help but feel a certain amount of tension in the room. Aziz Ibrahim was a full-time member of Simply Red but he felt strangely deflated. He was practically a popstar so why, as he walked home alone down Dickinson Road, did he feel more alone than ever? True enough, the band members had hardly welcomed him with open arms, but there was something else. He had had his first short measure of life in a successful pop group and all of a sudden he wasn't sure that he liked the taste.

Two weeks later, on 24 June 1987, Aziz Ibrahim flew to Italy where he would perform a PA in front of thousands. He was a popstar. Sure enough, it still felt weird. Back in England, Sylvan Richardson, with a look of concern painted across his features, took Aziz to one side and told him, 'Look, try and have a good time but be careful. You have no idea just what you are getting yourself into. If you think that my leaving was just a case of me not fitting in . . . it was much more than that . . . much deeper. This is a very odd group. You'll find that out very soon . . . be careful.'

Aziz was stunned and confused. On the one hand, a glorious opportunity – a chance in a lifetime – had just been handed to him on a plate. And yet somehow it just didn't feel so great. Furthermore, his predecessor, a man who he fully respected both as a musician and as an individual, and one of the most level-headed people he had ever known had actually warned him about the 'strangeness' within the band. It had to be more than a mere clashing of egos.

Like Richardson, Aziz immediately befriended sax player

Ian Kirkham and together they would hang out at the clubs, checking out the local fusion bands in each and every country on the strenuous world tour which followed. It was, as the initial rehearsal had indicated, a tour of strangely mixed emotions. The oncoming rush of excitement couldn't be denied, of course, but any sense of band solidarity didn't once extend to include Aziz. Although hurt, Aziz initially put it down to tour nerves.

'I soon noticed that everyone was acting strange,' he later said. 'There wasn't any sense of camaraderie. On tour, most of the time, everyone tended to act in a peculiar manner. In a kind of, "Don't touch me, don't come near me . . . I'm a really weird guy, I'm a genius." It was the strangest thing. There was, occasionally, just a hint of "all lads together" but it was pretentious and done for some professional reason.'

The alliance between Simply Red and Aziz was far from happy. The band's rhythm section, Chris Joyce and Tony Bowers, continually ignored him – although whether this was made worse by Aziz's own sense of injured pride is open to speculation. Fritz would remain aloof, strange, on his own, while Tim Kellet, although nice enough in Aziz's books, was far too close to Hucknall to be trusted. And that was the rub. This band, Aziz discovered, was Mick Hucknall and assorted musos.

'Mick was a particular kind of character,' he said. 'And we all had to fit in and gel with this Hucknall personality. In fact, Hucknall actually expected us to adopt that same brash, and as far as I'm concerned, unattractive personality. We were supposed to be loud-mouthed Mancunians and were, quite genuinely, expected to treat people in the same way that Mick treated people. I don't care what people think of me for saying this but I worked very closely with Hucknall and I'm telling you now, and I'm telling the readers of this book, that Hucknall is a clever guy, very intelligent but he has no concern for other people at all. Well, that's how it seemed to me. What's more, to expect me to step out of character and adopt exactly the same attitude . . . it was just bizarre. It was worse than bizarre, it was completely, utterly insane. It stunned me, it really did. Mick Hucknall had absolutely no idea how to treat other human beings. It never entered his head that he might actually gain something by learning how they feel, by finding out how they wished to express themselves. It would have made the music, I feel, much richer, much more interesting. But you were just shunted in there, much too quick, and told to play. That's not what I call a band . . . no way is Simply Red a band.

'I knew exactly what Sylvan had meant. Mick would only become a nice guy when it was in his favour to be that way, to a press guy or someone he was hoping to gain favours from.'

It was an odd period. The band's music was slowly becoming softer. The edges of hard funk were receding naturally in favour of more ballad-based sweetness. It was simply a natural progression into a far more commercially viable format, into the big league perhaps. But Simply Red wouldn't have been Simply Red unless the band themselves believed, however naively, that the changes were merely part and parcel of a musical maturity. The change was affecting everyone. Hucknall, volatile at the best of times, seemed particularly prone to temper tantrums during this tour. Aziz, a live musician boasting an enthralling natural exuberance, didn't exactly help to placate a band who were, if only under the surface, just beginning to question whether they were slipping into blandness.

One night, in Canada, the entire band submitted to Aziz's enthusiasm and went to a gig featuring the fusion outfit Tower of Power.

'The gig was storming,' gasped Aziz. 'They were absolutely brilliant and everyone knew it. But Mick kept shaking his head saying, "This band are not happening, man." It was incredible. I looked at Ian Kirkham who just smiled. Ian knew how good the band were . . . and yet all the other members of Simply Red suddenly started to agree with Mick. That put it into perspective for me. He was controlling their tastes, absolutely. One member of the band, in particular, was just a complete "yes man". It was pathetic. And that's why I didn't fit in. Sure, I like the same things as them. I liked James Brown, Sly Stone . . . all that stuff. But I liked lots of other things too. People began to say I was too rocky but that wasn't true. That came out of the fact that I wasn't snobbish towards rock music. I could enjoy the good stuff. Mick never liked that. He didn't want me to listen to heavy rock. You had to be a part of this band who were sliding towards blandness, that was the score. It was so stupid . . . Mick's favourite guitarist was Keith Richards for God's sake. How rocky can you get? I did my job for them . . . and then some.'

Around this time, just to confuse the issue further, Elliot seemed to be blowing hot and cold with Aziz. 'One minute he'd say, "Yeah, loved that solo Aziz" and the next day he'd have a go at me for the way I stood onstage. You could always tell when Mick had had a go at him. That really cracked me up.'

Elliot was, perhaps, correct to be concerned about the onstage persona of Aziz who quite openly took a little of the shine away from Hucknall. Aziz realised that, to all intents and purposes, the core of Simply Red was the professional relationship that existed between Mick and Elliot. Elliot represented Mick . . . and anyone who threatened that partnership could begin counting their days as a member of Simply Red.

It ended, of course, in tears. Returning from Brazil, Mick Hucknall went down with throat problems and a string of UK dates had to be cancelled. Aziz simply sat around in his Longsight front room waiting for the call to go to Montserrat – a studio later to be totally destroyed by Hurricane Charlie – to commence the recording of *A New Flame* under the guidance of Stuart Levine. Reunited with the Manchester music network, Aziz was soon aware of rumours that he had been ousted from Simply Red. Ignoring these whispers, he concentrated on performing within the funk unit Gina Gina and soul band Kiss Like This.

But as time passed, Aziz's phone stayed silent. Finally he phoned Andy Dodd at So What who informed him that he shouldn't worry, he was very much still a part of Simply Red.

'Maybe Andy Dodd really didn't know,' mused Aziz. 'That was possible . . . *anything* was possible with that band. But I had had a strange feeling for some time that Mick didn't want to continue working with me.'

As his mate Ian Kirkham was duly summoned to Montserrat, it began to dawn on Aziz that the rumours were true. Bursting into the So What offices, confronting a startled Dodd, Aziz demanded to know the truth.

'Don't worry, we'll be in touch,' replied Dodd. But, of course, that summoning phone call never came.

Chapter 17
Men, Women and Living Legends

As 1987 dawned, it had become blatantly obvious that the Simply Red bubble was not going to be allowed to burst. *Picture Book* had spent a cool eighteen months regularly inhabiting high chart positions, nudging towards the record books, and gaining the kind of esteem one had forever associated with the likes of Simon and Garfunkel.

In America, Hucknall, if not the band, had hoisted himself beyond the mere scope of another popstarlet. He had become a distinctive and recognisable figurehead, a star, a face that even living legends would love to be seen with. If, back in Manchester, Hucknall's credibility decreased in inverse proportion to his wealth, the opposite happened in America where success is universally applauded. But as far as the Hollywood glitterati were concerned, Hucknall was positively left-field. The cynic could be forgiven for suggesting (and Manchester was brimming with cynics suggesting just this) that Hucknall was becoming a trendy 'bit of rough'. It was a neat way for ageing American songsters to scrape away a chunk of credibility for themselves. This, however, was far from the truth. Although never one to shirk a party or an invitation to socialise with fantastically famous faces in the full glare of the circulating paparazzi, Hucknall had never allowed himself to drift too far into such dangerously shallow waters.

Nevertheless, he just loved to tell stories. 'Diana Ross gave me a kiss, foookin wild,' he boasted, during a brief return to

Manchester. If pushed a little further, he would gladly expand the theme, telling how he had swapped 'Hello darlink . . . mwahh . . . mwahh' style greetings with Tina Turner or Grace Jones. (That Diana Ross name drop, incidentally, is a typical Manchester popstar response. New Order had perfected this method years earlier. It was the understanding that affectation is acceptable as long as it is packaged in a suitably gruff Mancunian manner.)

Odd stories also began to flow freely from Simply Red's increasingly high-profile Stateside sojourns. Following one particularly successful gig, the band, buoyed by the ferocity of the audience reaction, fell into an impromptu jam in a late-night hotel room. Such boisterous musicianship didn't, however, go down too well with another of the hotel's guests, Frank Sinatra. Needless to say, a particularly dangerous-looking body guard was sent to abruptly terminate the source of the late-night hilarity – which he succeeded in doing. Hucknall's socialising, while hardly bolstering Hollywood's mighty sycophantic vortex, was achieving minor legendary status.

Then there was the strange case of the NATO general. Hucknall had, unwittingly at first, dated the general's daughter and soon found himself in attendance with the general himself. 'This general was not at all like I imagined. He was really hip. He knew a lot about music and he seemed to be, generally, very much into Simply Red. He was also quite high up in the Star Wars project.'

Musing over this odd liaison with Manchester-based journalist Andy Spinoza, Hucknall admitted that he had stumbled across the farcical goings on that took place at the very summit of the US hierarchy immediately after the shooting of President Reagan.

'You know when Reagan was shot and Alexander Haig went on TV sweating and saying he was in control?' he asked the expectant Spinoza. 'Well, this guy [the general] told me that Haig and Casper Weinberger were at the TV station for the press conference and they were arguing furiously about who actually was in control. So they raced each other up this spiral staircase and Haig got there first and went straight on the air with Weinberger looking on but frightened of going on. And that's why Haig was sweating like mad.'

Other absurdities occurred. Sauntering down an American hotel corridor, Hucknall found himself squinting in disbelief at the flamboyantly clad figure shuffling towards him. It was, unmistakably, Miles Davis. Hucknall was, for once, visibly awestruck. The figure moved closer and just as they were about to pass halted, before pointing a long, twig-like finger in the direction of Hucknall.

'Hey err . . . I know you,' drawled Davis, with the strength of charisma that most religious icons would kill for. 'Simply Red . . . right?'

Hucknall nodded vaguely in the affirmative.

'Hey man,' continued Davis, 'I love that album . . . keep at it.'

Such praise wasn't confined merely to Hucknall. In Minneapolis, an enormous black man grabbed the arm of Tim Kellet on the way back to the dressing room. Although alarmed, Kellet fell into an embarrassed hush when his assailant told him that he was the best trumpeter he'd seen since the golden days of Dizzy Gillespie. Such praise, while obviously not the product of mere pop infatuation, is certain to affect a young English boy for whom names like Gillespie still carry the aura of legend.

By 1987, two years into their great adventure, Simply Red had grown used to the traumas and trials of life on the road, in the record company's offices, at gigs. Defeating the madness and not letting it get to you was, to date, their greatest achievement. As pompous as it may sound, Simply Red, unlike I suggest some high-level rock acts, did have one great leveller, one constant, dominating reason to exist. People would openly laugh when they mentioned this, but it was undeniably, irrevocably the truth. The one constant was the wholesome worship of music. By 1987, as the Simply Red hyperbole had reached fever pitch, that one stabilising love had become more important than ever. Whatever his social failings, true or invented by envy, no one could ever seriously doubt that Hucknall and the band were motivated not by a lust for fame

but a lust for music. That could not be denied. The profundity
of this love was hinted at by Hucknall in a February 1987
article written by John McCready in the *NME*. Following on
from Sylvan Richardson's statement that, 'The music has been
the one constant', Hucknall added, 'Music helps us to know
where we are. When we are travelling, the major priority is
how good the sound system is in the car, or on the bus, or in
the house where we are staying. If you can rely on music, it
keeps things in perspective. We are stuck in the middle of
Alabama in a fucking bus and . . . just thinking about all
that . . . seeing what was going on around us . . . all the
madness of Los Angeles, New York and even Europe . . . I
stayed with the music. In a way it has always been a bit of an
escape for me.'

In a typical Hucknallian paradox, the singer has gone on
record in a number of interviews to slate Alison Moyet
venomously for her chart-topping and career-saving rendition
of *That Ole Devil Called Love*. Even Hucknall might be
tempted to admit privately, it wasn't such a terrible version –
though whether Cole Porter would rejoice in the reworking is
a matter of some conjecture. Nevertheless, it obviously
offended Hucknall's ferocious respect for timeless jazz melodic
masterpieces. One would have thought that, after saying such
a thing, he wouldn't wish to attempt something so similar and
so soon. But that is just what he did. He placed a call through
to Derek Brandwood at Yellow Two Studios in Stockport and
asked a simple question. 'Do you know that piano you've got in
the studio? Well, is it in tune 'cos a lot of the time they aren't,
are they?'

Having received a healthy reply in the affirmative, the
studio was duly booked for a night session for the recording of
the old Cole Porter classic, *Every Time We Say Goodbye*.
Hucknall liked Yellow Two. The studio was very much a
bastard offshoot of the famous Strawberry Studios situated
just around the corner, and both had been built largely from
the financial rewards of 10cc. Yellow Two even featured the
old Strawberry mixing desk, an infamous monster lovingly
restored by chief engineer Richard Scott and once responsible

for 10cc's *I'm Not In Love*. (The song was a legend within the darkened subterranean circles of the recording industry for its intricate harmonious tape loop which featured, during the recording, four Strawberry employees and a passing builder all holding vertical screwdrivers around the room, around which circulated the tape loop.)

But Hucknall was fond of Yellow Two for other reasons. The studio area was, by the standards of the mid-eighties, enormous and with a little imagination was almost reminiscent of the big band radio studios of American mythology. Perhaps even more to the point, the studio's size made it the perfect venue to record appalling team songs. Much more important to Hucknall than New Order's *Shellshocked*, it was here that *Glory, Glory Man United* was recorded to celebrate the team's Atkinson-inspired FA Cup meeting with Brighton, in 1983.

Yvonne Ellis, who as one-time partner of local engineer Chris Nagle had established herself as an engineer/producer of considerable local repute (and, furthermore, had extensive knowledge of the Yellow Two desk), was booked to take care of the recording. Initially, it was regarded as little more than an experiment, a demo possibly inspiring a further recording for the next album. Hucknall would be accompanied by the cello of Eleanor Morris.

The next morning, as Brandwood was entering the studio, a bleary Hucknall was staggering out.

'Well, how did it go?' asked the genuinely interested Brandwood.

'Bloody brilliant, mate,' replied Hucknall. 'Bloody brilliant.'

He was right although, whether even the hyperenthusiastic Hucknall fully understood just how excellent that Yvonne Ellis inspired recording was remains unknown. Suffice to say, some months later Brandwood received a call from a record company flunkey in America, who said, 'Listen man, we've tried to rerecord that song, *Every Time We Say Goodbye* for Simply Red's album . . . we have the best studios in the world here, yet we just can't match it. How did you do it, man?'

Hucknall's allegiance with the politics of the left intensified with the news that his father, Reg, had been dismissed from his job at the Stockport barbers.

'I feel so bad,' said Hucknall. 'He'd been in the job for thirty years. He's just one of the thousands of people over forty who will never work again.' Not that, rather sweetly, Hucknall would be about to shower his father with riches. 'He's his own man,' stated the proud son. 'I wouldn't want to insult him by offering him money.'

Hucknall's period back in Manchester – in the very plain £30,000 home he had bought and would still own five years later – was darkened by another, unfortunately predictable, incident. He had received a death threat from an anonymous telephone caller. Not one to shy away from a confrontation with such a fool, he screamed down the phone, 'Come round here and I'll kick your head in!'

The indignant Hucknall said later, 'I thought it was just pathetic. It is just people trying to be noticed. It doesn't bother me. I can look after myself. I don't expect to be treated like a normal person. I go down the street and people ask me for my autograph and I give it to them. I don't want to be driven out. I want to live in Manchester and it will be a sad day if I leave.'

The writing of *Men And Women* was to offer Hucknall what would soon be regarded as the ultimate soulboy pose. Through the connections afforded to him via WEA, Hucknall managed to secure a writing stint with the legendary Motown songwriter, Lamont Dozier.

Dozier's name, of course, had been sandwiched awesomely between the two 'Hollands' to form the most famous songwriting trio in popular music history. His musical story had begun, naturally, in Detroit in 1962. Lamont Dozier had previously recorded as Lamont Anthony for Berry Gordy's sister company. On joining Motown as an artist he was to enjoy no noticeable success. Dozier literally 'fell in' with the two Holland brothers, Brian and Eddie. Brian, an engineer, had coproduced the Marvelettes' 1961 standard *Please Mister Postman* while Eddie had achieved a minor Motown hit with *Jamie* in 1962.

The three began working together as a production team. It

was an unlikely and, history tells us, unprecedented partnership. Nevertheless, something clicked. Their diversity of experience paid off. Brian took control of the mixing desk and took charge of the guitars and keyboards, Eddie looked after the lead vocal leaving Lamont Dozier to orchestrate the rhythm section and backing vocals.

More importantly, at least as far as this story is concerned, the three also nurtured a similar approach to songwriting. Dozier would normally begin working on a basic melody while Brian Holland would attempt to place it within a certain structure. Dozier would summon forth a title (most important, of course, because the title sets the mood and feel) and the pair of them would take their work to another Motown staffman who would write out the chords (Holland Dozier Holland could not write music). After this and after the basic track had been laid down, Eddie Holland would finish the lyrics. The song would be passed before Gordy and the Motown quality-control team before being allowed to go into the studio, whereupon a suitable artist would be picked.

It was an astonishing system and one which was wide open to charges of 'production line' tactics. Legend tells it differently. The Holland Dozier Holland system proved to be genuinely magical and produced, between 1963 and 1966, twenty-eight American top twenty hits, including twelve number ones. Nobody in the history of popular music had ever managed to capture basic human emotion so effectively and within the scope of a two-and-a-half minute pop song. They were helped, of course, by an available and hungry array of talent that defies all comprehension. Lamont Dozier would be the first to admit that their success owed so much to this outrageous ocean of genius.

The system threw up some fascinating anomalies. The Supremes' first big hit, *Where Did Our Love Go?*, was the end product of a story that was not untypical of the Motown studio. Holland Dozier Holland had originally planned it for the Marvelettes. Gordy, wishing to improve on the Supremes' poor run of one hit from five releases, assigned the song to Diana Ross and Co. Dozier was incensed.

'We had already cut the track,' he told *Rolling Stone*

magazine, 'and because Gladys [Horton, of the Marvelettes] was singing it low, like she does, the key was written real low. And it was actually too low for Diana. But this song that was in the wrong key was what gave Diana Ross her sound. 'Cause before then, they had always put Diana in the clouds and, to me, she had always sounded very thin up there. But because of the way the key was cut, she had to sing it low and it came out very sentimental, very sexy.'

Mick Hucknall, needless to say, adored such stories. Motown for him had been the ultimate songwriting stable, perhaps even more important than the Beatles. As a youth, he had been profoundly affected by the magic that existed in labels which sported the names Holland Dozier Holland, and now he found himself in a position to explore what actually went on behind that inspiring façade. Even more incredible, he actually had a chance to get in there himself and actually become a part of Dozier's history. How his heart must have skipped a beat when he realised that the next Simply Red album might well contain a songwriting credit which would read 'Hucknall/Dozier'.

And so it was an uncharacteristically nervous, plainly awestruck Hucknall who drifted into the Motown network, carefully building a relationship with Lamont Dozier. Hucknall was stunned to discover that Dozier had been an admirer of his ever since he first heard *Holding Back The Years*. Hucknall remembered himself, brash and bullish, aged seventeen, sitting in his freezing cold bedroom and casting his adoring eyes over his Tamla Motown collection. Even then he consciously studied the structure of Holland Dozier Holland's timeless nuggets – and wondered if, one day, he might write songs of a similar standard. And on his notepad, amid the hurried swirls of biro doodles, were the words and chords to a song that would one day sit at number one in the States, alerting the ears of Lamont Dozier himself. Who would have thought it?

Even Hucknall, whose overt self confidence had helped him to transcend a thousand barriers from tap room to dressing room, was noticeably stunned by the welcome he received from such a Motown legend. His reticence was understandable. The more he heard about Dozier's songwriting methods, the more he worried that he might be getting out of his depth.

He had so much to live up to, such stories – Hucknall had long since become an expert on the tales of Holland Dozier Holland. For instance, there was the incomparable partnership between Holland Dozier Holland and the Four Tops and, in particular, the tale behind their first number one. It was July 1965. A rival company to Motown, the daunting Columbia, had realised that it had Four Tops material in its back catalogue and decided to re-release the 1960 Four Tops Columbia record, *Ain't That Love*. Berry Gordy, upon hearing about this, immediately set Holland Dozier Holland to work on a rival single. It was written before noon, rehearsed with the band in the afternoon and by mid-evening the Four Tops had completed their vocals. The record, *It's The Same Old Song*, was rush released in order to deflate the Columbia effort. *Ain't That Love* peaked at ninety-two while *It's The Same Old Song* reached number five and went on to become a Four Tops classic.

This was the kind of story that had succeeded in all but dismantling Hucknall's veneer of self confidence. He need not have worried. As heroes often do, Lamont Dozier turned out to be astonishingly approachable. More importantly, he seemed to be just as eager to work with Hucknall as Hucknall was to work with him. In fact, the only thing which marred their initial sessions, as Hucknall would later explain to amongst others Paul Gambaccini, was Dozier's hyper-enthusiasm and capacity to work on multitudinous projects, all at the same time.

'With Lamont, his head is moving so fast that you have to kind of slow him down. He is like writing and in the space of like five minutes he would be working on three separate songs. You have to slow him down and say, "Let's just work on that one a minute . . . and then see where we get." You could imagine the other two guys [Holland and Holland] putting it into order because melodies . . . music just kind of streams out of him but if you don't kind of get it controlled quickly, it's gone.'

The fact is that, once past the initial sense of awe, Hucknall found Dozier remarkably friendly. 'He's a musician,' Hucknall told *The Face*. 'Musicians don't fuck around with all this bullshit. They judge people by what they can do not by who they are.'

The two Hucknall/Dozier songs, *Infidelity* and *Suffer*, would both suit the mood of the forthcoming album (*Suffer*, in particular, involved an ear-bending vocal blend between a baritone male voice and Hucknall's more familiar howl). Neither would be destined for individual greatness, but they would serve as strong, colourful additions to an album that would enjoy a far greater 'groove' feel than its illustrious predecessor.

Back in England, as the rumours appeared initially in the music press and later, when proven, in the diaries and gossip columns of the tabloids, it all seemed so effortless, so perfect. Hucknall was working with Lamont Dozier. So what? Surely, the cynics voiced, this was just a clever bit of hype, a way in which to raise Simply Red above the British designer soul status? After all, what better way to silence the purists than to pair Hucknall with one of their true icons? And it must be said that there was more than a hint of truth to that.

Mick Hucknall might have seen it as an opportunity from heaven. Elliot Rashman saw it slightly differently. It would, he knew, establish his band's true credentials. No longer would they be considered just another passing pop phenomenon. And who could say that Hucknall wouldn't stay up there along with the Rosses, Gayes, Kendricks and Ruffins? Who could say that this new liaison wouldn't be the first step from star to legend for Hucknall? For Lamont Dozier this was another job. He liked to work with the best and as far as he could see, and despite snippets of cynicism in the quality American music press, Mick Hucknall was the best of the new singers from either side of the Atlantic. What's more, if *Holding Back The Years* was a true indication, he might also be one of the best songwriters. Not being at all versed in Hucknall's background and certainly knowing nothing at all about Manchester's punk years, the paradox was not particularly visible to Dozier. Hucknall was another great singer. It was as simple as that.

★ ★ ★

Mick Hucknall was no longer a daffy Dentonian with silly hair and a slick voice. Things had changed. *Picture Book* had laid out the base and scope of Simply Red. As Charles Shaar Murray would soon note in the increasingly influential *Q* magazine, 'There is probably a sizeable overlap of ownership between Sade's *Diamond Life* and Simply Red's *Picture Book*. Despite their obvious differences in style and outlook, both represent the penetration of British designer soul into the US marketplace.'

How Mick Hucknall would loathe that sentence. Murray, always one of the clever commentators, had effectively delivered the most telling back hander possible. As the comparison between Sade and Simply Red lay in their audience rather than their musical approach – which couldn't have been further apart – Hucknall would have accepted this as a compliment to the skill and shrewdness of Simply Red's marketing. The label 'designer soul', however, carried with it far more sinister connotations. More so, because it appeared in *Q* magazine – a publication feverishly devoured by so many Simply Red devotees – rather than the *NME* which could be reasonably expected to detest Simply Red. But Hucknall and Rashman were worried to the point of paranoia. They knew that the greatest threat to their credibility would lie within those two telling words – 'designer soul'.

The Right Thing, although failing by miles to emulate the success of *Holding Back The Years*, reached number eleven in the UK and twenty-nine in the States and nowhere in Singapore where, incredibly, it was banned due to the alleged offensive nature of the lyrics.

The video was joyously simplistic. The straight filming of a mock concert in a hall which looked suspiciously like an unatmospheric leisure centre which had borrowed the red velvet drapes from the local bingo hall. Equally, the crowd's ecstatic dancing had an air of stage-managed glee about it – rather like the crowd at some cheap daytime television quiz show in Anglia or Wales. Nevertheless Hucknall, sporting a cartoonish round black hat, danced supremely throughout even parodying the song's heavy bagful of sexual assertiveness. Even though Kellet, who looked as though he was marching before a conquering army punching the air with glee, detracted from the overall effect, the video's simplicity proved refreshing and acted as an effective platform for the song. The irresistible key change at the end was gloriously seized upon by the strutting Hucknall, before a fleeting vision of a sexual coupling flashed all too briefly before our eyes.

The record's chart placing had been assisted, however, by the fact that it was a 'doublepack' single, which included for the fourth time on vinyl – fifth if you include the Frantic Elevators – *Holding Back The Years*. Also included was Hucknall's stunning rendition of Ray Charles' *Drowning In My Own Tears* – without doubt a nod back to the Roger Eagle record collection.

The Right Thing was the perfect album enlivener. Apart from being quite the hardest funk that Simply Red had thus far attempted, it was also a vivacious song, saucily marrying gospel hooks with sexual assertiveness. Its appearance hardly helped calm the kind of Hucknall-as-stud image which had plagued him ever since the *NME*'s Alan Jackson had sat down at his typewriter. It was also, and quite deliberately, not the kind of song that would go down too well with the feminist fringe, although Hucknall was intelligent enough to realise that only the hopelessly fanatical would take genuine offence. Hucknall knew that nobody could seriously challenge the song's 'right on' credentials without also attacking practically the entire James Brown repertoire (if not the entire spectrum of rhythm and blues and, for that matter, soul and jazz). Such an argument would be futile, nevertheless, in the more sexually sensitive areas of home town Manchester, Chorlton-cum-Hardy and West Didsbury. For instance, lines such as these would cast the singer as figure of hatred: 'In the middle of the night, when the time is right, I'm gonna do the right thing', with the band growling absurdly, in the background, 'Geeet offfyer bacckkk boooaayy . . . get on toooaaap boaaaay!'

Somehow, one could never envisage the hipper, cooler, more liberally acceptable (at least in those days) Morrissey warbling his way joyfully through such lines. Hucknall relished the spark of controversy and the song was destined to become, on record at least, his most refreshing and ecstatic performance.

Hucknall's credibility with the green-shoed, rainbow-jumper-wearing fraternity was undermined further by his more outlandish outbursts. Although still reeling, at least in Britain, from the backlash to Jackson's article, he tended to inflame matters further by his candour. 'I think most other popstars who pretend to enjoy romance are just shagging around,' he boldly stated before, perhaps more dangerously, attacking the good sense that generally prevailed in the age of AIDS awareness.

'I could never use a condom,' he unwisely spouted, before adding seriously, 'I've never met a man who could. They're horrible. They take the pleasure out of sex. It becomes like cattle. I'd imagine I was a bull if I was doing that. It's like you're being stopped from breeding. And I don't like girls being on the pill. It worries me what they are doing to themselves.'

The undeniable fact that the subject of AIDS was a constant factor in the area of love and sex was acknowledged even by Hucknall. 'The most positive thing about AIDS – and you *have* to be positive with a disease like this – is that it's going to bring back romance,' he declared to startled journalist Andy Spinoza. 'Not romance like a Sunsilk advert or in a Mills and Boon way, but real. Because the experience I have encountered over this year is that you are getting the chase. And just courting – knowing somebody for three weeks – and not touching them. And getting to the stage when you want to touch them so much and you just go "OOOOOHHHH" and completely melt. 'Cos that was something that's been ignored. *Then* you have the blood test.'

If Hucknall's frankness and playful sexual references had angered the right-on crowd, they had certainly excited those at the opposite end of the media spectrum – the tabloid vultures and popular disc jockeys. *The Right Thing* had them all feverishly scrambling for the sex angle. To them, Hucknall's voraciousness cast him as a lecherous, beery slob. It was a downmarket image that Hucknall detested – nevertheless it sold records. *The Right Thing* helped to push Hucknall's face firmly into the tabloids, effectively transforming Simply

Red into a household name for the first time.

Radio One morning DJ, Simon Bates, by completely and deliberately ignoring the slice of humour to be found in *The Right Thing*, had set the rather pathetic tabloid ball rolling by pronouncing, 'Saucy Simply Red are setting dance floors alight with their extremely suggestive new single, *The Right Thing*. It's real smutty, that's why I like to play it so much.'

The *Daily Mirror*, warming to the theme with the speed of a halogen hob, continued the smut angle. 'If you listen to the lyric, you'll understand why everyone's getting so hot under the collar. Dance floors up and down the country are packed with couples who understand exactly what naughty Mick's getting at.'

Three months earlier, but still echoing in the mind of Hucknall and most certainly Rashman, *Times* critic David Sinclair had attended Simply Red's gig at the Hammersmith Odeon. The timing of the review had been crucial, for it had coincided exactly with Hucknall's period of self doubt which had followed the unfortunate 'designer soul' tag. If Sinclair's review is an accurate reflection of that night rather than the exercising of the critic's prejudices, then the doubt had showed through.

> By gathering virtually the whole gamut of trad black music style into one sweet pop package, the band have come up with a product as popular as sliced bread and of about the same anodyne texture when compared to the wholemeal source of their inspiration. In performance their strongest card was Hucknall, distinctive in voice and it was clear from the lack of interaction between band members and the way the stage was lit that he was the star of the show. Despite the long tuft of hair making his locks look like Bobby Charlton in a high wind. But although he sang forcefully and with grace during *Heaven*, there was a lack of emotional resonance in most of the material. Similarly, the band failed to gain adequate purchase for him to impose his personality on the over-ambitious range of style. The jazz swing of *Sad Old Red*, heavy funk of *No Direction*, gospel forces on *Right*

Thing. Such a cavalier approach to idioms, any one of which would take most artists a lifetime to master, resulted in a superficial, if pleasant environment.

The look of concentrated relief on bassist Tony Bowers' face when the band had successfully negotiated a long free-time break near the end of *Heaven*, illustrated a lack of experience which was emphasised by the aspirations to musical sophistication. If nothing else, *Holding Back The Years* made them the first band in my experience to induce couples to waltz romantically in the Odeon aisles.

This review was not forgotten either, for it had perceptively or luckily honed in on a streak of paranoia within the band. Had they been spreading themselves too thinly?

Their paranoia was not unfounded. From the outset, Hucknall had known the kind of tightrope that he was about to walk. His early reaction to the smoothness of Levine's work on *Picture Book* had not been entirely based on naivety. Although Levine had been, with stunning success, polishing the music to suit the largest available audience, he had also been creating a record that the young Hucknall, were he not involved, would surely detest. The furious rush of hyperbole that had engulfed him post *Picture Book* had not managed to quell his true fear completely. Had Levine really created the sound of designer soul? Is that how the average James Brown fanatic viewed the band? If someone was to tell Hucknall as he began to write the songs that would form the follow-up album *Men And Women*, that, despite his efforts to the contrary, Charles Shaar Murray, one of the most respected rock critics on the globe, would still be labelling Simply Red as 'designer soul' he would probably have gone back to waiting on tables in the Broomstair Working Men's Club. For the very point of *Men And Women* was to prove that Simply Red, if you will forgive the bluntness, still had balls. Mick Hucknall wanted to make a record that reversed the expected slide into lucrative blandness. He wanted to make a bold, funky statement. A record that would manage to fulfil record company expectations, gain the sales and yet still, somehow, challenge the casual listener.

This album would be different, harder, braver, funkier. Stuart Levine would be replaced in favour of Alex Sadkin. He was responsible for the funkier edges of Tom Tom Club, Grace Jones (a mediocre artiste turned extraordinary by the sheer force of the surrounding musicianship and production), Duran Duran (ditto) and a notable section of Bob Marley. The sound that Hucknall sought would be solid, menacing and on ballads, lush rather than winsome, beauteous rather than pretty, passionate rather than enticing. Sadkin approached the band with, as Hucknall put it, 'open ears'. He seemed less determined than Levine to impose himself on the music. Hucknall immediately informed Sadkin that he wanted his voice brought very much to the fore.

'I think my voice has improved by just doing concerts,' he asserted. 'It's got a bit richer, a bit deeper.'

This was not egotistical naivety. Hucknall's voice had been enriched and trained by sheer hard work. The rough, Mancunian edges had been transformed naturally into a smooth, melodic growl. The album's title came to Hucknall quite early in the writing process. *Men And Women* – it was simple enough, an easy option perhaps. A number of songs about love, sex and pain (not hardship this time around, for that would hardly seem suitable) gathered together under the umbrella *Men And Women*, and could reasonably be expected to have universal relevance – from spotty necking sessions behind asbestos garages to thirtysomething divorces. In truth, though, many of the songs would be personal to Hucknall.

'A lot of the songs are about things that I have experienced over the past year, about relationships I've not been able to fulfil because of the work I've been doing . . . like being in a country for two weeks and then having to leave it,' he said, perhaps looking tentatively forward to the next five years of 'gypsyfication'. The simple fact was that life as a top international pop singer was hardly filled with opportunities to sink into a stable, steady, lasting relationship. The problem for Hucknall was professional as well as personal. The bulk of his audience would be entering deeper and deeper into a single relationship. Any kind of songwriter hoping to continue to reflect their lives would surely have to experience similar feelings, similar frustrations.

Hucknall strongly desired to transform Simply Red into a mature pop act, one which would become enriched with age and, hopefully, would capture emotional complexities previously rarely achieved by such a commercially successful outfit. This desire cut against the grain of the rather tiresome punk ethic – still sported, strangely, by Radio One's John Peel – that good pop music can only be made by incompetent acne-infested teenagers. This was rapidly becoming a terribly dated concept. In fact, just as Simply Red were emerging, the music industry had started to re-invent itself with the help of the compact disc market. The revelation was that the old Beatles, Dylan and Zeppelin fans had not died at all but were still very much in evidence, still desiring new product and were seemingly with brass in pocket.

As Hucknall was himself no longer in the first flush of youth, he fully recognised the importance of appealing to the ageing pop market. The very best pop songs, he always believed, were not confined to any particular age group. One of his loves, extraordinarily unhip at the time, was the batch of late-term Abba songs, *The Day Before You Came, Knowing Me, Knowing You and The Name Of The Game,* all of which were unusually adult in approach as far as lightweight pop songs were concerned. Perhaps *Men And Women,* with its intended lushness, would convey a similar maturity?

A review of *Men And Women* in the Manchester listings magazine, *City Life,* which hinted that the album fell way short of Hucknall's ambitions, hit a sore point, similar to Murray's, causing Rashman to explode into a furious rage. The writer of the review, Bob Dickinson, wouldn't know the full extent of his crime until many years later. But as far as album sales were concerned, the thoughts of the likes of Murray, Sinclair and Dickinson, however perceptive, were wholly ineffective. *Men And Women,* complete with hard-edged pretensions, soared to number two in the UK.

The oddest aspect of popstardom is the effect that the measure of stardom has not on the artist but on the more vulnerable sections of the audience. This is especially apparent when bands have, despite their musicianly capabilities or artistic pretensions, only recently surfaced in the thinner, cheaper, younger, brasher downmarket magazines. It is to do with image. It is possible, for instance, for a band to score a number of hits and never really make an impact on, say, the readers of *Smash Hits*. But Simply Red's visuals, their elegant, colourful slick suits, inelegant mass of red curls, neat ties, striped shirts and distant pouts, would have made it virtually impossible for the band, even if they wished, to be placed ineffectually in such a glossy format.

Simply Red surely welcomed the fact that, by mid-1986, a sizeable teen pop audience had attached itself to the band. This wasn't a problem, far from it. It seemed to be the case that Simply Red's audience base was fairly broadly spread from thirteen to fifty, perhaps with a slight break in the suede jacket/black Levis period around studenthood. But the most fascinating and rather comical effect Simply Red had surely surrounded their teen following.

It was fascinating not least because the band were offering a wide range of musical styles and references, all of which were hastily swallowed by teens not noted for the discerning nature of their taste. It was most odd, for instance, to catch a young, giggly daughter breaking away from her maths homework to skank around the bedroom to the controlled dub sounds of *Love Fire*, or gaze dreamily at the Simply Red poster in the flush of a crush, as *Every Time We Say Goodbye* drifted across the room. The level of sophistication provided by the music belied the image. It is a matter of some conjecture whether or not these teens would have attached themselves to the band had Hucknall displayed all the vocal prowess of a Beastie Boy and the band had been a manufactured dancing troupe, churning out a couple of one-dimensional pop albums before fading fast. It is, of course, rather condescending to describe the teen market in such a way. It is also something of a generalisation. Nevertheless, within the offices of WEA more than one meeting took place concerning the size and influence of the more transient members of Simply Red's audience.

In Manchester, as the British tour reached the Free Trade

Hall, the breadth of the band's audience was to prove faintly comical. As one local newspaper dryly remarked, this could be the first band to appeal to the parents *and* their besotted, spotty offspring. As it happened, the besotted, spotty offspring commandeered the first five rows, falling into intensely irritating squealing fits whenever Mick, or Tim, or Tony glanced in their direction. At the front it was like the Beatles at Carnegie Hall. In the circle it was more like a Tangerine Dream gig. (I, needless to say, found myself somewhere in the middle.)

The concert began rather badly as the entire spectrum of audience largely ignored the spirited, though ultimately forgettable support act, Live For The Weekend (a Manchester band managed, significantly, by the lively John Barratt. As manager of Syncopation, he had crossed swords with Rashman back in the Poly days. Here, any trace of antagonism had vanished. Hucknall and Rashman had strongly desired that a local Manchester act should be selected as support. Live For The Weekend being suitably funky and not too flash – and not too good either – would be just about perfect).

For the teens, however, only Simply Red would do. Even Hucknall seemed genuinely surprised when his raincoated introduction, the bandless *Every Time We Say Goodbye*, was greeted with fleeting snatches of teen hysteria. It was hysteria that bubbled on the brink of disaster later in the evening as the band ploughed vivaciously through *No Direction*. It was frankly bizarre. Those in the audience older, wiser perhaps, who had seen Simply Red from the early days at the IYY Festival, if not before, cast bewildered glances in the direction of the girls and looked genuinely abashed every time the screaming reached fever pitch. Mostly, they just wondered whether or not they should have attended such a gig; whether it would have been more rewarding to have driven down to the Band On The Wall to catch some small-time, low-key jazz. This after all was an out and out pop gig. They needn't have worried. The teen phase would pass all too soon. The unlikely scenario of Mick Hucknall as teen pin-up would fade too. Even Hucknall had felt rather embarrassed by that one.

'I must admit I never saw myself as a pin-up,' he joked. Then he added defensively, 'Look . . . some people say I'm ugly. If that is the case, then that's my problem. But I don't look at it that way at all. I don't see myself as anything, really. I wouldn't want to have film star looks, that has never appealed to me,' and then mysteriously, 'I channel my energies in other ways.'

Worryingly for Rashman, *Men And Women* just failed to dent the US top thirty, effectively exploding the bubble of expectation. Simply Red had not, as the success of *Holding Back The Years* had prophesied, reached the upper echelons of the US rock hierarchy – not yet.

The tabloid hyperbole was hardly welcomed by Hucknall, although obviously relished by the record company. During the series of interviews involved in the pre-*Men And Women* promotion, Hucknall found himself becoming more and more depressed as journalist after journalist honed in on his alleged hedonism. It was absurdly naive of him to expect anything else, of course, but he did long to talk about the music.

Only in *Melody Maker*, which had not committed such a crime, was he able to fully vent his opinions to a grateful Caroline Sullivan.

'I don't think there's enough talk about music. Particularly from the people in your field, with your type of newspaper . . . the last thing they seem to talk about is the music. It's usually connected with what your sex life is like, whether you like football . . . the in-depth thing about everything except . . . music. Maybe they think that discussing things about music and tracks on albums is boring. Nobody has asked me about this album. Nobody has asked me about the tracks, anything connected with the songs on the album. Nothing. It's got to the stage where, perhaps, journalists' companies are guided by younger execs and people who have not much concern for the music itself, but the marketable potential of someone's image . . . The papers try to take a line on me.'

During the recording of *Men And Women*, Hucknall had been constantly set up by over-zealous journos. One photograph appeared in the *Daily Express* showing Hucknall with a topless woman. What the subsequent article failed to mention, however, was the obvious fact that Hucknall was looking the other way. In fact, to his apparent dismay he wasn't even aware of the incident until he saw the paper.

'While I was looking the other way, she undid her shirt and I didn't even get to see her tits for God's sake. I'm seen with a topless in this fucking newspaper and I never even saw her tits.' He concluded with the comical though unwise comment, 'She could at least have given us a flash . . . but I'd have been horrified, actually.'

It was just another one of the unreal situations the average popstar has to face especially during the days when tabloid editors had, at last, discovered the true power of youth culture. Distinctive young creatures like Hucknall would make great copy. The music media did, at least, attempt to form a critique on the music. To the tabloids, of course, the music wasn't of the remotest importance. For sure, they loved to shower Hucknall with superlatives whenever reviewing a live show, for instance. But it was merely a case of build 'em up for the kill. In tabloid land there is no discernible difference between Simply Red and, say, Bros. They are pop fodder to be exploited, to be exposed. Who cares what the band sounds like? This might seem obvious, indeed it is obvious, but Hucknall had spent most of his life in total awe of the best of popular music and just wasn't, and still isn't, capable of understanding this basic concept. It hadn't registered at all. The simple fact is that to many people and certainly to the people who scribble tabloid gossip, music plays no important role at all. Mick Hucknall might as well be Princess Diana. It just didn't matter what people did. As along as they were there in the full glare, then all manner of stories would unfold.

I was once befriended by a typically astute tabloid hound. She was a bright woman who would one day write her own pop column and publish a particularly revealing portrait of Hucknall's childhood. She stated openly, proudly even, that she not only knew absolutely nothing about popular music but had absolutely no desire at all to learn. Not only did this not matter but, in her view, it actually helped to distance the writer from the subject. Tabloid mentality is suitably mocking of any aspirations of aesthetic worth. Tabloid hacks would one day scramble their collective exposés together and even write books about Hucknall. This is what truly horrified Hucknall – not the exposé, but the total lack of importance or understanding of his music. For a man wishing to be taken seriously, this would be the ultimate indignity.

Since the days of *Picture Book* Hucknall had been developing a small, but growing reputation as a newcomer to the London nightclub scene. He was depicted, for example, at the *Sun's* White Hot Club Party at London's sycophantic hellhole, the Limelight Club, in the company of Maria Whittaker.

'Is that who she was?' he asked, incredulously, in *Melody Maker*. 'I just remember this woman with the M62 coming out of her chest. Well, we do go to the Limelight. We go out on the piss to the Limelight because we get free bottles of champagne, but we are not going there anymore because I'm pissed off with being implicated with a drug thing that the *Sun* did, on the drugs allegedly available at the Limelight, they just said I was there.'

There were no real drug allegations in the *Sun*, just a legally safe condemnation by association. The fact is that Hucknall, although by no means a stranger to the softer drugs on the rock'n'roll circuit, has always taken a hard line on coke and heroin, which only increased the irony. Hucknall had been horrified by the downmarket heroin outbreak in Britain in the mid-eighties. Like most people, he was shocked to read about drug pushers hanging about outside comprehensive schools.

In his youth, the drug scene, although widespread, had been considerably less serious. Even the well-known 'drug dens' in most towns had consisted of little more than a few dowdy hippies sitting down smoking cannabis to the sounds of Hawkwind and Gong. This was the environment in which Hucknall and his punk peers grew to detest any kind of speculative tabloid stance which was all too quick to label people who sampled the odd joint as crazed druggies. But, alas, by the mid-eighties things had worsened and Hucknall, alongside most of his ex-punk contemporaries, was quick to adopt a furiously indignant stance against the new wave of truly dangerous drugs, from heroin to the horribly underestimated (at street level) ecstacy.

'I was astonished when I first got into the papers,' continued Hucknall in the *Melody Maker* interview. 'I thought, God what would they want to write about me for? Prince and Madonna and Nick Kamen are popstars. The idea of them doing it to me. It just kind of woke me up and I thought, "Jesus". Makes me think I'm next on the ladder of writables.'

For Hucknall, the best thing about going to the Limelight was the chance to meet a few more of his genuine heroes, in particular Bobby Womack. As the vultures circulated with intent, Hucknall and Womack fell into deep conversation. More than anything else, he saw that as justification for his attending and partaking in cheap champagne. But when Hucknall spun around, wielding his cane with apparent intent outside the Limelight, screaming, 'Why don't you all just fuck off?' he was surely guilty of incredible naivety. Nobody provides free champagne just to have the pleasure of seeing two musicians sitting down and talking about chord sequences. The whole point of going to the Limelight is to enjoy being seen in one of London's premier media goldfish bowls. The Limelight was a place where people would go to get publicity, not hide shyly away from it. If Hucknall had truly desired a secret meeting with Womack, then fifty city centre restaurants spring to mind. The Limelight was tabloid land, and to enter it was to play the game.

Men And Women, despite criticism from the likes of Murray and Sinclair, reached number two in the UK. This, of course, was immensely satisfying to Hucknall who was happy to silence his critics. He was ecstatic – and Rashman dumbfounded – when the success of *Men And Women* unexpectedly lit a fire underneath the sales of *Picture Book* which sensationally climbed right back to number two. This was the kind of curious anomaly that happens to major acts, not young funky pretenders. Simply Red, in producing a hard-edged album that the record company had feared would be less of a commercial success, had restaged their initial splash, albeit unintentionally. *Men And Women* had fulfilled Hucknall's artistic desires, it was crammed with contrasting styles and wasn't in any sense a 'safe' record, and yet it had not only far exceeded sales expectations, but had significantly increased Simply Red's fan base.

As *Every Time We Say Goodbye* moved up the charts in December 1987, dutifully providing the band with a continuing high profile it also introduced the voice of Mick Hucknall to an almost entirely new audience via the medium of Radio Two. I use the word 'almost' because *Holding Back The Years* had nestled quite comfortably amongst the likes of *Sixteen Tons, King Of The Road* and *Four In The Morning*. But *Every Time We Say Goodbye* was an entirely different matter. This was a recognised Radio Two jazz classic. What's more, the startlingly obvious fact that the Simply Red version was every bit as good as the original, possibly better, hoisted Hucknall above and beyond the category of another popstar. It was rather like being filed away in a dusty library of esteem. The name Simply Red, if not Mick Hucknall, had actually managed to break free from the mass of modern pretenders, as far as the older listeners were concerned. Simply Red fans might not have noticed this breakthrough and it might not have had the record company execs turning cartwheels of delight, but it was immensely important, none the less.

Hucknall arrived back in Manchester after working in Japan, Australia, New Zealand, Canada, America and Europe in mid-December primarily to perform at the city's proud converted railway station, G-Mex. Following this a quiet, homely spell of Christmas indulgence was greatly anticipated.

The date at G-Mex, Simply Red's first appearance in that huge upturned bean can, was the beginning of a relationship between band and venue which would become, to say the least, notoriously tempestuous. Rashman took Hucknall to have a look inside. Even by the standards of some of the huge venues he had performed at throughout the world, the singer was astonished by the ex-station's awesome cavernous proportions. He wandered alone, noting the resounding echoes of his footsteps. A worry? Perhaps, but the reports he had from fellow artists who had performed in the venue, especially from the previous year's Festival Of The Tenth Summer had been favourable. This had been a Factory Records organised event featuring the best of Manchester and related talent to have risen since the early days of punk. The best, that is, except one.

'Well it feels all right,' he said. 'But I can't tell whether or not it will be possible to generate an atmosphere in such a place.'

The cold fact was that, atmospheric or not, G-Mex was simply the only Manchester venue big enough to house the band. Apart from anyone else, the entire band and their families still lived in Manchester, and the relatives' presence alone would account for over two hundred free tickets. During the few days prior to the gig, Hucknall spent a considerable amount of money transforming his Old Trafford house into something approaching an impenetrable fortress. A sad fact, but the house had become well known, especially to local thieves who couldn't resist the magnet of a famous, wealthy owner who spends most of each year away from home. Consequently, it had been broken into at least eight times during 1987.

If the long-term future of Simply Red was beginning to look terrifyingly burdened with responsibility, which is the dark accompaniment of superstardom, then the immediate future looked comparatively restful. Mick intended to spend Christmas as simply as possible back in Denton. 'I will get all sentimental and gooey . . . drunk and maudlin,' he said, before resignedly adding, 'I will probably get my eczema back.'

The skin irritation to which he referred (which he had inherited from his father) could arguably have saved Hucknall from the inevitable tortures of too many years drinking far too much alcohol. Although hardly ready to extol the virtues of teetotalism, he had swapped a good amount of alcohol intake for swigs of Evian water. This wasn't an entirely virtuous switch. In fact it was motivated by necessary vanity. A doctor had recently informed Hucknall that his somewhat unstable skin condition was entirely related to his alcohol intake. Cutting the hard stuff out completely wasn't at all necessary he was relieved to note, but a general reduction as far as his skin was concerned certainly was.

After Christmas, Hucknall took great pleasure in spending

a month in the slow lane. Hanging out at the Hacienda probably did little for his eczema or his mental state. The clientele at the Hacienda, as far as Hucknall was concerned, were worryingly young looking, raucous and irritatingly vociferous in their dislike of wealthy redheaded superstars. 'I hate foookin' Simply Red . . . they are shiiite!' one extraordinarily intelligent young hedonist spat in Hucknall's face. Replying politely, 'I'm very sorry you don't like it,' Hucknall ushered himself out of the Gay Traitor cocktail bar and moved his entourage upstairs where, at least, the horrendous booming noise blanked out any possibility of further attacks. It was during moments like this that one could understand why a public figure should wish to retire to some remote, sunny corner. But Hucknall remained determined to defend his right to live life as normally as possible.

'I'm not going to let a few assholes stop me from going out. I enjoy Manchester. I enjoy being in the city, day and night. It's a place where I like to ride my bike or maybe get drunk in some dark corner. Most people are pretty cool . . . it is generally a pretty cool city . . . but the problem is that the few wankers that exist will always hone in on people like me. I just hope people understand sometimes, when they call me arrogant, when they say I'm aloof . . . that it isn't always my choice to be that way. Sometimes you are forced into a corner. I don't enjoy being a star . . . I don't, I really don't. I haven't changed my view that, just because I write and sing a few songs, that makes my life somehow more important than somebody who is an expert joiner. It doesn't. I know this. I have come to terms with it. But certain other people haven't . . . well, at the end of the day, that's their problem, not mine. Having said all that, I must state that most people in Manchester are generally great with me. Some people might be sick of me but most of them aren't that much fussed.

'When I am away from Manchester, I miss the home life. I miss not being able to cook in my kitchen. I also miss not being able to go down Rusholme for a curry. You have no idea how much I have longed to step into, say, the Sanam Sweet Centre. Sometimes, I think that Manchester has the finest Indian restaurants in the world. It's true. I could be in LA with all those wonderful eating places within easy reach of me geographically and of my pocket. Yet can they do a decent korma? You can get much better on Wilmslow Road . . . no doubt about it.'

Hucknall was slowing down in anticipation of the huge amount of energy he would soon need to write his way through another album. Nevertheless, he did spend time working on a song called *I Am Going To Lose You* to be featured in the forthcoming Roman Polanski film, *Frantic*, starring Harrison Ford. There had been talk of Hucknall writing directly for Miami Vice star Don Johnson although, at the time, this had been one of the many projects that began life on the lips of hyper-enthusiastic managers and agents and petered out to nothing. However, Hucknall had met Johnson socially on a couple of occasions, the most notable being at the Grammy Awards ceremony in Los Angeles. A strikingly volatile trio was set up when Whoopi Goldberg had joined Hucknall and Johnson, most people in the immediate vicinity being struck dumb by their unstoppable barrage of guffaws. Hucknall suggested that Johnson and Goldberg were naturally suited and should team up as a double act.

Chapter 18
A New Flame

The absurd rollercoaster effect that had defined Simply Red's singles history to date continued in February 1988 when the heartening success of *Every Time We Say Goodbye* was followed by a predictable flop. *I Won't Feel Bad* was backed with Hucknall's soaring *Lady Godiva's Room*, which would surely have made a cleverer and resolutely more memorable choice of A side.

The problem would seem to be obvious. *I Won't Feel Bad* was clearly a groove tune. It was terrific, kick-along funk, not without hooks, but not without distinctive singing either. One cannot imagine a song more capable of injecting a little heat into a concert set, or enlivening an album, or even making a dancefloor shudder (or, for that matter, featuring on the flip side of *Holding Back The Years*. Interestingly enough, both *I Won't Feel Bad* and *Lady Godiva's Room* had previously found themselves on the other side of Simply Red's biggest hit to date). But as a top selling single? It was simply never on. The only real excuse for its release, other than contractual obligation, could be that it was the antithesis of *Every Time We Say Goodbye*, thereby demonstrating that Simply Red were one of the more diverse chart bands around. Certainly, one could not imagine such a gulf of styles within the work of Simply Red's peers, like Dire Straits or Chris Rea. It peaked at sixty-eight, effectively highlighting the fact that, despite being one of Britain's top acts, absolutely nothing can be taken for granted. It probably didn't cause too much consternation within the Simply Red camp, for the continuing worldwide success of

Every Time We Say Goodbye and the album's sales it continued to generate, would certainly carry the band happy
towards the next album without seeming to 'fade' away, which
is always the great fear.

The lack of budget afforded to the accompanying video
probably spoke volumes for the confidence that both band and
record company had in the song. Sometimes, even with top
bands, it seems that a video made on the cheap is the only
logical tactic. *I Won't Feel Bad* was such a video. Shot mainly
during a Rio De Janeiro soundcheck, it concentrated on
Hucknall scratching his head, berating the band, joking and
singing to a ghostly stadium, lightly peppered with
bewildered-looking staff. (Whenever English film crews go to
Brazil, one can be sure that the camera will linger, at some
point, on brown female bottoms wobbling along beaches usually with Sugar Loaf Mountain in the background. Unfortunately, in its refusal to break with this tradition the video for *I
Won't Feel Bad* could have doubled as a downmarket televison
holiday report.)

The video was notable for just two reasons. Firstly, it
features quite clearly Aziz Ibrahim on guitar, by silencing
those who believed he had been unceremoniously shunted out
of the band *before* the Brazilian trip. And secondly, it includes
the only known video appearance of Elliot Rashman sitting at
a desk, looking as pensive as ever before a large gig. By the
time the video had spliced neatly into actual concert footage,
the song's allure had been lost. The viewer is made to feel
faintly resentful. Who, after all, really wants to see popstars
filmed in exotic locations, even in such a documentary manner?

The Brazilian connection was strengthened in March 1988
when Simply Red performed and Hucknall shared the stage
with, on separate occasions, Simple Minds and Duran Duran
in front of feverish audiences of 130,000 or more. Although
nominated for a Brazilian 'Best Foreign Act Award', Hucknall
played down the honour by briskly stating, 'I don't particularly like the rock'n'roll scene.'

This anti-star stance still managed to charm the Brazilian
audiences who were more used to seeing their popstars arrive

in helicopters or stretch limos. Indeed, both Duran Duran and
Simple Minds managed to fulfil such fantasies by hiding
behind a plethora of apparently necessary minders. Hucknall
had different ideas though. In a statement which seemed
endearingly bizarre to the Brazilians, Hucknall wandered
freely about the crowd on his own, chatting politely to the
endless barrage of stunning Brazilian girls while eating pop-
corn.

Aziz's somewhat untimely departure was cruelly heralded by
the announcement that his replacement would be a musician
of exotic background.

Heitor Pereira – affectionately dubbed Heitor T.P. by
English acquaintances unwilling to wrestle with such a sur-
name – joined the band partly due to their ongoing affection
for Brazil. Heitor, aged twenty-four, hailed from the small but
intense musicians' scene in Rio De Janeiro. Heitor was already
a star in his native country, albeit of a profoundly upmarket
nature. He was well known as one of if not the superlative
guitar player in the country, and Mick Hucknall became a fan
before even considering Heitor as a possible Simply Red band
member. Heitor's talent was uncanny. Fluent in all styles, his
ability is probably best demonstrated by the fact that, in
October 1988 as the band members of Simply Red were back
home furiously rehearsing in readiness for the arrival of their
new guitarist, an awestruck Rashman exclaimed that he,
'Likes to relax by playing Bach fugues on the guitar.'

Hucknall was excited by the addition of Heiter *and* by the
upgrading effect he had on the rest of the band. In a sense it
had refuelled Hucknall's thirst for, above all things, quality of
musicianship. The fact that Heitor had taken the band onto
another musical plain with ease, caused Hucknall to look
deeper into the basic structure of the band, and wonder in
which other departments things might also improve. However, rumours that there were more Simply Red changes on
the way were strongly denied by So What Arts and it was
claimed, however superficially, that as a unit Simply Red had
never been stronger.

By autumn 1988, a strange web of Simply Red rumours,

partially fuelled by lazily scurrilous press reports, had begun to take hold. One national newspaper in particular was responsible for the stories. 'Mick Hucknall,' it pronounced, 'is not interested in being a popstar or media figure anymore.' It was rather like saying that Brian Clough was no longer interested in football. It was a ridiculous notion excited perhaps by Hucknall's snubbing of a particularly precocious Fleet Street hack. Nevertheless, the story sprouted further reports that, for instance, Hucknall and the band had turned their back on Manchester and would, it was said, spend the rest of their days in some warm foreign clime, probably Italy.

'This is a complete tissue of lies,' stated Rashman. 'They will be back in the UK shortly. We are Mancunians and are not moving anywhere.'

The rumours undoubtedly revolved around the fact that Mick and the band were living in £60 a week rooms in a block of flats at Gallarate, near Milan. It was an arrangement of convenience rather than intent. The band had moved there to be with bassist Tony Bowers whose wife, Antonella, had just given birth. They had also booked into a nearby rehearsal studio, steadying themselves for a forthcoming tour of Spain (a fact which contradicted the reports that Hucknall had opted for a reclusive life in a 300-year-old Italian mansion).

However, Simply Red did surprise a number of people, fans and critics alike, by failing to play anywhere outside the Iberian Peninsula in 1988. The fortunate and grateful Spanish and Portuguese were the first fans to taste Simply Red's new material.

Ironically, this was the very period when the band's Mancunian roots seemed to be at their strongest. Hucknall was practically fighting to spend as much time as possible in his Old Trafford home. Chris Joyce had just bought a terraced house in Heaton Chapel, near Stockport. Tim Kellet was firmly housed in Trafford while Fritz McIntyre, perhaps the most naturally nomadic of all of them, had been house-hunting in the unlikely leafy suburbs of Marple, near Stockport.

During the time in Milan, Mick Hucknall wrote the songs and pondered upon the cover versions that would, six months later, gel together to form the new Simply Red album. It was a nervous time for quite clearly Simply Red had reached a major turning point in their career. Although their success had been, in many respects, nothing short of phenomenal, it had still been patchy. The blame for this quite possibly lay in the comparative 'hardness' of *Men And Women* (compared that is, to acts of a similar worldwide stature who would have regarded such musical diversity as downright reckless and naive). Perhaps Hucknall had spent too long writing for himself – exploring the musical virtues that turned him on? That massive audience out there, hovering around Simply Red, especially after *Holding Back The Years* and *Every Time We Say Goodbye*, had still to be fully seduced.

If it was to realise its full commercial potential, Simply Red's music would have to be able to settle within the everpresent cloud of 'muzak'. It would have to go with the flow – totally, unreservedly, regardless of what the critics said (who were mostly completely irrelevant as far as Simply Red were concerned anyway). Hucknall shouldn't be writing for himself and certainly not for Charles Shaar Murray. He would have to write completely for – to pluck two names at random – Dave and Pam, a thirtysomething couple from Essex, or the Fylde, who work in insurance offices or maybe in computer programming. Although the credibility of Dave and Pam might be nil in the eyes of the essentially naive music press, they would have no musical prejudices whatsoever. Furthermore, they didn't know nor wish to know anything about the origins of music and, to be frank, why should they care? Dave and Pam wanted to pay £11.99 for a compact disc that they could slip on quietly, tastefully after dinner, or in the car, or while doing the ironing, or on holiday in Antigua. If it gently touched their emotions, if lyrics occasionally seemed particularly relevant to them, so much the better. They wanted quality, not innovation.

It would be two years before Hucknall would become fully intimate with the likes of Dave and Pam, by which time his maturity would have lifted him and the band way above the ridiculous and juvenile notions of musical credibility.

But one thing was obvious, the next album would be softer, smoother, more relaxed, classier perhaps, and certainly far

more mature than the disparate *Men And Women*. The new
record would be closer, in feel and in pace, to *Picture Book*
than *Men And Women*. Hucknall's idea was that it would be a
development from *Picture Book* that would incorporate what
he considered to be the best bits from *Men And Women*.
Perhaps predictably, it would be made up of predominantly
love songs.

The most significant aspect of the new album, which was
eventually recorded in the incredible setting of Montserrat's
Air Studios but prepared in Gallarate, was the re-
establishment of Stuart Levine as producer. The work in
progress would take the title *A New Flame*, after Hucknall's
refreshing opening song, extolling nothing more revolutionary
than the madness that accompanies a fresh love affair.

The songwriting connection with Lamont Dozier was to be
cleverly deepened by the inclusion of two more Hucknall/
Dozier songs: the sprightly, assertive *Turn It Up* and the
lovely, lilting *You've Got It*. The former song, lyrically speaking, at least, was wholly at odds with the mood and feel of any
album that Dave and Pam might wish to own. Hucknall's
lyrics, which proved to be overtly anti-Thatcherite, sat
unnervingly within the structure of Dozier's bouncing rhythm
and uneasily among a set of songs deliberately glossed by
Levine presumably to assume an aura of absolute ease, of
almost arrogant understatement. There were times on the
album when the gloss would fail to be challenged by Hucknall
vocally and musically. During such moments, the album
would seem submissive and would surely attract the charge of
blandness. (The song *More* springs most readily to mind for it
soon became symbolic of Simply Red at their weakest. It was a
song that caused even Elliot Rashman to have his doubts.)

But the album would be spiced not by aggression but by
touches of sheer awesome quality. It was Hucknall's idea to
cover the Harold Melvin and the Blue Notes classic *If You
Don't Know Me By Now*, primarily because he, 'Just thought it
was a beautiful song.' It is hard to imagine an admittedly
beautiful song more perfectly suited to set the tone for the
new, super smooth Simply Red. The song, originally a wigs'n'-
flares seventies hit, would be plucked straight out of the

fading memories and dusty record collections of the Daves and Pams and, when given Levine's delicate treatment, would surely carry Simply Red straight back into the heads of those who had been tempted by *Every Time We Say Goodbye*. The reaction to the song, however, would annoy Hucknall for people would begin to press home the mistaken opinion that, 'Mick Hucknall is a great singer . . . but not a great writer.' The flames of this argument – which began with *Every Time We Say Goodbye* – were fanned somewhat by the release of the album's pilot single *It's Only Love*, a Jimmy and Vella Cameron song that contained just enough delicacy to gently tease the radio listeners out to the record shops. (To be honest, when placed among the often discordant crackle of general chart noise, the song's arrival on the play lists came as a blessed relief. It sold well, too, reaching a surprising number thirteen in the UK – surprising because the song's subtlety, although an aesthetic attribute, did not seem to forecast a massive hit.)

Another collaboration was to appear on the album with Joe Sample, keyboard master of the Crusaders who never managed to better their extraordinary single *Street Life*. The song, *Enough*, poignantly glimpsed into an affair at the very moment of breakdown. It was, perhaps, only fitting that an album predominantly filled with love songs and sporting a title cut that extolled the wonders of falling into a new affair should finish on such a downer.

The album was preceded in the UK charts by the subdued *It's Only Love* single which, peaking at thirteen, hardly had the record book scribblers feverishly tapping the calculators. Hucknall's newly polished understanding of his own audience would be proven, however, when the album swept all before it aside and arrogantly shunted to number one, silencing those who had, to Hucknall's fury, been predicting his impending demise. Considering the runaway success of *A New Flame* – commercial rather than critical – Hucknall was, if one was to believe the music press, quite the embodiment of carefully constructed naffness. Not that he cared a jot. He was a world away on a different plane, launching into a relationship with his audience that would have few parallels. The following tour dates, obviously set before the album's release, seemed positively minuscule.

17 February	Dublin Stadium
18 February	Maysfield Leisure Centre, Belfast
19 February	Barrowlands, Glasgow
20 February	Playhouse, Edinburgh
21, 22 February	Apollo, Manchester
28 February, 1 March	City Hall, Newcastle
3 March	Spa, Bridlington
4 March	Opera House, Blackpool
6 March	BIC, Bournemouth
7 March	Arena, St Austell
9, 10, 11 March	Wembley Arena
13 March	Centre, Brighton
16 March	NEC, Birmingham

Compared with what was to come, these dates, Wembley Arena and the NEC aside, seem almost quaint. It was almost the last chance to see Simply Red in an atmosphere of comparative intimacy. For band and audience, such a luxury would soon be lost forever.

Three days before appearing at Manchester Apollo, Hucknall, Joyce and McIntyre booked themselves into the ostentatious Britannia Hotel in Piccadilly. Partly for secrecy but mainly in the spirit of lampoon, they signed the hotel register under the names Flotsby, D. Corleone and F. Douglas. Needless to say nobody was particularly fooled by this and, more than once, it was remarked just how the name 'Flotsby' seemed to suit Manchester's favourite flame haired singer.

The hotel staff, thoroughly schooled in the idiosyncracies of popstar guests, merely exchanged knowing looks when the trio's ground rules were delivered to them. Nevertheless, the rules did seem a little out of the ordinary. Nobody, for instance, was allowed to knock on any of the doors of their fourth-floor rooms and no member of the housekeeping staff was allowed to use a vacuum cleaner within earshot of the resting musicians (this was particularly emphasised). Indeed, the band were most adamant that their rooms should be situated in the quietest part of the hotel. As one hotel

The hat, walking cane and Lowryesque swagger. Simple, distinctive imagery, with a hint of northern grit. (*London Features International Ltd*)

Mick Hucknall's birth certificate.

THE FRANTIC ELEVATORS

**Voice in the Dark
Passion
Every Day I Die**

Mick Hucknall's vinyl debut. The
archetypal late seventies indie single.

Sunglasses and dour expressions.
The gangsters of soul? (*Pictorial
Press Ltd*)

On promotional duty. Note the reluctant gaze of Sylvan Richardson (far right). (*Syndication International Ltd*)

Onstage at the International Youth Year Festival, Platt Fields, Moss Side, Manchester in 1985 – a launch-pad event, for both the band and the burgeoning Manchester music scene. (*Courtesy of* City Life)

The demands of stardom can be wearying. Hucknall is patient . . . up to a point! (*Syndication International Ltd*)

Backstage at the 1987 Grammy
Awards, Shrine Auditorium, Los
Angeles. (*Pictorial Press Ltd*)

Onstage at New York's Ritz. (*Pictorial
Press Ltd*)

With Ashford and Simpson. (*Pictorial Press Ltd*)

Performing at the San Remo Festival, 1986. (*Pictorial Press Ltd*)

At the London premiere of the Chuck Berry tribute movie, *Hail, Hail Rock'n'Roll* in 1988. Hucknall – the rebel reformed – hangs out with the elite. (*Syndication International Ltd*)

Coping with the paparazzi. (*London Features International Ltd*)

Pugnaciously shunting through Heathrow. (*All Action*)

At the tennis. In later years Hucknall sought solace through a variety of friendships with sports stars. (*All Action*)

Concentration during the recording of *Stars*. (*Val Wilmer/Redferns*)

Goofing about onstage – a vision of style and elegance? (*All Action*)

Accepting applause – the consummate performer. (*Rex Features*)

Mick and the band post *Stars*, by now well accustomed to graciously accepting awards from a grateful music industry. (*David Koppel/All Action*)

Onstage at Monte Carlo, 1992. (*London Features International Ltd*)

employee remarked, 'Some of the chamber maids were simply terrified of going anywhere near their rooms. Mick Hucknall, after all, has a reputation for losing his temper. It was lovely to have the band staying in the Britannia but, I have to admit, it wasn't particularly easy to bow to their every wish.'

Oddly enough, Hucknall – or Flotsby – insisted that his room, although on the same floor, was situated as far away from the other two band members as possible. There was considerable anguish among the hotel staff when it was discovered that Hucknall was a little too near to Chris Joyce's room for comfort.

The So What operation's desire to diversify and perhaps utilise their now considerable talents were mainly hampered by the sheer weight of work created by the dominance of their main act. Hucknall's apparently invincible devotion to Rashman and Dodd naturally had to be reciprocated at all times. The idea of So What Arts developing into a full-scale operation, dedicated to the nurturing and prospering of other artists, had always appealed to Rashman, Dodd and indeed Hucknall. Throughout his career, he continued to express a desire for his success to help to subsidise other musicians in some way. But this, of course, is often easy in theory. The reality is that if Rashman and Dodd really did wish to take such diversification towards a logical conclusion and create a management team with a number of hit artists on its books, then the unique and distinctive nature of the operation would be lost. After all, there is a world of difference between a set up wholly dedicated to the promotion of one massive act, and the more conventional notion of a team acting as the nucleus of many artists. After all and friendship aside, did Rashman and Dodd really want to risk loosening the ties with their main act however slightly?

The solid bond between So What and Hucknall was probably put most forcibly to the test during the height of the 'Madchester' explosion of the late eighties. Suddenly, Simply Red and So What were no longer lone stars, not even in their own office block. The Madchester explosion, born from the innovative stirrings of the Hacienda-centred rave circus, had provided the city with an internationally famous music scene. By 1989, Manchester was awash with homegrown pop stars, many of whom, hardly believing their luck, had caught the wave of hype and were riding towards success that would elevate them stratospherically above their deserved status. At one point the city's G-Mex venue played host not only to acts the size of Simply Red, but also to Happy Mondays, Inspiral Carpets, 808 State and later James.

It was madness, of course, and couldn't possibly last. Nevertheless, as the world tuned in, the businesses from the inside and on the periphery of the Madchester scene burst into life. Record pluggers, promoters, management teams, downmarket clothes designers, club owners, disc jockeys, T-shirt pirates, writers, photographers – and, of course, a whole mass of artists.

At So What Arts one fact began to hit home. The Madchester scene – the biggest musical revolution since Merseybeat – which had temporarily wiped out the smugness of London had exploded completely without the help of Simply Red or, more worryingly for Rashman, without So What Arts. Huckanll's only true contribution towards Madchester was to be often seen charismatically riding his pushbike through the city centre. A famous *NME* Readers' Poll for 1989 saw the Stone Roses, Happy Mondays, Inspiral Carpets, 808 State and Morrissey sweeping the board. This was a game that Simply Red were just not involved in. To a ridiculous degree, the world had gone Manchester crazy. Young folk in voluminous denim jeans would arrive at Piccadilly Station from London, Newcastle, California and Japan and scurry about the city centre, clutching *A to Z*s, asking bemused Mancunians directions to supposedly legendary local rock landmarks. Most of these strange new 'tourists' were motivated by endless tales of Happy Mondays' hedonism, or Stone Roses' gormlessness or Morrissey's preciousness – but were many of them even aware that Simply Red had come from Manchester?

Common sense, of course, suggested that, not only would the bubble soon burst and most horribly, as it did, but that Mick Hucknall and Simply Red had risen on to a plane way above such trends. It had occurred to the wisest of the acts, those whose Madchester success hadn't occurred during their first flush of youth, that an enormous backlash was rapidly approaching and it might be wise to distance themselves from faddish Madchester. The band James – the oddest success story of the scene – were among the most experienced musicians from the city. They were a band who had musically developed slowly, carefully and often in the face of a cruelly chequered history (battles with the record company, etc.). Their back catalogue was rich in quality and in many respects they seemed most unsuited to the role of Madchester popstars. Nevertheless, the little kids who scurried about the city seemed all too willing to wear James's T-shirts.

The band had been most effectively managed by Martine MacDonagh, the girlfriend of lead singer Tim Booth. They openly desired, however, the services of a management team with a deep understanding of the international music business network. Not without certain reservations on both sides, Rashman became associated with James on a management level. It was a major challenge, at least as a tester of the strength of the Rashman/Hucknall partnership. What it wasn't, however, was a particularly perceptive move. James had lost their footing with, ironically, Sire Records and had released material briefly on Rough Trade. But they now looked certain to pick up their career and evolve into one of the most stable selling units in the country. A safe bet? Possibly, but James were and are musicians of extreme seriousness, of great dignity. Wholly dedicated to their art, they could never be effectively managed by a team with conflicting interests.

It was to end in tears. Rashman's honest desire to turn James into a band who could go with the flow of a record company's marketing plan, rather than react against it at all times, unsettled the band. Tim Booth, in particular, soon found his artistic pretensions offended by Rashman's cool business head. 'I'm not one of your plastic popstar puppets,' screamed Booth, in a final confrontation.

Some time later, after James – once again managed by MacDonagh – had become quite preposterously enormous, Rashman sent Booth a fax. 'Welcome to the world of plastic popstar puppets,' it read.

★ ★ ★

Despite the somewhat humbling fact that *A New Flame* had gone platinum in the UK and Simply Red were just beginning to look like a band capable of joining and remaining in the company of the likes of U2 and Michael Jackson (a possibility that just wouldn't be admitted by the jealous hordes of Manchester), the nerve centre of So What Arts remained distinctly seedy. They were still based – and as I write, still are – within the downbeat office complex at 48 Princess Street, Manchester.

The office block is typical of Manchester. Once grandly sitting among the astonishingly ornate warehouses at the very hub of the Industrial Revolution they had, like the rest of Manchester, fallen into ghostly disrepair. They had been rescued by property developers who transformed them swiftly into downmarket offices. As such, they attracted a number of perhaps romantic, certainly 'optimistic' businesses. One-room insurance brokers, private detectives and a whole splattering of small-time operators from the fringes of the burgeoning music business. Pluggers and promoters, indie labels and established indie groups. (The Fall's label, Cog Sinister, was housed in there, as was Tony Michaelides' apparently unstoppable promotions company, Hacienda DJ Dave Haslam, and Playtime Records owner, Paula Greenwood.) Such activity gave the complex a dusty Bohemian atmosphere. It was a perfect home for the indie dream but a rather odd place to find the headquarters of one of the world's top bands with such a sophisticated, elegant, stylish image to uphold. While it never seemed unnatural for the legendary Mark E. Smith to be seen filling the kettle in the dirt-encrusted washroom, meeting Mick Hucknall, garbed in a raincoat and dragging his bicycle up there just didn't seem right at all. In one sense, Hucknall couldn't win in Manchester. Although dour Mancunians, understandably perhaps, could often be heard moaning about Hucknall's wealth, they were also rather confused by Simply Red's apparent lack of noticeable opulence. Apart from Hucknall's about-town scruffiness, it didn't escape people's notice that Rashman still resided on unlovely Didsbury Road in Stockport's Heaton Mersey while Dodd remained encamped a mile away among the decayed glamour of Brownsville Road.

Despite continuing rumours that So What were about to up and leave and relocate in Salford Quays, if not Milton Keynes, Rashman and Co. seemed to revel in the seediness of it all. Perhaps it was because of a naive lust for credibility. Whatever, So What Arts never seemed to find any reason to leave this crumbly base.

Rashman and Dodd, needing an escape valve from the occasionally suffocating atmosphere of Simply Red, wished to find some kind of musical involvement outside the band. Blessed with decent capital, they saw no reason why they couldn't kick start a record label which would operate on a purely aesthetic rather than commercial basis. Why couldn't they subsidise the kind of music that, in the increasingly hard times of the late eighties, hadn't a hope in hell of attracting serious interest from the majors. Rashman had 'unplugged' the sixteen-track recording studio which was situated in the snooker room at the back of his home in Heaton Mersey, and had transferred it to a pristine new studio in Denton. Apparently, the idea was to allow struggling songwriters to make demo tapes free of charge.

'Creative people need a medium to work on that's low on overheads,' said Rashman. 'There are a lot of frustrated musicians involved in this venture who do work for us instead of having to pay for studio time.'

It was alleged that this oddly benevolent venture would follow on into the intriguing notion of an acoustically minded record label. Whatever, it was an indication that Rashman, in particular, was keen to prove that the phenomenal success of Simply Red wasn't just a case of an individual lucky break. As ridiculous as this charge might seem, it had been known to reverberate around the more cynical areas of Manchester. There had been talk of the utter 'selfishness' of the So What operation; the fact that every single act hones down to pushing not even the whole band, but just one man. This was, perhaps, a necessary selfishness. Nevertheless, reasoned Rashman, there was no reason at all why Simply Red couldn't be seen to help other musicians. It might even prove to be fun – lucrative or otherwise.

★ ★ ★

However unhip Simply Red might have become at street level, at teen level, after U2 they were just about *the* band to be seen with, at least as far as Hollywood superstars were concerned (especially after Simply Red had ecstatically nudged into the number one singles spot in America, for the second time. This most coveted and precarious position was brought about by the US public's love of *If You Don't Know Me By Now*).

Whenever Simply Red passed through Los Angeles, for instance, Hucknall would find himself endlessly bouncing from screen idol to screen idol. It was quite absurd, although Hucknall chose not to scoff and treated every last one of them with extreme courtesy. After all, when the sycophantic circle around you begins to include the kind of screen and song legends who would have made Hucknall's aunties swoon years before, then you can be reasonably certain that you have truly arrived.

The list of confirmed Simply Red fans was growing to an embarrassing degree. Diana Ross, Mick Jagger and Diane Keaton were the latest to publicly declare their love of Mick and the band. Diane Keaton must have been a particularly strange one for Hucknall who had declared his love for Woody Allen's glamorous sidekick in the early eighties after seeing 'Annie Hall'. While Simply Red performed at a high-profile concert at the Los Angeles Roxy nightclub, the stars streamed in from down the road Beverly Hills and Bel-Air, clutching their special passes. After all, it was a social 'event'. Points were there to be scored in the glare of paparazzo. Jack Nicholson was among the most notable and surrounding him were an illustrious gang who included Debra Winger and Harry Dean Stanton.

Following the gig, Nicholson invited Hucknall and crew for a drink at his private club. 'Winger was wonderful and charming,' stated a clearly besotted Rashman. Stanton, somewhat the worse for wear, tried unsuccessfully to stand on the tables, while Nicholson spent an hour chatting intensely to Hucknall. He told Hucknall that his latest project was about jazz in the 1940s and the pair swapped anecdotal tales of meetings with ageing musicians from that era.

'When these old guys say that there is nothing in pop music with any substance,' . . . said Nicholson, 'I play them Simply Red.'

Back in Manchester, Hucknall's devotion to Manchester United was severely tested by the club's 'red' tape. Wishing to wear his sporting heritage on his back, Hucknall wanted a complete football kit in the sixties style of Manchester United, à la Best, Law and Charlton. (Following an upsurge in cult appeal, such items became readily available and, with their sky blue opposite, enjoyed a brief spell as fashion items in the early nineties.) Hucknall made several phone enquiries to Old Trafford but to little avail. The disembodied voice at Old Trafford steadfastly refused to offer any assistance other than a curt, 'Try the club shop.' The club shop, however, couldn't help either. 'I would have paid, handsomely,' Hucknall said. 'I'm not a freeloader. I just wondered if it was possible to buy the style of kit worn by George Best.'

A letter from Hucknall to supporters' club chairman, Barry Moorehouse, still failed to work and it was only when the story began to surface in the *Manchester Evening News* Diary that the club began to respond.

'I'll see if we can dig out a replica kit,' stated Moorehouse, before adding, 'if we can't, I'm sure we can fix him up with a present-day kit.'

Mick Hucknall always had a soft spot for Manchester's Ritz ballroom. He had been slightly disappointed back in 1985 when the band's pivotal gig had been transferred to the International.

The reason for this fondness lay rooted in the club's long, impressive history because the Ritz is no shallow disco. The acclaimed 'springy' dance floor had been talked about for generations and, on that very stage, many of the greats of swing, be-bop, R'n'B and rock had performed during the early years in their development. When Joe Jackson brought his Jumping Jive jazz band to the Ritz in 1982 (Jumping Jive was a thoroughly enjoyable Jackson project involving a swing band who tastefully aped the record collection belonging to

Jackson's father), Jackson remarked with considerable awe, 'This one is called *Five Guys Named Moe* . . . and, just think, this was probably played once in this hall by the original musicians.' Hucknall was also open to sensing such ghosts. The Ritz might have had a chequered past but it was possible, at least for someone with Hucknall's nose for musical reference points, to feel the aura of greatness.

In November 1989, Mick Hucknall gleefully returned to the Ritz's DJ box every Tuesday to revive his legendary Black Rhythms night from his days spent at Manchester Poly Students' Union. It was a high-tech operation. Hucknall, never without taping equipment, made up his disc jockey reels on a portable state-of-the-art DAT machine at his home in Old Trafford. He was very fond of making impromptu DJ appearances be it at the Ritz or a club in Toronto or Japan, and he simply plugs the DAT machine in. Interestingly enough, Hucknall's old Black Rhythms evenings at the Poly, which had been taken over by DJ Andy Sage, were still a successful regular event in the city. And so, for one month only, two rival Black Rhythms evenings clashed entertainingly in the same city.

At Whitworth Street's most famous junction at night, a queue often snaked from the garage-like doors and intimidating low-key façade of the Hacienda, around the corner and almost within view of G-Mex. This queue had become a Manchester cliché. Even standing in it, anticipating the rigours of frantic nightlife to come, had itself turned into something of a cult. Although most of the kids in that queue failed to realise it, it was an absurd parallel of the Hollywood hierarchy. In creating the Hacienda door policy, Factory had instigated the most obnoxious system imaginable. It was a system where the guest list reigned absolutely supreme even if all one had to be to get on to it was a second cousin twice removed of a bass player who once guested with an obscure Factory act, Crispy Ambulance. Nevertheless, the kids in the queue would gaze adoringly at those who would drift casually past, arrogantly accepting the nods of recognition from the box office and bouncing staff before disappearing enigmatically through to the pulsating interior. The queue stood and aped, apparently content to fulfil the necessary though lowly role of 'punters'.

If the guest-listed freeloader was a popstar or a recognisably famous face, this pathetic divide would seem all the more profound. At best, this social statement was simply good fun, a bit of glitter in the night – very eighties, very Thatcherite, too. At its worst, it blatantly displayed all that is distasteful and unacceptable within the youth culture business. It did not square well with many of the popstar guests who would so often love to spout left-wing rhetoric for the benefit of some journalist. And to the poor nightclub fiend, blowing his dole money on the entrance fee, there could certainly be more soothing visions than the rather smug-looking photograph of Factory boss, Anthony Wilson, which glared down from the rear of the ticket office.

To many of the punters, one of the more familiar sights of this weekly queuing – other than the entertainment provided by busking Factory act, Rob Grey – was Mick Hucknall, garishly suited or heavily raincoated, drifting ghostlike down the line. Hucknall had become out of necessity an absolute master at passing by the gawping eyes speedily, before recognition was followed by abuse. Hucknall was a regular Hacienda attender since breaking out of his Frantic Elevators period of isolation.

In the mid-eighties, as the club slowly began to fill up – just prior to the Dave Haslam-inspired revolutionary Thursday nights, when all hell was let loose – Hucknall, by this time a rising star, was the club's most commonly spotted famous face. It was difficult to miss Hucknall, difficult not to stare at him as he marched across the dance floor, his ornate walking stick held aloft before him. This bizarre sight established him as resident popstar 'poser'. It was a widely known and greatly exaggerated image, but not one that was particularly flattering. In some circles it induced open hatred, but what could he do? Hide away in a Spanish castle? Dress all in black and send flunkies to replenish his forever empty glass? Hold court in the club's most inaccessible alcove? Not dance? Surely, to choose any of these would be rather more 'popstar' than to queue up with everyone else for a drink and to continue to gyrate on the dance floor, as was his wont.

Nevertheless, he was a noted master of pose and he certainly took great delight in living up to that image. In fact he would positively glow as he bypassed that queue. But this pose was never more in evidence than the day when Hucknall famously arrived at the Hacienda, in mid-Madchester boom-time, accompanied by a large and familiar-looking blonde woman. As Hucknall and friend weaved their way downstairs to the Gay Traitor bar, recognition began to register on many of the faces who, no doubt, had spent time glued to mildly erotic fantasy Red Sonja. Mick Hucknall, for God's sake, had taken Brigitte Nielsen into the Hacienda. It was a preposterous thing to do. A challenge, perhaps, to those who regularly accused Hucknall of overt posing.

The truth is that Nielsen, who had like most people read endless tales of the now internationally famous Manchester club, simply wanted to taste the energy and see for herself the nocturnal nucleus of all the Madchester fuss. The request had come from her rather than from Hucknall, who was well aware of the kind of attention the couple would surely have to suffer. Nevertheless, it was a most brilliant piece of PR and one that would still be talked about years later when the Hacienda would resolutely celebrate its tenth year in the face of the collapse of Factory Records.

Hucknall's relationship with Brigitte Nielsen had been published – and no doubt blown out of all proportion – by the tabloid press prior to the Hacienda appearance. Although the couple had spent considerable amounts of time together, apparently on both sides of the Atlantic, and were not afraid to be seen in nightclub situations, any romantic notions can be put down to media exaggeration. Hucknall, however, was not entirely averse to fanning the flames a little. When a *You* magazine reporter stated that she didn't really believe the rumours, he mysteriously replied, 'Yeah, well, it's true. I could tell you a lot of things about her . . . She's big, huge, domineering. That's my type. No the silicone don't put you off, it were very well done, very sexy. She's misunderstood. People have got the wrong impression of her. A lot of what she is like is down to Stallone. What a weird trip that guy is on, man, I'm telling you.'

Chapter 19
Stars

By 1990, Rashman, as creatively entrepreneurial as ever, had instigated plans for the filming of a one-off television concert to be held in a suitably eccentric, though uncharacteristically small hall. The basic idea would be to compile a one-hour television film intended to signify the end of a chapter in Simply Red's history.

'It can bring all the qualities that TV can bring to a live concert,' stated Rashman. 'We'll be building special stages and gangways to get all the best close-up shots.'

The chosen venue couldn't have been more bizarre. It was the basement theatre of Manchester's dominant gothic, though somewhat ignored, architectural beauty the Refuge Building. Situated opposite and towering above Oxford Road's hyper trendy Cornerhouse gallery, café bar and cinema complex, the Refuge Building, with its deep red tone and tendency to cast long, magical shadows, had long since gained a cult admiration society from the many students and BBC employees who stared in awe each lunchtime whilst nibbling carrot cake.

Rashman and Dodd knew that a televised gig in such a place would instantly become one of the classic evenings of Manchester's musical history. They set up a new company, specifically created for the task of making this estimated £200,000 film.

The show was destined to be seen only by a couple of hundred lucky entrants and would surely cause congestion problems by attracting hopeful ticketless fans by the coachload. 'We could fill it with our friends alone,' said Rashman. 'But we would like to get real Simply Red fanatics there. We are still working out how to do that.'

Another minor scuffle broke out, at least in the local Manchester media, when Sky Television expressed an interest in screening the proposed film. Upon learning this, Hucknall hit the roof, apparently objecting to working with any organisation directly associated with Rupert Murdoch. 'Sky won't get a look in,' declared an adamant Rashman.

Unfortunately, the Refuge Building plan proved too ambitious and collapsed when enquiries from unnamed potential buyers caused the owners (Skillion, who had paid £4½ million for it in 1980) to kill Rashman's plans abruptly. It was a terrible blow which left Rashman very angry after eighteen months' preparation – he'd even negotiated the overseas rights. Skillion's back-out came late, too late for the snowball to stop rolling. The special set, for instance, had already been designed and was on the verge of installation.

Rashman's anger was not aimed purely at Skillion: 'It's taken eighteen months because we wanted to do it in our home town,' he told the *Manchester Evening News*. 'The city council were no use in finding us a venue. They are just not using their own buildings or promoting the modern cultural heritage of Manchester . . . and yet Liverpool City Council were able to offer us a warehouse specially done up for the purpose right away – and they are supposed to be bankrupt and dead.'

This outburst was deliberately pointed at the time when Manchester City Council was running a PR campaign designed to prove that the city was capable of hosting the Olympic Games. One official in particular, the week before, had stated on the local news programme 'Granada Tonight' that claims that Manchester was a city run in tune with the vibrant youth scene and cultural heritage of area were 'not just the usual load of hot air'. Rashman's words were a direct contradiction of such a notion.

All of which left Rashman and Dodd scrambing around for another suitable venue. They were forced to settle for the fitting, though considerably less charismatic Manchester

Polytechnic which would provide the strangest of homecomings. Only 200 fans would be allowed in. What's more, the televison deal was put on hold for a while in favour of a special concert video.

The chosen video company was the oddly named Big Star in A Wee Picture, run by producer Jo Homewood – although the entire project lay in the balance until the last minute. A deal was struck with the Poly literally two days before the filming. Before the ink was dry, technicians moved in to build stage effects in the Polytechnic's Capitol Theatre.

On the night, the band minus Hucknall all arrived, with tremendous affectation, in separate limos. Hucknall, on the other hand, chose to saunter his way on foot.

'He's just as bloody scruffy as he always was when 'e was nobody,' commented the security guard.

'I don't see why I should change now,' replied Hucknall.

Between March 1990 and November 1990, the tour-weary Hucknall demanded time off. *A New Flame* might sound like one of the most effortless pop albums of all time, but the promotional demands placed on a performer of world standing are enough to make even the most level-headed popstar seriously begin to doubt both his sanity and stamina. Hucknall made good use of the extended holiday to relax, travel loosely around the globe with few schedules to interrupt his flow, and visit friends. No hint of work was allowed to disrupt his relaxation. The tight crippling chains that bound him to the role of 'superstar' were allowed to slacken. The simmering ego, forever threatening to explode into self-destructive fire, was well and truly dampened. It was a terrifying situation he had got himself into with a mighty weight of responsibility which hadn't been allowed to be lifted from his shoulders. Despite his seemingly boundless self confidence, the cracks had started to surface.

It was time for him to reflect, not merely on what had happened to him during the last, fantastic six years, but also on what had happened before then. Had the personality he used to be become mixed up with the person he now was? Had the crazy hyperbole that forever surrounded him really taken its toll? The idea was simply to sit down and think, to try to assess the past and the future and find some kind of perspective.

The fact that his was a situation that most people, let alone most aspiring bands, would gladly swap a couple of limbs for didn't help Hucknall at all. Nobody knew more than he did that he had been quite outrageously lucky. Lucky to have the talent and drive in the first place, lucky to be able to get himself into that position and lucky that the market forces responded to staggering perfection. Nevertheless, there is a downside to such luck, a downside to fame that is made all the more dangerous by the general public's complete lack of understanding. To be top dog is fine, but it carries with it not just responsibility but a terrible isolation. Who, after all, could Hucknall turn to for advice? Who else had ever been in the same situation? Other rocks stars generally seemed to be completely wrapped in their own worlds. This was one reason why Hucknall sought the company of famous sportspeople. Footballers, in particular, liked Hucknall. Much to Simply Red's embarrassment, their music had long since found itself snuggling into the in-car CD rack of the archetypal British professional footballer, most often next to Chris De Burgh, Chris Rea, Dire Straits, Phil Collins and just possibly U2.

Tennis star Steffi Graf was another friend. Catching a glimpse of Mick Hucknall skipping jauntily down the Champs Elysees, accompanied by an equally lightheaded Steffi Graf, was just about all the tabloids needed. Steffi'n'Mick – an item? Reports gushed into the sillier gossip columns. Hucknall, it was widely reported, was, 'Completely besotted with crises-hit tennis ace, Steffi', etc. It was a difficult and embarrassing press wave which in truth had little to do with Hucknall at all. Graf had been recently knocked out of the French Open. She had looked decidedly and uncharacteristically ruffled throughout the tournament, and had been swamped with allegations that her father, Peter, had had an affair with Playboy beauty Nicole Meissner. The sports press, sensing a chink in what had seemed to be such impenetrable armour, searched for every possible method of unsettling the tennis star. It was a lot for a twenty-year-old to take, even one as naturally unperturbable as Graf. Being a big fan of Simply Red she had sent Hucknall a ticket for the French Open. Hucknall, arguably more able to handle such intense media pressure than Graf, had simply agreed to escort her around Paris and they had become platonic pals.

Stories of a love match, ridiculous as they were, were probably best dismissed by Elliot Rashman, who noted in a statement to the *Manchester Evening News*, 'If you think about it, they are not exactly a good match are they?'

There were a few, apparently hugely enjoyable musical excursions during this period. Perhaps this was a chance for Hucknall to flex the muscles of his fame for his own enjoyment rather than merely the promotion of his product. He took great delight in guesting as vocalist on veteran saxophonist Andy Hamilton's debut album. In Milan, looking charismatic and at ease, he duoed with his old hero Barry White. Their performance of *Let The Music Play* naturally went down a storm. He drove over the Alps (stopping about once every fifteen minutes to swoon at the stunning scenery) to catch his 'good friends' Quincy Jones and Miles Davis at the Montreux Jazz Festival. The jazz fraternity had started to clutch Hucknall to their hearts by this time.

There were other refreshing activities. Hucknall had made a brief reappearance as a Manchester disc jockey at Manchester's wonderful Ritz a year previously (and had accepted virtually every given opportunity to act as guest DJ in many clubs across Europe). Now he decided to take the opportunity of another stint behind the turn tables. This time he took his DAT cassette and black vinyl collection to Manchester University's purpose-built music venue, the Academy. DJing still came naturally to him. It was, after all, a perfect opportunity for him to share his current influences, to show off perhaps, and occasionally stun people by the disparity of his listening habits and tastes.

He was aware of the strength of the DJ cult, especially in Manchester since the Madchester days. Hucknall had seen many old acquaintances – Mike Pickering at the Hacienda, Dave Haslam at the Hacienda and following a less than amicable split at the Boardwalk – and a whole mass of others. It dawned on Hucknall that, had singing and art not dominated his early eighties life, a third occupation would surely have presented itself. For Hucknall's Black Rhythms evenings would certainly have gained an immense cult following, even if he hadn't achieved superstardom.

For Hucknall it was just another aspect of performance. An easy aspect, perhaps, although any twinges of guilt he might have felt when standing back and merely spinning the discs was tempered by the knowledge that he was helping to push what was, to his mind, excellent and often unfairly obscure music. Even in 1990, he took his DJing activities very seriously indeed.

'There's a whole black music heritage that goes back to the forties that's really significant and is going to be remembered as being significant, so it's nice just to show some of it and review it a little,' he said. 'My DJing collection just covers everything that I think is really danceable, including relatively undiscovered dub reggae which has been named as being an influence by a lot of major musicians around now. Sometimes the diverse nature of my collection surprises even me. Having said that, I do tend to keep harking back to the seventies. It's incredible how much some things released in the seventies sound so contemporary right now. So much has actually been sampled by the house thing that you occasionally hear something and think, "Oh yes . . . I've heard that before." It happens all the time to me . . . I suppose it always did, but it's more apparent now. This is a really weird phase in popular music. As we drift into the nineties, the music in our heads is profoundly old fashioned . . . and so much seventies stuff.'

This quote, which appeared in *Record Mirror*, could be most aptly applied to Manchester's band of the moment, Inspiral Carpets, perhaps the most obviously representative of all Madchester contenders. Would a derivative musical stance offend Hucknall's musicianly approach?

'Well, I think the beauty of it is that it doesn't often sound like it is intended to sound,' he continued. 'Perhaps if they have got too good at sounding like something old fashioned it wouldn't work too well. It sounds, actually, quite original and some of it actually sounds very good indeed. There's always going to be that emulation period for any band. I think I went through the same thing in 1984 when you are obsessed with a certain mental idea of what you want to do. If you listen to the first two Stones albums, they are like R'n'B covers verbatim, then later on they move out and become more original. I think the best bands from the Madchester thing will continue and slowly find their own true niche. There is nothing wrong with that. We are now past the really energetic period in this city. It's reaching a point now when the really interesting music will start to stand out a little bit from the mediocrity that is created by trends and fashions. In the sixties only a few bands got through. The same thing happened with funk, and the same thing is going to happen with this.'

It was ironic that the concept of the next Simply Red album would be developed, at least in part, from this period of rest and reflection. He spent time, some of it back in Manchester, watching up-and-coming bands and the bands of the Madchester boom, watching how they were coping as fame swept in to turn their lives around.

Once again he admired the solidness and calmness of the sports stars who, with the odd notable exception, tended to accept their stardom with grace and wisdom. He spent time with the England football team the weekend before they played in the World Cup in Sardinia. He became particularly friendly with Gary Lineker and Chris Waddle.

'I really respect sportspeople,' he said. 'It's a very different life to mine but they still have to have discipline, and I have discipline when it comes to my work.' Popstars traditionally seemed to allow the whole process to make them go crazy. Indeed, the classic rock cliché, from the Rolling Stones to Happy Mondays, was simply to revel in such craziness (à la Spinal Tap).

Hucknall was fascinated by the fact that, had the Frantic Elevators encountered fame, they would have been completely torn apart, physically as a band and emotionally as individuals. They were pretty wild to begin with. He knew too, that had the young Mick Hucknall become a star his personality would have mutated into something quite horrific. The thought frightened him.

Mick Hucknall thought a lot about 'stars'; three kinds of stars. He contemplated his own stardom and how it always threatened to ruin him.

'The only crisis I've had was dealing with fame,' he told *Q* magazine's John Naughton, 'which is the weirdest trip you can ever go on. Some people, like Madonna, love it. She wants to be loved by the whole world but when anyone plays one of my records in a club, I'm embarrassed. Fame is a funny thing. Women have a complete mistrust of you because you are famous. It's very difficult to get someone to trust you 'cos they always think you are going to be with someone else.'

Such thoughts would ricochet around his head. With a bottle of wine beside him he looked up and away from his crazy existence towards a different kind of star.

'Well the thing about looking up there,' he reflected, 'is that it fulfils so many questions and answers in itself. It's the future, it's the past, it's mythology, it's science, it's romance, it's anything you want it to be.'

The stars represented for Hucknall the ultimate form of escapism. He believed in their indefinable magic. Taken at face value, looking up at the stars and gleaning the inspiration for the next impending body of work is an acutely hippyish and dopey activity. But Hucknall was well aware of this. Nobody, more than he, understood just how excruciatingly precious a star-gazing popstar would seem. However, he was quite willing to risk the ridicule. The plain truth was that the stars seemed like the only place he could look that wasn't tainted by his own fame. The stars were refreshing, humbling, awesome and inspiring. Hucknall looked to the stars, possibly in desperation.

Stars played a third role in his life. He had spent so much time in Europe since *Money's Too Tight* that he was transformed politically into a staunch pro-European. His 'stars of the European Federation' tattoo was no mere whim. He was serious. His interest in the European Community had been fired by his time spent flitting freely across Europe, from the apartment in Milan to the house in Old Trafford. Having accepted and revelled in Italian culture, he had long since openly regarded himself as profoundly European and to such an extent that his detractors thought him pompous and shallow. After all, it's all very well to spout rhetoric about the importance of Euro-bonding when you can afford to treat it as your own back yard. It's a little different when you are stuck in Britain on the dole, in Denton perhaps, only to see Britain's role humbled by the absurdities and anomalies of the EC. Common sense might point to the Community's long-term benefits, but Hucknall, swanning around in a pro-Europe T-shirt with his stars tattoo, couldn't see that the British were becoming scared, paranoid perhaps, about the possible under-mining of their own identity. Did we really need pro-EC popstars to carry such a banner, possibly against Britain's wishes? If seen as a PR campaign, Hucknall's pro-European stance was certainly unwise. The reaction against him and the band's music was most effectively summed up, in a typically vitriolic outburst, by hack Julie Burchill who displayed about as much love for Simply Red as she did, week after week, for the powers that be in Maastricht.

'On second thoughts,' she concluded, after slamming Huck-nall for stealing his musical influences from America rather than Europe, 'the music of Simply Red is perfectly suited to the powers that be in Maastricht. Smug, bland and very boring.' As brilliant as ever, Burchill was, of course, not really attacking Hucknall at all but irritating the huge body of *Mail On Sunday* readers who were, she knew, avid Simply Red devotees.

However, the image of a completely pro-Europe Hucknall was not totally accurate. Although strongly stating the case many times for economic union, he held many reservations too.

'Federalism is something that might come about if it's handled sensibly in the space of twenty or thirty years when people are comfortable with the idea, when they've retained their own strong sense of identity and they feel happy doing it that way. That might happen. But the idea of it happening in the next five years I find quite frightening. I think there should be cultural independence within each country and then in issues like social welfare, legal things . . . they at least have the court. The European Court Of Human Rights . . . but the idea of him [Delors, presumably] running the government from Brussels, telling the British people what to do I think is just plain wrong.'

These thoughts and feelings would simmer a while, as Hucknall tried to, 'Do as little as possible for a change.' Rest and relaxation was never really on, though. Perhaps before he even consciously sat down, pen or guitar in hand, the next album had begun to write itself. Even his unusual state of relaxation would play a role, and would be detected within the softer spaces of the work.

Most people (at least people in the real, commercial world and not in late teendom) regarded *A New Flame* as the ultimate Simply Red album. It was up there alongside Tina Turner, alongside Michael Jackson – well, almost. From a fan's point of view, it had been close to perfect. A lovely post-dinner smooch.

Hucknall knew this, but he also knew that *A New Flame* was flawed. Even Elliot Rashman was heard to admit that he had his doubts about it. Regardless of the fantastic sales, wasn't it just too damn slick? And where could a band go from there? Further into muzak? Softer, weaker, more bland? Hucknall wasn't daft. Although he remained extremely proud of *A New Flame*, he realised that the album contained certain danger signs. He didn't believe it to be bland at all, but there was a road opening up before him which would, should he choose to tread it, take him towards complete, absolute and deadening safety. Furthermore, he was being openly encouraged to step on to that road. Simply Red could have produced another three albums, all virtual copies of *A New Flame*. It would have been simple, effortless, a fantastically lucrative slide into mediocrity.

Simply Red's ticket into the next millennium was booked and just waiting to be picked up. What's more, after the traumas and hardships of the past ten years who could really have blamed Hucknall – who wanted to slow down anyway – from taking the easy way out? All he would have to do would be to carefully select two or three cover versions and hang the next album on those. *If You Don't Know Me By Now* had established for the band a reputation for producing sublime covers. The fans expected it and even the critics seemed to forgive it – more than that, they were extremely happy to cast Hucknall in the role of 'supreme singer. The best cover artist in the world.'

But that wasn't enough for Hucknall. It misrepresented him. He wasn't just a great singer. This might be enough for most people, but Hucknall felt insulted by the tag. By throwing the accent on to his singing, his performance, he felt that his writing was severely undervalued. This wouldn't do at all. After all, he had written *Holding Back The Years*, and he was the man who wrote *Maybe Someday* – not just pretty pop tunes. He was capable of creating true beauty, something of genuine emotional quality. He could cut across all those pitiful musical barriers. What's more, Hucknall was beginning to feel like a true writer. Melodies and lyrics would form in his head. The cocktail of his thoughts had already started to fall into the discipline of song. It was almost automatic, natural, certainly 'meant to be'.

There would be other differences between the old band and the new era which, he hoped, would be ushered in by the launch of the next album. The band would change. It was time. Simply Red would be painfully upgraded and the legacy of fired musicians would continue. At long last, as many envious Manchester musicians would say, Chris Joyce and Tony Bowers would be asked to leave. When asked whether such a process would hurt him, Hucknall would just shrug and offer the lightweight explanation, 'It depends on the person.' Perhaps he would think back to the day, in the So What office, when Sylvan Richardson said he was leaving. Hucknall couldn't forget that day because, just as Richardson stepped out of the room, Hucknall glanced out of the window to see a parade float crawling up Princess Street. The float contained a skiffle band and there, playing bass, was Mog. Such stories would be left to haunt him. He had dedicated himself to the music – and music, as always, was the master. Hucknall had no choice. After all, he was already excited by a young Japanese drummer.

The elegant, refined Gota hailed from Kyoto, Japan. He was raised in a household filled with an awareness of music and the intensity of musicians. His father was a classical drum master. At the simply appalling age of one, Gota received a traditional Japanese drum from his father who encouraged the tot, quite openly, to begin rhythmic banging. A somewhat subliminal, if well-meant influence continued when his father pinned an Art Blakey poster on the wall. The young Gota, by this time in the middle of enthusiastic boyhood, promptly became a jazz buff.

But even Gota's father couldn't steer the boy clear of teenage distractions, as typical in Japan as in America or Britain. Wearing his musicality on his sleeve, he swiftly fell in with a troupe of Bohemian hippies who schooled him in the ways of the West – long hair, rock music and further English/American influences. Before long he would discover the delights of the local nightclubs and slowly become acquainted with the fast-moving trends of dance music, which became his greatest passion. Through his links with dance DJs and the general Japanese in crowd, Gota met producers Nellie Hooper and from Bomb the Bass, Tim Simenon.

He became the drummer, or drum programmer, with Japanese outfits Melon, Plastic and a bizarre reggae band called Mute Beat. It would have been easy for him to stay firmly entrenched in the hopelessly insular and ineffectual (on a worldwide basis) Japanese music scene. However, natural ambition pushed him towards London.

It was Nellie Hooper who proved to be the all-important contact, and soon Gota found himself introduced to and programming the drums for such massively influential artists as Soul II Soul, Seal and Massif. Within the musicianly circles of the London dance scene, Gota's innovative prowess began to turn influential heads. The unforgettable and hit-making programmed instruments on Sinead O'Connor's massive hit, *Nothing Compares* 2 U, were the work of the busy Gota.

He had an impressive CV. But arguably nothing amongst that lot could have fully prepared him for the day when Mick Hucknall asked him to join Simply Red.

★ ★ ★

The next album would surprise a lot of people. It would be a massive album – *massive* – the biggest of Simply Red's career. More importantly for Hucknall, it would discredit this notion of him being a 'great singer, average writer'. The only way to achieve this was to make the next album, the biggest album, contain no cover versions at all. It would have no safety net, no easy option hit singles. It would be entirely self penned.

Work had already begun. Hucknall gathered together his influences – personal, emotional and political. He would put a lot of himself into the writing, more than he had ever dared to show before. It was a dangerous thing to attempt. He risked being ridiculed or being thought pompous, perhaps. The very idea of using his feelings as the basic concept for a body of work would seem alarmingly pretentious. More worryingly, as far as the record company were concerned, he risked creating an album incapable of producing any major hits at all.

Hucknall was poised to write his finest song to date. It was a song that he would claim (and about fifty per cent of his fans would agree) would be superior even to *Holding Back The Years*. *Holding Back The Years* had long since become a classic, rubbing shoulders with the likes of *Hey Jude* or any one of a plethora of Beatles' hits. Out of Simply Red's three-album history, one can only pluck a couple of songs from the pack that compare, in terms of soaking into the psyche of the general public, with any one of twenty-odd Beatles songs. Hucknall would surely agree that it is an interesting measure of the true might of the Beatles. On the other hand, and again Hucknall would agree, writing songs for the sophisticated 1990s audience is a whole different ball game to penning love songs in the 1960s.

The song was simplistic, in terms of composition if not musicianship, while its subject matter was quite stunningly tender. Hucknall had been moved by the fact that a lot of his friends, including both his managers, had become parents. He was fascinated by the change in Rashman, in particular, who now seemed to be living a life light years away from the hippyish hedonism of the Hebden Bridge days. Rashman couldn't even bear to watch horror videos where children were involved. He had become, as all good fathers are, hopelessly, selfishly over protective. Many of Hucknall's other friends, just edging into their thirties, also seemed to have crossed a barrier and were moving into a different period of life with different goals, different values.

He was more than well aware that the importance of pop culture, pop music and, even more specifically, Simply Red, had faded considerably. Their new arrivals had become the new, all-encompassing focal point, and all of a sudden the fact that their friend Mick just happened to be an international superstar just didn't seem that important. It was a humbling though valuable experience for Hucknall. It had dawned on him that his friends wouldn't always be able to make time to fit him in whenever he was in town. He had to respect that they, too, were immersed in busy lives. Although they might still rejoice in his success and enjoy his music, he couldn't expect them to regard it as anything other than a tasty diversion. To think otherwise would be truly pretentious, truly arrogant.

It was a crossroads for Hucknall. Many lesser stars, upon reaching this point, decide to take the route of bolstering their own egos at every available opportunity, by believing their own press releases, by believing the sycophantic hordes who surround them. Hucknall would choose a more dignified, musicianly road. He would strive, even further, for pop perfection, all along knowing that he might be the only person in the world to whom achieving such perfection would be at all important.

The song was written in an imaginary, almost surreal way. Hucknall imagined a guy – a friend perhaps – sitting in a room on his own watching his child at play. While he is doing that he is reflecting on how his life has just dramatically changed. The song was written during the Gulf War and Hucknall's imaginary friend is sitting there, thinking that there aren't many things out in the world to believe in. But he believes in the child playing before him.

The song was called *For Your Babies*. It was Hucknall's tribute to his friends, his way of telling them that he really knew that himself, Simply Red and the music paled into insignificance when compared to his friends' family life. It is an extraordinarily complex and personal emotion, succinctly captured within the lyrics that flow so effortlessly over one simple, gorgeous song. A great song – perhaps Hucknall's greatest – and he knew it. With this scenario in his mind, Hucknall sat down with an acoustic guitar and strummed to reflective lyrics conjuring the image of a child at play. The chorus, in particular, depicted paternal hope. It may not have been poetry, but it was a long, long way from *The Right Thing*. It's a long way from *Holding Back The Years*, too. Hucknall had written a profoundly adult song. Whether he was aware of it or not, he had also written a song that could well become a thirtysomething anthem. It was quite spectacularly suited to the core of his audience. Cynics would point out that, from conception to eventual hit single, it was always destined to make regular appearances on Simon Bates' 'Our Tune'. It was *that* kind of song. Hucknall would take that as a compliment.

The initial stirrings of *Stars* saw Hucknall moving on to a new plateau as far as songwriting was concerned. Interestingly enough, as it began in that period of relaxation, it was very much a case of the songs going to Hucknall rather than Hucknall going in search of the songs. It was, if you will forgive the element of pretension, an organic process.

'The way I view my career,' he said, 'is that it's just really about a musical growth . . . I guess, somebody's life story, a little like a diary. The music is improving and I am just trying to articulate myself as best as I can. The idea about being a classic songwriter . . . is something I am trying to attain. I want to be that. I am trying to be that.'

Respect was now the spur. Hucknall was taking himself one step beyond popstardom. In his eyes, although possibly unattainable, he would be the new Berlin, Sondheim, Bacharach, Lennon. Maybe such things just were not possible in the nineties. But songwriting, arguably for the first time in his career, had become his primary obsession.

It is difficult for someone like Hucknall, writing softly for mass appeal, to filter his more extreme political thoughts and feelings into his mass market music. Most bands in such a position – U2 spring to mind with *Sunday Bloody Sunday*, for

example – opt for passionate sounding ambiguity which is
something of a safety precaution. Hucknall had never really
accepted the irony that Simply Red, a band named partly after
a political leaning, were always viewed as being politically
neutral. He never felt comfortable with such a harmless
image, despite his success in nurturing it.

His song, *Freedom*, was entirely based upon the feelings he
experienced when visiting East Berlin. His reaction was
typically British. He found it quite unfathomable. He couldn't
understand how people could be subjected to such an austere
lifestyle and for so long. His working-class background seemed
full of riches by comparison. The profound lack of opportunity
astonished him. Once again, it was a humbling experience.
Here were regular people who, by geographical accident, were
completely denied the basic freedoms that Westerners take for
granted. The impression that East Berlin made on Hucknall
before the wall crumbled was vast. He just left literally
thanking God that he had been born in the right part of the
world.

The song, *Freedom*, is the basic expression of that astonishment. It is one of the most basic, obvious songs in the Hucknall
repertoire.

However, as blatant and simplistic as *Freedom* was, the
song *Wonderland* would prove to be Hucknall's most overtly
political statement to date. Not that the bulk of Simply Red's
middle-aged, casual following – the Daves and Pams – would
notice. They wanted 'prettified' tunes. Hucknall knew this and
duly wrote one – a gently lilting melody, skilfully crafted to
soothe the work-weary minds of Dave and Pam. It was proof
that Hucknall had nurtured an intimate understanding of his
audience. Along with *For Your Babies*, especially, *Wonderland* proved to be that most fragile of pop creations – a gentle
melody carrying a profound, factual message. Not a hint of
innovation was in evidence. In fact, it was the proof that
Hucknall had fully come to terms with the commercially
imposed boundaries that stretched around the scope of his
songwriting, but was stubbornly determined to make as much
as possible out of what was allowed.

The critics who would wait pathetically in line would obviously despise such tactics, but frankly this had long since been the least of Hucknall's worries. Critics do not buy records and the kind of people who take any notice at all of British critics, whether in the *NME* or even *Q* magazine, were most certainly not the Daves and Pams of this world. Dave and Pam would make compilation tapes in readiness for long car journeys. They would record Chris De Burgh's *Lady In Red*, Clapton's *Wonderful Tonight*, Phil Collins' *In The Air Tonight* and perhaps most interestingly, Chris Rea's *Road To Hell* (a song which might be regarded as a fairly close relation to *Wonderland*).

Mick Hucknall wanted to write at least two songs from this evolving album that would join this company on Dave and Pam's compilation tape. He had long since discovered that Dave and Pam were the most powerful people in the music biz. They were the genuine, unprejudiced, solid punters. If they didn't like it they would never return. If they played it in their Ford Scorpios, they would also make trips to the NEC or Wembley to see Simply Red in action. The band would become a part – a romantic part perhaps – of their lives. They must not be upset. The critics might scoff, but Dave and Pam knew exactly what they wanted and, as they wouldn't go within a million miles of a review in the *NME* the critics' opinions wouldn't matter anyway.

To please Dave and Pam and yet still find room to air a genuine political viewpoint is no easy task. In writing *Wonderland*, Hucknall managed to achieve this. Whether or not Dave and Pam would ever actually tune in to the reasonably explicit lyric is another matter entirely.

Wonderland proved to be an out and out attack on Margaret Thatcher and Thatcherism. Once again, a dark message would lie beneath the prettified exterior, more so than anything Hucknall had previously written. He knew that Dave and Pam would hardly notice, in fact they could be forgiven for thinking it to be a modern fairy tale song, about contentment perhaps. But if the song's feel tended to wrong-foot those who would only use it as background, one half-hearted ponder on the lilting lyric line would put them straight in no uncertain terms.

Hucknall seemed refreshingly uncluttered during *Wonderland*, by his most obvious and some would say suspicious paradox. The song is about the new, post-Thatcher Britain. This Britain had finally awakened from its slumber to realise that, alas, the matriarch had vanished, leaving nothing but shock and despair. Hucknall noticed that a violent change had affected the psyche of the British public, who far from extolling the glories of Blighty were scurrying backwards, terrified of the next mortgage payment. The Thatcherite dream, always a scam in Hucknall's view, had ended in the worst possible manner with a mealy-mouthed, inadequate replacement, a decidedly shaky opposition and, for the first time in Hucknall's lifetime, a genuine, universal belief that things were never really going to get better. In fact, terrifying as it may seem, things might get worse. It cannot have been too far from Hucknall's mind as he wrote those lyrics, that the role of an expensively garbed superstar might be put into question in a society apparently in the process of crash landing. *Wonderland*, if nothing else, was a statement that through it all Mick Hucknall's natural political stance had not changed one iota. It still remained with his dad and Nell in Haughton Green, Denton.

The softness, however, would seep too effectively into some of the songwriting. *Thrill Me* was destined to become pure formula, loved by the Daves and Pams, but hated by the cynics. *Thrill Me* positively flirted with blandness. It was a song that, from the moment of writing, was destined to be profoundly 'muso'. Like the worst aspects of jazz funk, it would be admired mainly by dull people who studied bass lines or drum patterns and would hang about in music shops, talking about Rickenbackers and Gibsons.

Timing the release of an album from a band of the magnitude of Simply Red might seem to be all important, especially in days of recession when pennywise punters become increasingly selective in regard to their listening habits. Serious sales damage could occur if, for instance, two sizeable acts with large crossover audiences find themselves releasing long-awaited CDs within weeks of each other, let alone days.

For Rashman and Dodd, and their record company East West, finding a suitable gap in the 'heavy traffic' of new releases would, one would think, be a delicate and difficult operation. With *Stars* set to go, they were worried that U2 (to all commercial intents and purposes, Simply Red's main competitors) were also set to release *Achtung Baby* amid a quite astonishing amount of publicity. Strangely, nobody knew what was happening with the increasingly enigmatic Michael Jackson but also awaiting liberation from the warehouses sat Dire Straits' *On Every Street*. Rashman spoke to Dire Straits' manager Ed Bicknell about whether these major artists should make concerted efforts to try to avoid appearing on the racks at exactly the same time. Everyone seemed to be curiously unresponsive towards Rashman's notion of a kind of industry 'traffic light' system which would ensure that no damaging commercial collisions would take place. Everyone that is except Bicknell who simply stated, 'This is the date we are going . . . don't come out on the same day.'

In the end such fears were unfounded. *Stars* shot immediately to number one, and remaining there one week later began to look instantly formidable. The recession, it seemed, far from denting the sales potential of Simply Red actually helped it. The theory behind this seems altogether too simplistic to be true but can possibly account for the apparent ease with which Simply Red have always managed to court phenomenal success. If music fanatics are forced by recession to cut back to, say, one album per month as opposed to four, then they will opt for the record which offers them two things: a guarantee of quality and, most importantly, the widest scope of music. With Simply Red the punter is offered a delicious cocktail of jazz, funk, blues, soul, reggae and ballads. Simply Red offer, as far as diversity is concerned, unparalleled value for money when simple economics dictate to the consumer.

Speaking to *Q* magazine's John Aizlewood, East West managing director, Max Hole, no doubt in a condition bordering on ecstasy, expounded another couple of theories.

'This hasn't happened overnight. Simply Red have built up a solid fan base. They are one of the few groups that people will buy an album without hearing it, because Simply Red are equated with quality. Secondly, Mick Hucknall is a great singer, the best of his generation, black or white. He can sing an average song and make it great. With great songs you are on to a clear winner. Simply Red are acceptable to everyone.'

Not true, although it is easy to see why Max Hole might think so, considering the contributions Hucknall's art has made to the East West bank account. The swell of dislike which for so long remained prevalent within the more left-field areas of the pop industry, and *especially* in Manchester, teetered on the brink of mass hatred as *Stars* swept all before it on its direct line to the number one spot. This antipathy was voiced more eloquently than ever before in the wave of British press reviews which greeted what was to become the biggest selling British album for, at least, the next two years. It was the ultimate paradox. It was also obvious to anyone above the age of six that *Stars* was a quite magnificent achievement – anyone, that is, who didn't either harbour a grudge or openly fear the risk of losing credibility. Of course, the possibility of the latter terrified the rock critics. How could anyone live down the shame of being the only serious rock critic in Britain to be seen applauding the likes of Simply Red? The streak of pure snobbishness that has remained intact within the British rock media and its ardent readers since the days when the *NME* was a sixties record business ad-comic showed no signs of abating, even during these post *Q* magazine days, when tastes had broadened considerably.

Andrew Collins of *NME* said in his review of *Stars*:
This is the sound of some technicians desperately fanning some of the smouldering ashes for people with central heating. And there's a rip off of *Jamming* on it, called *Model*: And how much do we need that, Eh? (4 out of 10.)

Nick Coleman of *Time Out* meanwhile said:
Hucknall's shaggy John the Baptist thing would be less irritating if he actually had something to evangelise. But no, he will go on and on and on about what a bastard job the evangelist's is, what with all the chicks, the loveless

duplicity and the way, 'this society don't care about nobody else.' Thing is, you just *know* that Hucknall reckons it's saying something important, something about life, love and blocked pores, probably. He goes on and on about looking in the mirror, any road up.

Of one thing we can be certain, Hucknall's desire to find a space for himself, a respite, room to manoeuvre, would have to wait. The promotion for *Stars* lay oppressively before him. Anyone who thinks that life in a huge pop band is an easy ride, money for nothing, might be interested to cast their eyes across the following tour itinerary.

STARS WORLD TOUR 1992

January

5–12	Eire	Dublin	The Point
13	UK	Belfast	King's Hall
16	UK	Aberdeen	E&CC
17–18	UK	Manchester	G-Mex Centre
20–21	UK	Birmingham	NEC Arena
23–24	UK	London	Wembley Arena
26	UK	Sheffield	International Arena
27	UK	Glasgow	SECC Hall 4
28	UK	Sheffield	International Arena

February

15	Sweden	Stockholm	Globe
17	Norway	Oslo	Spektrum
19	Denmark	Copenhagen	Valby
20	Germany	Bremen	Stadhalle
22–24	Germany	Hamburg	Alsterdorfer Sporthalle
26	Germany	Stuttgart	Schleierhalle
27–28	Germany	Munich	Olympiahalle

March

| 1 | Germany | Frankfurt | Festhalle |

2–3	Germany	Hanover	Musichalle
4	Germany	Berlin	Deutschlandhalle
7	Germany	Wurzburg	Carl-Diem Halle
8	Germany	Mannheim	Maimarkhalle
9	Germany	Kiel	Osteehalle
11	Germany	Saarbrucken	Saarlandhalle
12–13	Germany	Dortmund	Westfaienhalle
15–16	Switzerland	Zurich	Hallenstadion
17	Belgium	Brussels	Fôret National
19	Holland	Rotterdam	Ahoy
20–21	France	Paris	Zenith
23	France	Toulouse	Palais des Sports
24	Spain	Barcelona	Palacio De Los Deportes
27	Spain	Madrid	Pabeilon Del Real Madrid
30	France	Marseille	Palais des Sports
31	France	Grenoble	Summon

April

1	Italy	Turin	Palasport
3	Italy	Rome	Palaghiaccio
4	Italy	Naples	Partenope
6	Italy	Modena	Palasport
7	Italy	Forli	Palasport
9	Italy	Milan	Forun
10	Italy	Florence	Palasport
12	Austria	Innsbruck	Olympiahalle
13	Austria	Linz	Sportshall
15–16	Austria	Vienna	Stadthalle
18	Holland	Arnhem	Rijnhal
19	Holland	Rotterdam	Ahoy
20	Belgium	Brussels	Fôret National

May

19–20	USA	San Francisco	Warfield Theatre
22	USA	Los Angeles	Universal Amphitheatre
23	USA	San Diego	Convention Centre

| 30 | USA | Houston | Southern Star Amphitheatre |

June

1	USA	Atlanta	Fox Theatre
4	Canada	Ottawa	Congress Centre
5	Canada	Toronto	Kingswood Music Theatre
6	Canada	Montreal	Theatre St Denis
10	USA	New York	Central Park Summer Stage

July

2	Denmark	Funen	Midtfyns Festival
4	Germany	Cologne	Mungersdorfer Stadium
8	Switzerland	Montreux	Montreux Jazz Festival
11–12	UK	London	Wembley Stadium
18–19	UK	Manchester	Old Trafford Cricket Ground
25	UK	Gateshead	Gateshead Stadium

August

2	Eire	Tipperary	Feille Festival
27	Israel	Tel Aviv	Hayarkon Park
29	Israel	Jerusalem	Sultan's Pool

September

4	Greece	Athens	AEK Stadiu
17–18	Australia	Sydney	Entertainment Centre
20	Australia	Brisbane	Entertainment Centre
22	Australia	Newcastle	Entertainment Centre
25–26	Australia	Melbourne	Palais Theatre
28–29	Australia	Melbourne	Palais Theatre

October

1	Australia	Adelaide	Thebarton Theatre
3	Australia	Perth	Entertainment Centre
6	New Zealand	Auckland	Logan Campbell Centre
9–10	New Zealand	Wellington	Town Hall
12–13	New Zealand	Christchurch	Town Hall
16	Singapore		Indoor Stadium

November

2–4	Hong Kong	Coliseum	
21–23	UK	London	Wembley Arena
25	UK	Manchester	G-Mex
26–27	UK	Sheffield	Arena
29–30	UK	Sheffield	Arena

December

1	UK	Sheffield	Arena
3–4	UK	Glasgow	SECC
6–8	UK	London	Wembley Arena
10–12	UK	London	Wembley Arena
14–16	UK	Birmingham	NEC
18–20	UK	Birmingham	NEC

Sitting in his office at Granada, television producer Bob Dickinson was painstakingly piecing together the ingredients for the weekly local listing programme, 'What's New'. He made his regular weekly call to music business promoter Neil Ferris, at the infamous Ferret and Spanner plugging company. The original reason for the call is lost. This is probably because, halfway through the call, Dickinson was astonished at the message he was receiving.

'I nearly dropped the phone,' he said later. 'I couldn't believe that people I knew reasonably well could be so touchy.'

During the conversation, Dickinson had quite casually mentioned that Steve Locke at Granada had approached WEA with a view to making a film about Simply Red. Granada had already made similar films with Inspiral Carpets, Happy

Mondays and James. It would be, as was usually the case, a coproduction. The deal would be quite simple. If the record company were favourable they would come up with a sum of money to finance the project, and Granada and Warners would agree the rights between them. Granada would film a live event and provide a guaranteed transmission. The record company would receive the video retailing rights. It was a perfect arrangement and, at least in the Granada camp, there was an air of optimism about the film.

Coproductions had, by this time, become fairly commonplace though still somewhat controversial. Tina Turner's special video, 'The Girl From Nutbush', was made by PMI and the BBC with EMI. Sony had agreed to pay for a Manic Street Preachers video while an Eddi Reader special, initially screened in Scotland, was heavily backed by record company funding. Whether or not it is ethically correct for a record company to fund what looks to all intents and purposes like an investigative documentary is still open to debate. Simply Red's record company, East West, became closely involved with the video's production. When *Music Week* – the British music business bible – challenged Stuart Prebble, Head of Factual Programmes at Granada about the dubious ethics of the Simply Red venture, he replied, and not unreasonably, that the production was a 'Celebration (arts programme), not a "World In Action".' Which is fair enough, though one wonders just where the line might be drawn. The Simply Red programme was eventually filmed at a gig in Hamburg and spliced with numerous snatches of Hucknall in interview. It attracted just under four and a half million viewers.

Back at the beginning of the project, Dickinson was merrily explaining his way through the plans and stressing just what a fine idea it was when he noticed that Ferris had gone unusually quiet. Indeed, Ferris was extremely concerned by Dickinson's enthusiasm. He informed the Granada producer that Elliot Rashman had, at the start of the deal, laid down an unbreakable proviso. He read this out: 'Under no circumstances would Simply Red go ahead with anything at Granada if it included the involvement of Bob Dickinson.'

Dickinson, clearly stunned by this, asked Ferris if he knew the reason why this should be.

'Apparently,' came the reply, 'Elliot has never forgiven you for something you wrote about them years ago in a magazine.' Dickinson couldn't for the life of him remember writing anything remotely offensive about Simply Red. On the contrary, he had written the band's first live review in the *NME* (at a time when the band were just beginning to attract A & R interest and badly needed positive press, which it had been). Furthermore, nobody else at the *NME* had the faintest idea who Simply Red were and, until Dickinson's review, weren't in the least bit interested in finding out. There had been other snippets but those too, as far as Dickinson could remember, were firmly on the side of the band.

The only thing he could think of was his short and somewhat indifferent review of *Men And Women* which had appeared in *City Life* and had, in effect, merely mirrored the way many of the band's more left-field followers were feeling at the time. What stunned Dickinson so much was the absurdity of the situation. Here, on the one hand, was a band of international standing, a band who regularly battled with the likes of Michael Jackson and Dire Straits. And yet, they had been deeply upset by a mild panning they received in a tiny review in a local what's on magazine some four years previously. What kind of paranoia was this?

'Perhaps,' offered Ferris, 'if you wrote some kind of apology and sent it to Elliot, the band might reconsider.' Dickinson, with respect to Ferris thought the suggestion was stupid. 'You can't undo the past,' he said. 'And, anyway, it's a free country . . . I wasn't going to be pushed around by some arrogant pop group.'

Dickinson told Ferris that although he wouldn't under any circumstances make an apology for writing an objective album review, he probably wouldn't be involved in the recording in any case. He visited Granada's legal adviser, Catherine Buchanan. In the interests of a healthy relationship between the band and Granada, a document was drawn up to confirm that Bob Dickinson quite categorically would have no involvement in the filming of Simply Red.

* * *

As the Granada filming appeared over the horizon, Rashman
found himself with an unusual problem. A severe ear infection
had made it impossible for him to fly unless wishing to disobey
doctor's orders. He had to get to Hamburg though, and he set
off on the rather awkward drive from Heaton Mersey to
Harwich where he intended to board the direct ferry to
Hamburg. On reaching Harwich, however, Rashman, who
was seeking a relaxed, painless crossing to ease his ailment
found the ferry brimming with excited Simply Red fans. It was
all too much and reluctantly he climbed back in the car and
proceeded to Hull where a ferry took him to the Hook of
Holland. Unfortunately, this meant that he had to endure a
six-hour drive to Hamburg, where he arrived literally minutes
before the filming of the concert began.

Elliot was looking forward to a five-day sea cruise to the US
on the QE2 later in the year.

Basil Yablonski was the only Russian member of the Simply
Red fan club. When the fan club were invited by the band to
attend the filmed gig in Hamburg en masse, Hucknall was
keen to extend the invitation to Yablonski. There was to be a
meet-the-band session after the gig and Hucknall desperately
wished to use the event to make personal contact with
Yablonski, so much so that he instructed his management to
send $200 to Yablonski's address in St Petersburg. Unfortu-
nately, Yablonski didn't manage to make it to the event and it
was generally assumed that he had, understandably, used the
money to help survive the Russian winter. Granada director,
Steve Locke, later said, 'I thought he'd used it to buy 10,000
acres of land in Siberia.'

But with the episode almost forgotten, a rather touching
letter arrived at Simply Red's Manchester offices. Fan clubs
are often much maligned because of their traditionally fawning nature. But when a situation like this arises, it can only
highlight the fact that the best fan clubs are actually capable
of bridging that vast gulf between artist and follower. In a
heartfelt letter to Simply Red and fan club members, Yablonski explained that the $200 had indeed arrived. Unfortu-

nately, due to the crippling red tape of the visa system it had proved impossible for Yablonski to have his papers approved in time. He would use the $200 hopefully to cross the political barriers and meet the band one day. Rather touchingly, Yablonski quoted the words to Hucknall's *Freedom*, the song quite obviously carrying for him a special poignancy.

As the tour proceeded and the Old Trafford Cricket Ground gig passed without major incident or criticism – without major praise too – Hucknall, no doubt buoyed by the possibilities involved with playing to such enormous audiences went decidedly against the musicianly trend to 'get back to the small clubs, to a more intimate atmosphere'. This seemed a little unnatural. After all, hadn't Hucknall been reared on a diet of music that would traditionally be best when performed in tight, little, smoky clubs? And surely nothing could be further away from his level of influences than stadium rock?

But Hucknall was drawn towards the big show. He simply 'got into' the idea of performing in front of 9,000 plus. He relished the grand scale and also the often forgotten fact that it isn't merely a question of band-performing-to-passive-audience at such venues. In fact the reverse is often the case. When huge crowds sing along to the choruses it creates the kind of vibe that, as Hucknall said, 'You just can't get in a small club.'

He was, of course, anticipating the progress of Simply Red to stadium band. Their initial taster of such a massive scale show came in Rio when they performed in front of 70,000 people, alongside the likes of Tina Turner. The band, although terrified before the event, had felt considerably encouraged by the sheer power of the crowd.

Another factor which pointed towards a future spent enjoying cavernous arenas was the consistent fact that Simply Red's fans – who as always ranged from eight to eighty – had been at all times a completely trouble-free mix. The spirit of conviviality had become synonymous with Simply Red's live shows to such an extent that the band had attained legendary status among the strange subterranean world of the rock road crews where the band were known to be a nice, soft gig – a good, trouble-free earner. That fact is, perhaps, a terrific and largely unparalleled tribute to the band's fans.

Any notions that Hucknall's aura of self confidence or, if you are on the receiving end as journalists so often are, 'downright arrogance' might have mellowed with age or wisdom or life on the road would, by all reports, seem to be unfounded. Throughout the tour, Hucknall would simply power his way through confrontations, both with the media and fans who pushed their luck a little too far.

Hong Kong, later in the year, would prove typical. The local press had heralded the arrival of Hucknall with the kind of fervour one might expect for Michael Jackson. Because of this, and because the requests for interviews were staggeringly numerous, Hucknall reluctantly agreed to hold a press conference. It was not, however, an affair that would be remembered for the mutual respect and amiableness between the star and the press core. True to form, Hucknall spent most of his time berating the poor hacks, lecturing them on the right kind of questions they should ask musicians and openly moaning about the fact that he would much rather have been elsewhere.

At one point, Hucknall halted the conference and, as one journalist noted, 'In a tone of unbelievable petulance', complained, 'I find it incredible that we've been here for fifteen minutes and that no one has asked me about music, I really do.' When one reporter was unwise enough to voice a rather stupid comparison between Hucknall and Paul Gascoigne, Hucknall cut him short with an understandably curt, 'When did you last have your eyes tested?'

'I think he's a very unhappy man,' theorised ex-Manchester journalist, Michael Mackey. 'I don't know why he held a press conference if all he wanted to do was play the part of reluctant rock star.'

The tension was appeased, if only a little bit, by Hucknall's statement that Hong Kong was a very 'Funky Town', which echoed his feelings about Hamburg – and one can see the connection.

All major pop bands bar none, during their rise to prominence and beyond, leave behind them an unholy trail of ghosts. Ghosts who are often but not always embittered and sadly envious. They might be ex-band members, ex-managers, ex-agents, ex-promoters, indie label owners, small-time video production companies. Many of them will have good reason for their bitterness. As the big time arrrives so do a variety of strange, powerful forces, all jostling for position, and any claims for reimbursable services are generally mocked as small time. It is to the credit of Rashman and Dodd that they remained in power from demo to superstar stages.

Musically, as this book testifies, Mick Hucknall's background lies scattered with ghosts. The Pete Bests of Simply Red continue to stalk the streets and studios of Manchester, exchanging wise, wry smiles whenever their ginger-headed collaborator of yesteryear is ushered in before the media as he is, more and more. And this strange club of ghosts is still growing.

Thankfully, most people have prospered in the wake of their involvement with Hucknall. Especially those like Richardson or Aziz or Bowers and Joyce who contributed noticeably to a band in flight. Nobody can doubt that their particular reputations were considerably enhanced by the association.

For others, however, whose involvement failed to provide even the merest hint of fame, it is difficult to assess whether they have been able wisely to put the whole episode down to experience, and even take pride in Hucknall's success.

Few people, it seems, know quite how David Rowbotham felt. His was the weirdest position of all. He contributed so much to the earliest Simply Red incarnation – almost as much as Hucknall – and yet one has to search incredibly hard, even among the circle of seasoned Manchester musicians, to find anyone who knows that David Rowbotham had anything to do with the band at all. When his life ended tragically in November 1991, the violent nature of his death was splashed across the front page of the *Manchester Evening News*. Yet the newspaper was unwittingly subjecting Rowbotham to one final, hugely ironic indignity. The article completely failed to mention the fact that Rowbotham was a musician, let alone a one-time member of Simply Red. The story was big, albeit locally, but it could have been huge.

David Rowbotham had been living in Grangethorpe Drive, Burnage, with his common-law wife, Catherine Griffiths. They chose not to socialise too much with the neighbours, but they were well liked. They were also, by the standards of Grangethorpe Drive, eccentric to say the least. Rowbotham was known locally as 'Cowboy Dave' due to his taste for Stetson hats and fringed suede jackets. As Catherine was aged forty-five and Rowbotham still just thirty-four, they looked somewhat unusual as they skateboarded down the street together.

But the banner headline in the *Manchester Evening News* on Saturday 2 November 1991 was little short of chilling: 'LOVER IN AXE HORROR'.

David Rowbotham was found dead, surrounded by empty beer cans and a heavily bloodstained axe nearby.

Chapter 20
In The City

In Cannes, at the Midem music business gathering in January 1990, an ungainly gaggle of Mancunians wandered down a fashionable boulevard amid considerable glamour.

The dark-haired, elegantly besuited Elliot Rashman remarked that it was ridiculous that there was no event comparable to Midem in Britain. Yvette Livesey, a former Miss Great Britain, Piccadilly Radio reporter, would-be Granada Television starlet and close confidante of Factory Records boss Anthony Wilson, seized the moment.

'Well, I've been here a couple of times,' she said, 'and I've been to the New Music Seminar [in New York] . . . I see no reason why something like this couldn't take place . . . not just in Britain . . . but in Manchester.'

'Yes,' replied Elliot, 'but would the music business moguls based in London be willing to travel to Manchester?'

'Don't know,' replied Livesey, 'but it's worth a shot . . . if you'd support the idea, I'd like to run with it.'

The Holiday Inn Crowne Plaza ostentatiously decorates the Peter Street corner of Manchester's St Peter's Square. For many years, as the Midland Hotel, it operated proudly as the most classic hotel in the city – an ornate architectural gem, a genuine manifestation of the city's former prosperity. It did fall from grace in latter years, at least until the late eighties when the Holiday Inn Group rescued it from heartbreaking decay, undertook lengthy and costly renovation and provided it with one of the most stunning and largest reception areas of any hotel in Britain, if not the world. Since opening in 1991, it has gained a reputation as the natural home for visiting top businessmen, pilots, and Olympic officials who were dourly scrutinising the city centre and assessing the chances of Manchester hosting the Games. Despite a fair peppering of grandiose four-star hotels across the city centre, most of which were built in anticipation of the Olympic dream becoming a reality, it was the Holiday Inn Crowne Plaza which best captured the spirit of the early nineties, making pivotal appearances in Tony Warren's weighty tome, *The Lights Of Manchester* and providing temporary refuge for many visiting rockstars.

It was also the hotel which most resembled the big hotels of New York, specifically the New York Hilton and with its subterranean conference suites seemed like the perfect venue to hold an international music business seminar. Yvette Livesey – spurred on by Anthony Wilson and Simply Red managers Rashman and Dodd – moved into an uninspiring office in Manchester Town Hall and took on the daunting task of organising and squeezing music business craziness into a three-day extravaganza to be held mainly within the Holiday Inn's walls. Livesey attended meeting after meeting with the Holiday Inn management, the project at times verging on disaster.

'Of course, it will be a bit lively,' she suggested, before brashly admitting, 'and this being a rock convention, many of the delegates might smoke.'

'But Yvette,' came the reply, 'lots of our guests smoke. There is nothing wrong with that.'

'No I didn't mean cigarettes . . . I meant . . . they might . . . smoke! You know!'

The blank stares which met this remark came to typify the scale of the problem. Only the rather pleasing fact that delegates would be staying, eating and drinking within their walls, managed to overcome the hotel's possible objections (and, as it happened, nobody 'smoked' anyway).

Livesey had to soak up intense criticism during the run up to In The City, as the project was called, and it was to her credit that she didn't crack under the full weight of verbal attacks. Thankfully, the Rashman and Dodd camp at So What Arts – who were priming themselves for a major music business wrangle which they hoped would explode at the In The City event – provided Livesey with more than adequate support. However, the appearance of Rashman and Dodd alongside Wilson and Livesey in the local press shots which preceded the event certainly caused a few understandable ripples throughout Manchester.

The Fall's Mark E. Smith, an anti-In-The-City campaigner most effectively summed up the feelings of his camp: 'Basically, it's just an excuse for a bunch of industry fat cats to get together and talk about ripping off the artists.'

The In The City debate would effectively split the city in half. *City Life* magazine reported that Manchester City Council had subsidised the event to the tune of £25,000. Naturally, this didn't go down too well when the Council was forever apologising for cutbacks in local services. The fact that Simply Red were widely reported to be involved in the In The City organisation only served to inflame the sense of indignation felt not so much by ordinary Mancunians, but certainly by the legions of local musicians who were not invited to take part or perform at one of the gigs surrounding the event.

The debate, spurred on by a spirited anti-seminar article by Hacienda DJ Dave Haslam in *City Life* boiled over into a rather sordid and insular mess of bitchiness, both in print and at the Waterstone's launch of the self-indulgent Factory book, *The Hacienda Must Be Built*. I do not know if the music business delegates from across the globe were at all aware of what was going on. Whatever, it was not a good advertisement for a city which still saw itself as, to quote Anthony Wilson, 'The hippest town in the world'.

But Manchester's unhappy outbreak of bitching seemed like small potatoes compared to the music business furore which had been simmering for several months and would, if Rashman and Dodd had anything to do with it, come to a head during these three short days in Manchester's Holiday Inn Crowne Plaza.

The row was complex. A report in the *Mail On Sunday* stated that Mick Hucknall, among other big name artists like

Dire Straits and U2, were about to rebel against the central corporate bodies of the music industry who intended to force artists to accept royalty cuts when their music appeared on the new state-of-the-art format, DCC. In fact, Hucknall would soon refuse to allow *Stars* to be issued on DCC format.

The argument began way back in the days when compact discs were launched. Reductions in royalty payments to artists were sought for the CD format, and strangely this was accepted by the artists with little debate. But in 1992, the big-time managers led by Rashman and Dodd were determined not to make the same mistake again. The issue was, of course, deadeningly complex and of little interest to the general public who couldn't care less about the publishing rates of their favourite artists. But it is of more general interest to note that the DCC publishing row spurred Rashman and Dodd to instigate a new powerful body, the International Managers' Forum. A kind of high level union, this solid force was dedicated to preventing the kind of thing that Andy Dodd called, 'The great compact disc rip off' from ever happening again. The implications of this were tremendous. Rashman and Dodd knew that if they managed to get the forum on its feet and, what's more, if they actually managed to win the royalty issue which surrounded the DCC format, then as *Music Week* reported, 'A more long-term victory may be within their grasp.'

In short, Rashman and Dodd were instigating a battle to give managers greater powers within the strange hierarchical pyramid of the international music business. Putting it more crudely, they were after grabbing more money which is, after all, their job.

The situation led to wild speculation and ear-splitting rumours. One particularly absurd line of rumour speculated that Rashman and Dodd had set up the entire In The City seminar simply for their own devices as just another one of Rashman's Machiavellian plots, albeit of an incredibly elaborate nature. Of course they hadn't, but sensible theorising was in painfully short supply in mid-September 1992 in Manchester.

Walking into the Crowne Plaza on Monday 15 September

was, for all but the most hardened of music business types, a deeply unsettling experience. The hotel's stunning interior was awash with A & R men in black Levis; older, fatter, balder, richer figures garbed in absurd waistcoats; journalists and small-time television presenters downing triple vodkas together and swapping tales of punky times of yesteryear. Small clusters of record company execs and juniors cast nervous glances at the opposition – who looked exactly the same. Occasionally one would read the name tag pinned to some anonymous looking chest and realise that you were face to face with the chairman of CBS, or Dire Straits' manager Ed Bicknell, or you might bump into Led Zeppelin's mighty Peter Grant. Everything happened in the bar. In the seminars, the atmosphere remained generally deadening. Mostly, it would be bored panellists wondering what on Earth they were doing there standing on a rostrum and answering the drunken jibes of the delegates in the hall. The most fun one could have was to simply wander about, bouncing from one conversation to another.

Elliot Rashman was in evidence everywhere, or so it seemed. He was openly proud to see the leaders of the worldwide music business on his doorstep. It would be, he would later say, 'music business nonesense' but in truth he loved every second. Every time Ed Bicknell collared him in the corner and pulled him up on some point about the International Managers' Forum, he would simply bask in the drama of it all – and why not?

And on every spare table there was a leaflet to be perused by everyone, from New York nightclub owners to bewildered waiters. The leaflet read as follows:

A personal statement by Elliot Rashman and Andy Dodd.
So What Arts/Managers of Simply Red

As the managers of Simply Red we would like to register our protest against the intentions of the recording industry to reduce artist and mechanical royalty rates on DCC and any other future formats. Furthermore, we completely oppose the recommended packaging deductions for DCC and any other future formats.

We oppose these scams for many reasons, not least that the recording industry has not seen fit to even consult the artists or their representatives over matters that directly affect them. It's so damn disrespectful to the art that fuels the machine. How can we respect the BPI and the recording industry as a whole if it does not afford us respect?

We intend to fight these royalty breaks to the bitter end. This is no lost cause. We know that the majority of managers feel the same way. It is worth fighting to keep music alive, to create a thriving, creative community.

As a story, DCC does not hold much interest for the general public, some of whom will think it's simply rich pop stars moaning. However, the majority of families in the UK will come into close contact with a musician (a loose term) – as a relative, for instance, or as a friend – and they know musicians don't get any easy breaks in life. They work long and hard for their art. The popularist artform of the twentieth century.

Over all these contentious and complex issues, all we are really saying is:

We are fighting for our creative right. And for our rightful due.

We are fighting to improve our creative community. The more we empower the creative aspects of our business, the greater the music and the greater the entertainment.

15 September 1992

And that was the basic manifesto – simple, sharp, effective. It made people talk, and many of them became aware that arguably the most important debate in the entire kaboodle, certainly as far as Rashman was concerned, had begun some twenty-four hours earlier in the same hotel at the inaugural meeting of the International Managers' Forum. This event wasn't open to every prowling delegate or members of the press. It was Rashman and Dodd's coup, it was all managers together.

The first Parliament of Managers appointed a steering committee, due to meet again in October to draw up general policy and, in particular, policy pertaining to the DCC bust up. At the following press conference this committee refused to be drawn into any debate over DCC royalty breaks, but Rashman offered an intriguing glimpse into the real issues that would soon come into focus.

'It's not just about DCC,' he said. 'That's just a red herring. It's about all new technology, including MiniDisc and Digital Audio Broadcasting.'

Over 300 managers attended the first meeting that lasted four hours, overrunning by nearly ninety minutes. Rashman, in full flow, revelled in using the conference as a tool for his own devices. Strangely, considering the fact that the band he managed had been performing at outsized venues for a number of years, he spoke eloquently against the basic concept of the 'supergig'.

'Simply Red will never again play huge stadium concerts,' he announced, much to the surprise of the local reporters. It was a shock to hear such a statement, especially as Manchester still cherished memories of the two Old Trafford Cricket Ground dates that summer.

'The biggest complaint I heard from the summer dates was that people could not see it and they wanted video screens,' he continued. 'In most of this country, and in Europe, they are stood in a shed paying too much for T-shirts. The seats are not great and the venues are unwelcoming. People will still enjoy it because they are there for the music but we will never play them again.'

Rashman's illustrious In The City sidekick, Dire Straits' manager Ed Bicknell, was equally vehement in his condemnation of big pop events.

'The days of the Transit van, three guitars and a drum kit are long gone,' he said. 'I am in the building industry now. I sometimes go round the back of the stage now and say, "Why have all these people come to see a sound system and huge television screen?" Stars want not only top sound systems and lighting rigs but also pyrotechnics and even magical illusions as part of their stage set up. Every single act going out today wants to do better than the last tour they did and better than the other guy.'

While the cynics might scoff at the notion of two of Britain's top managers whingeing on and on about the problems involved in staging mega gigs, it was obvious that Rashman was in part voicing the artistic dissatisfaction of Mick Hucknall. Had Simply Red, as far as performance was concerned, spiralled out of control? Had the simple, aesthetic pleasure of seeing a good singer performing a good song – the basic premise of Simply Red – been lost in a farcical scramble to stage bigger, mightier, more spectacular gigs? Wasn't it all becoming a fiasco more befitting of some big heavy metal act? In a sense, yes, and it was this paranoia that would, later in the year, ignite the spark of a sordid little wrangle between Manchester's top band and Manchester's top live music venue.

Chapter 21
The Battle of G-Mex

Manchester, endlessly spouting about its Olympic aspirations and making the ludicrous claim of being 'the hippest city in the world' took an unlikely knock on Tuesday 13 October 1992 when the local press reported that the city's top pop group – and one band that had become synonymous with large-scale gigs in the city – couldn't stomach the thought of playing another set at G-Mex.

It was a curious outburst coming, as it did, just days after Simply Red had announced that they would indeed include one day at G-Mex in the forthcoming UK climax to their groundbreaking world tour.

'G-Mex is a lousy venue,' claimed Rashman. 'It's unfriendly and the box office is inefficient. It is acoustically inadequate and the facilities for the public are poor.'

Simply Red were not going to play Manchester at all, but it was at Hucknall's insistence that they should play just one date at G-Mex for the sake of the home city fans who couldn't travel.

'This is our city,' continued Rashman, 'and we wish there was a better venue. Our home town fans deserve the best possible environment to see Mick and the band.'

The attack, appearing in a prominent position in the *Manchester Evening News*, wasn't confined to technical jibes about the venue either. G-Mex boss, Frank Winter, also suffered criticism from Rashman.

'G-Mex is a difficult venue run by a difficult man. He has a reputation for being uncooperative,' he said, which hardly

283

instilled confidence in the minds of the Manchester fans who had just defied recessionary caution in order to see the band at the venue, especially as Rashman cited nearby Sheffield Arena as 'The best venue in Europe.'

The outburst outlined the problems facing a live band of Simply Red's stature and cast a significant shadow over Manchester's ability to accommodate such events. The political implications were immense, as if the city's one large-scale venue had been so savagely attacked by the top local band what did this bode for the future?

Frank Winter was incensed by Rashman's attack and replied, most venomously, on the North-west news programme, 'Granada Tonight':

'I think they [Simply Red] sounded off when they were in a difficult situation, trying to dig themselves out of a hole they had put themselves in. We held three nights for them, for twelve months, ready for them to do their concerts. At the last moment they decided that they were only going to do one. It can do anything, this building, and I won't have people knocking it. Particularly those who are trying to use it as a way of getting themselves out of trouble.'

Winter proceeded to provide a list of satisfied clients, including local girl Lisa Stansfield and George Benson. 'We even had a good crit from the *Manchester Evening News*,' he jauntily proclaimed, 'and that takes some doing.'

The feud, by now billed as the 'Showdown between Manchester's top venue and Manchester's top band', was handed over to *Manchester Evening News* editor, Michael Unger, who effectively fanned the flames of the argument in this surprising fashion.

'Manchester needs a proper concert hall for proper concerts. Like popstars, opera stars, whoever. It's no good to do that sort of concert in an exhibition hall. It's no good trying to do it on a football pitch or cricket pitch. We desperately need a concert hall better than Sheffield's or Birmingham's and we haven't got that at the moment.'

Andy Dodd issued a statement to deflate the argument which insisted that, 'We have shifted the other two nights to Sheffield which we prefer.'

By October 1992, *Stars* had become one of the classic pop albums of all time. Indeed, jokes about the album's presence in so many households of Britain abounded. Elliot Rashman had once stated, probably in a moment of bravado, that Simply Red would one day achieve a level of penetration that no other pop band could possibly hope to achieve. As Christmas 1992 began to draw near, Simply Red would seem to be getting close to this prophecy. *Stars* was set to become the UK's biggest selling album for the second year running and sales would naturally rise to meet the demands of Yuletide. (Not since Simon and Garfunkel's *Bridge Over Troubled Water* had any album managed to become the top seller in Britain for two years running). Surely, it would not be at all necessary to inject the album with a triple dosage of out and out promotion? But that is exactly what happened and one can only applaud So What Arts and East West for realising that British sales of *Stars* – which stood at 2.8 million – could, with a little application, be shunted way over the three million mark by the new year.

This was helped by the return of the band to Britain for the climactic flourish to the *Stars* world tour. Hucknall was back and apparently hungry to work hard at the painful process of gaining an even higher national profile. It had obviously been decided that it would be in the best interests of everyone concerned if the spotlight were to fall heavily on the man and his voice. The band would, at least in the eyes of the general public rather than the fans, fade drastically from view. Indeed it was not unknown, and for the first time really, for local radio DJs to regard Simply Red as a mere pseudonym for Mick Hucknall. This admittedly risible lack of respect for what had become one of the finest working pop outfits on the globe was surely furthered by the release of the Montreux EP. For the first time on record, this stop-gap release of genuine quality fully captured the awesome and much improved power of Hucknall's voice in live performance. It was quite simply the most evocative chart release in a year that will not be fondly remembered for producing a vast array of vocally oriented quality singles. (Its only competitor was the simultaneous release of Whitney Houston's *I Will Always Love You* which was still lodged at the top of the charts months after Hucknall and Co. had departed.) By focusing on the voice, the release immediately set Hucknall aside from Pete Waterman triggered dance pap, the all-engulfing wave of rap and hardcore, and the solid male-oriented mass of traditional rock – be it U2, REM, or Def Leppard. The EP made its point simply: Here is a great artist singing great songs. Anybody got a problem with that? Few people had. In fact, the refreshing notion of a singer simply performing great songs set the tills ringing and few people even complained when faced with irritating over-the-counter questions like, 'Which format would you require, sir? CD? Well, which version would you like?' In times of heavy recession, surely only serious fanatics would wish to own two musically identical but differently packaged versions of the same EP? (Apparently not. Enquiries made at three Manchester city centre record stores and London's Virgin Megastore revealed that many people had actually bought both versions. This startling discovery, if repeated across the country, made a mockery of the chart system and made East West appear, in view of the multi-packaging, strangely unconfident about the sales potential of such a splendidly unique product.)

The four songs, enhanced rather by the decidedly un-jazz-like whooping of the Montreux crowd, were Cole Porter's heart-rending *Love For Sale* with which Hucknall had opened the Montreux set, in stunning acappella style; *Drowning In My Own Tears*, the Henry Glover song which had been such a milestone for Ray Charles (and such a regular on Roger Eagle's record decks); the Bill Withers song, *Gramma's Hands* and the Hucknall-penned *Lady Godiva's Room* which sounded remarkably good in such esteemed company.

The deadpan prose of Montreux director Claude Nobbs' sleeve note succinctly captured the quality of the performance. 'What turned me on completely,' he wrote, 'was *Drowning In My Own Tears*, by Henry Glover which made me even forget Ray Charles' classic version.' Roger Eagle would have been proud.

The second prong in the attack to revitalise the sales of *Stars*, was the availability of Hucknall himself. The Montreux

EP simultaneously opened media doors in areas both of great esteem and chart pop. Everybody wanted a slice of Hucknall, from *Smash Hits* to *Arena* (he chose *Arena*, appearing on the cover of the December issue), from the *Sun* to the *Independent*, from the dire and dying 'Top of the Pops' to 'The Late Show'.

Hucknall allowed the popular media to write and say what it pleased, while he opted for the areas of esteem. He appeared on BBC 2's oddly successful weeknight arts package 'The Late Show' on Wednesday 18 November. On this, as fans reached for their video record buttons, he hesitated before sliding into a sublime accappella version of a song which Hucknall discovered on Chet Baker's *Let's Get Lost* album, originally recorded by Bing Crosby. Singing live without accompaniment on late-night television is the kind of thing guaranteed to give one's manager several heart attacks. But the supremely confident Hucknall handled the task with typical aplomb, even smiling smugly between lines as aloof, cynical cameramen circled for effect.

Twenty-four hours later Hucknall was back, this time ably supported by the full band, as part of Jools Holland's late-night, outrageously cute celebration of muso smugness, 'Later With Jools Holland'. This time he performed *Gramma's Hands* and *Drowning In My Own Tears* in rotation with Kirsty McColl and, one of Hucknall's favourites, Ann Peebles. It was a nice 'warmer' for the forthcoming British dates and, without doubt, the one aspect of promotion which Hucknall thoroughly enjoyed.

But East West were by no means leaving it at that, nor were they content just to allow the forthcoming string of British dates to swell the sales of *Stars*. They were determined to mop up the few remaining adults who were yet to buy the album. Hence the £300,000 television promotional campaign, featuring 'off the wall' commercials to be broadcast in all regions in the run-up to Christmas. Ably directed by John Carver for Leisure Process, the commercial featured two artists painting a huge mural and was only moderately identifiable as an advertisement for music. Until, that is, it became apparent that the artists were painting an outsize version of the sleeve from *Stars*. It was slick, intelligent and stylish. The three-week campaign would feature 150 such commercials across the country at peak viewing times, and would coincide with considerable advertising in both the national and the music press.

All this commercial activity contrasted sharply with the general state of the British economy. Despite keeping a concerned eye trained on world events, even Hucknall was stunned by the extent of the financial devastation that not only shouted from a hundred tabloid headlines but seemed etched into the state of the national psyche. The Britain they found at the climax of the world tour had darkened considerably since Simply Red had embarked on their eighteen-month voyage through the disorientating unrealities of superstars on the move.

As Christmas fast approached, the extent of the national despair had become unbearable. Computer game advertisements screamed as usual from fifty-six million television sets, doubtlessly causing consternation in the millions of families who had no idea just how they were going to meet the expense. It was also impossible to turn on the local television news in any region without being confronted by some dour-faced presenter soberly reading through a cruel list of the week's major redundancy stories. Following the astonishingly callous programme of pit closures revealed in October, the miners had taken to the streets once more. But this time the miners knew full well they would be sharing their uncertain futures with so many others. No longer could they command centre stage. The country was in this together.

Hucknall, who prided himself on his ability to tap into the British psyche – à la *Wonderland* – was genuinely shocked at the extent of the despair. The media which was the only industry to infringe constantly on the magical life of a star of Hucknall's stature was simply brimming with people living in a state of freelance terror. Nobody, he noted, really seemed to know who they were working for or whether they would be working at all after their present short contract. This whole mess was, even to Hucknall, deeply unsettling. He was well aware of the paradoxical nature of Simply Red's success.

Although he would proudly spout the sales figures of *Stars* and would hardly shy away from chatting freely about the album's immeasurable greatness, even Hucknall would have trouble squaring its success with the genuinely terrifying economic situation to be found in the British Isles, if not elsewhere.

In one sense, he felt quite moved, almost awestruck by the stubborn support shown by his fans. How many of the people who had so eagerly purchased *Stars* on CD, the Montreux EP and the two recent video releases were just one step ahead of impoverishment? How many people who had queued so resiliently for tickets to the twenty-two British shows – all sold out with telling haste – were sinking behind with their mortgage payments? Impossible to tell, but Hucknall was more than aware that in all truth people had more important things to think about than whether they would be able to afford some dumb pop show or not. But attend the shows, they did. So many people, all more than willing to join in the mass celebration of Simply Red's success. It was weird all right. Of course the alternative argument would assert that the harder the times, the greater the demand for the escapism of a night spent in a concert hall. But this is only valid when the price of tickets comes within the weekly budgets of those with smaller incomes. Frankly, to a huge proportion of British households, the act of buying pop concert tickets must seem unforgivably frivolous.

Hucknall, to his credit, had never been one to fall into the kind of overtly patronising, pseudo saintly clap-trap favoured by so many so-called left-wing popstars on guilt trips. Although the colour of his politics was well known it was more through his lyrics than any anti-government lashings in the press. In many respects, the true extent of his political fervour remains a soundly kept secret, no doubt filed next to his donations to or work for charity (which are not inconsiderable and he will not thank me for informing you). He knew that the people of Britain were hardly in any mood to accept the sympathetic waxings of some hugely wealthy popstar. Such a thing would surely be quite horrible and would hark back to the dreaded days of Red Wedge.

However, in the run up to the 1992 general election, Hucknall had appeared in a promo advertisement leering at the camera and pronouncing, 'I'm going to vote for Labour!') And, somewhat against his best instincts, he unleashed a tirade of Tory bashing in the *Daily Mirror*. He openly explained to *Mirror* journalist, Nick Gibson, about his willingness to stay in Britain and pay tax on an extra ten per cent of his earnings, come the dawn of a Labour administration.

'If the Labour Party win the next election they'll raise top taxes to fifty per cent,' he said. 'But I don't mind paying more money if it means the money would go to helping hospitals and pensioners . . . worthwhile things. It's a matter of principles. I want to see my tax money used to help other people in society.'

Of course, two thoughts do spring to mind when reading such a statement. Mick Hucknall would never have to worry about the size of the next gas bill. Secondly, his words might well have been rather more carefully measured than it might seem at first glance.

Twenty-four hours before Simply Red were to play their potentially volatile date at G-Mex, Manchester's music scene was severely rocked by a recessionary bombshell. The *Manchester Evening News* splashed the story across its front page. Factory Records, after fourteen tumultuous years, had finally collapsed with debts amounting to £2 million. A last desperate attempt to sell off fifty per cent, and then even more desperately seventy-five per cent, to Phonogram had fallen through and the receivers had been called in. Rumours raged in Manchester as well as in the music business in general. Although the entire, sorry scenario (unthinkable three years earlier at the height of the Madchester explosion), could be blamed on the general recession and the public's reluctance to buy the more obscure records, the main force of the blame came down on the heads of Factory's top band of recent years, Happy Mondays. The disappointing sales of their album, *Yes Please*, was the subject of the most vociferous speculation, although in truth this was merely the final straw. Opinions from deeply concerned creditors, mouthy local television presenters-cum-journalists and distraught artists peppered the local press and, a week later, the music press.

One hard fact remained obvious. In Britain in the 1990s, it was simply not possible to run any company in a romantically aesthetic or anarchic manner. Cold, commercial facts ruled the day and Factory Records, for all their artistic successes, just couldn't justify its eccentricities. The portents were far from good in the wake of this collapse, especially for young talent with a thirst for innovation. Symbolically, Wednesday 25 November 1992 could be viewed as the end of Madchester, although a very good case was made which suggested that Factory Records, far from being the main cataclysmic force behind Madchester was merely a lucky benefactor. The record company might have been over but the bitching, it seemed, lived on.

The ramifications of the Factory collapse were multitudinous, in rumour if not in reality. Even Elliot Rashman became dangerously embroiled at one stage when the future of the In The City music bash was called into question. The response to this speculation was swift. In The City organiser, Yvette Livesey wasted no time in pointing out that, 'There is no connection businesswise between Factory and In The City. Are we going ahead? Absolutely. After the first In The City, I spent three weeks taking phone calls from America asking, "What have we missed?" '

The Holiday Inn Crowne Plaza remained booked solid for a full five days for September 1993. In The City II would go ahead. The success of the first In The City was due in no small part to Rashman and Dodd's groundbreaking International Managers' Forum, destined to be forever linked with the initial Manchester event. Had Factory's closure sent In The City crashing into history then, by association, Rashman and Dodd's credibility would also have been seriously damaged.

Mick Hucknall, flamboyantly dreadlocked and bearded, was back in Manchester in time to catch the news of Factory, although offered no response when a local reporter asked for his comment. The singer was happy to be seen doing nothing more newsworthy than buying two green peppers in his beloved Safeway supermarket in Chorlton.

At G-Mex, the much-reported rift between the band and the

venue thankfully failed to materialise into anything serious, at least on the day of the gig. Faced with a venue that, to their minds, just wasn't suitable for large gigs, Simply Red performed the first half of the set from a mini stage set up in the centre of the auditorium. This innovative tactic worked superbly and even managed to break through the G-Mex mud. For the best part of a two-hour set, the band overcame the familiar lack of atmosphere within the venue. By the time Hucknall concluded the set with the words, 'Gunnight . . . see you at the next album', it was more than clear that Simply Red had won the battle of G-Mex. It was a slightly odd comment though, especially as Hucknall was about to take two years off from Simply Red and any planned release of the fifth Simply Red album lay lost in the murk of the distant future – three, possibly four years away.

And so 1992 was to end with a promotional flourish. It was difficult to tune into television or radio for long without encountering Mick Hucknall's voice, if not sweetly surging through song then brashly laying down the law in conversation.

Veteran crit/journo/jock/expert/celeb Paul Gambaccini managed to pin Hucknall down for long enough to produce an interesting, although rather confusing hour-long Radio One special. It was a somewhat gushy little number as the Great Gambo, hamming it up as ever, made the whole thing seem so damned dramatic. Gambo's climactic flourish was centred around the DCC row and Hucknall's statement that Simply Red would not, in future, recognise the format. It was undeniably a big story, but not for the Daves and Pams who would surely be tuning in, possibly to be slightly fazed by the sheer broadness of Hucknall's rhetoric. To them, as Rashman had hinted, DCC was at least for the moment the dullest imaginable issue. After all, they had only recently converted to compact disc (repurchasing the first three Simply Red albums along the way). Nevertheless, Gambaccini honed in.

'The two new formats that the music business is bringing in, the digital compact cassette, the upgraded quality of tape cassette and then the mini disc . . . and you have made the decision not to have *Stars* released on DCC. Reason?'

'Well,' sighed Hucknall, 'the DCC in fact is only really the lid on the can of worms. What has actually happened is . . . it's opened up the can of worms that bring in a whole series of questions about the morality and the fairness of what the music industry is now. Now, I've heard Mr Oberstein and these people in magazines saying "Well, why should Mick Hucknall care about what's going on, he's got lots of money in the bank. He's a rich guy, what's he got to be worried about?" Well, what I've got to be worried about is that when I stop doing this there are a whole series of generations that are going to follow me that can be put into a much better situation financially by creating a basic standard contract in order that they get what their fair whack is.

'Basically, when I go into a recording studio and make my records, when that recording is finished, I don't own that recording. That recording is then owned by the record company. I've paid for it. I've paid for all the recording costs, and yet when I walk out of that room, they own it. Now, for me, a recording company is a company that sells records. They have absolutely no right to own those records because I wrote them. I sit there in my room with an acoustic guitar and write these songs. Now how can anybody say that they then own that piece of me? And this is the issue, I think, ultimately. It's one of the issues, anyway. I will irritate the next Labour government about it. Because I think it is a fundamental human right and the sooner Mr Oberstein and Mr Dickens get off their high horses and come down and start talking to us, the less they will probably have to pay.'

The prospect of a growing body of major artists irritating their respective record companies about all kinds of subjects connected with the rights of musicians was tentatively floated by Gambaccini, and surely reflected the major story from across the Atlantic which centred on the battle between George Michael and CBS/Sony. It was a huge hint at trouble to follow.

'It's going to be an interesting couple of years,' remarked Gambaccini.

'It's going to be a *very* interesting couple of years,' laughed Hucknall.

Quite what Dave and Pam made of that one can only speculate. Hucknall had, however, displayed a degree of curious naivety. The idea of major artists negotiating for greater rights for all musicians is not at all a bad one, and it would seem perfectly natural for the DCC row to become the catalyst for this. The idea of a standard record contract for *all* artists is also quite interesting. However, the fact that Simply Red had recouped all initial advances, promotional and record- ing costs is to miss the point.

Certainly, from the viewpoint of a successful artist, casting a retrospective glance over the contractual elements of his early career, Hucknall is perfectly correct. Successful artists do eventually pay for absolutely everything, right down to the cocktails quaffed by greedy journalists at press launches. To believe otherwise would be to be well and truly naive (although many rockstars are still incredibly unaware of this fundamental fact). However, what Hucknall neglected to mention is the equally relevant fact that advances and record- ing costs doled out to most artists who are attempting to embark on lucrative careers are never recouped, simply because the artists in question do not become successful.

In slating the record companies, Hucknall failed to mention the huge risk factor which hangs heavy over every contract offered to an untried artist. In a sense, as the system stands at present, the smaller untried artists are effectively subsidised by the likes of Simply Red. To alter the system of recoupable advances would possibly make record companies even less inclined to take the risk of taking on a new artist, which would surely act against Hucknall's objective. If *Picture Book* had failed to sell and Simply Red had been dropped from Elektra's books, then the record company would probably have been cast as an evil, capitalist organisation with little respect for artistic endeavour. But it would have been Elektra, not Simply Red, who would have had to live with the costs of sending the band to Holland, drafting in producer Levine, recording a full album, promoting the subsequent singles and album, and paying for the production of a series of videos – none of which come cheaply.

Chapter 22
'I Hate the White Soulboy!'

'This white soulboy tag that comes with Simply Red. As the years go on and on I start to find it more and more ridiculous and absolutely amazing as life goes on. Because, what is Elvis Presley? What is John Lennon? What are the Rolling Stones? What have every single white act ever been? Deep Purple? Led Zeppelin, they were all completely entrenched in black music, *completely*! All their first records were basic imitations of black music. So why single out Mick Hucknall as the white soulboy? It's utterly ridiculous. So I wish they would just go away and stop being so silly . . . You could even say that about Frank Sinatra, that he wanted to be Nat King Cole. So please guys, wake up!' Mick Hucknall said to Paul Gambaccini in December 1992.

The white soulboy is dead – long live the white soulboy. The white soulboy is not the young man who befriended Lamont Dozier or revived *If You Don't Know Me By Now* so exquisitely, but the much younger boy, aged thirteen, who fell in love with music and, living in the North, found himself surrounded by a scene that might as well be forever tagged soul. It was the black music – that filled the local discos, that had been studiously copied by the bands of Merseybeat, that had been so perceptively promoted by Roger Eagle – that was merely the nucleus and perhaps the catalyst.

To be a soulboy was to become 'something' and not just be the grubby urchin playing with pushbikes down on the canal or the little girl nurturing bland crushes on pretty-boy popsters. Its roots, at least in England, belonged to the 'Mod ethic'. It involved a pride in appearance, a desire to possess those trousers, polish the shoes, pin the Prince of Wales scarf in the barathea pocket. It was not rebelling blindly against anything and everything but making the system work in your favour. Keep your head up, search for your vocation, nurture it, take no crap.

It was a reflection most certainly of black urban America where those who were regarded by the white rulers as downgrade, downbeat, low class would create the best music, produce the finest athletes, and outsmart, outdress and out-think their 'white' superiors to such an extent that white achievers of the future would have to glean their inspiration from the genius of black America. Jazz, blues or, the most general term of all, soul.

Mick Hucknall could have been the scruffiest, drunkest, most obnoxious, most useless slob in Denton – that path was wide open to him, and so inviting it must have looked. But he loved to sing and dance and dress individually. All around him, especially in the North, the music of black America was soundtracking people's lifestyles, inspiring pride. It influenced so many, from the flash young boys who scissor-jumped to the sound of Arthur Conley to the young girls who would shuffle so expertly in discos from Stoke to Silverdale; from those who would endlessly polish the mirrors of their Lambretta GP200 scooters to those who would climb into Burton suits, place their feet in shiny black leather brogue 'Royals' and go to the job interview.

Mick Hucknall was one of the luckiest of all. The talent he never doubted turned out to be genuine, unique. He found his passion and never lost his respect for it. Against the odds, he pursued the vocation of his dreams and made it across the divide with his dignity intact.

He's not a popstar, not just a musician, either. He's a soulboy, no doubt about it.

Chapter 23
Summer 1993

With a twist and a wiggle and then another twist, Mick Hucknall skirted the penalty area at Old Trafford, surrounded not by adoring, vociferous hordes, but by a few cynical photographers. Nevertheless it cannot be denied that Hucknall, whose celebrity status had gained him access to that hallowed turf, felt a surge of pride as he scampered around on the improved Old Trafford pitch which would soon see, amid a frenzied tumult, Giggs, Cantona, Ince and the other Reds parading the inaugural Premier League trophy. Manchester United were, as in the sixties, the top side in the country, not just in gate receipts and supporters club membership, but in footballing prowess.

It seemed apt that Hucknall, himself triumphant after completing one of the largest and longest world tours in rock history, should openly link himself with a club so huge and, at long last, so successful. Glory days were back in Manchester, and the town was celebrating. Hucknall was happy to see his gleeful exploits on that Old Trafford pitch adorn the front pages of the local press, even at the risk of scorn from his own manager, whose sporting allegiances still had a blueish hue.

It seemed like a perfectly symmetrical 'end of story' too. United, back there after so long and Hucknall, playing around – in the cleanest sense of the word – in public, apparently happy to have wrenched himself free of the stifling machinery that entraps a huge pop band. 'Well, he's all but retired,' claimed a spokesperson from So What Arts when taunted with the question, 'Well, what's the old bugger up to, anyway?'

Neighbours of Hucknall's Old Trafford residence certainly began to see more and more of him, his flash of hair catching the eye as he clambered into his blue Mazda, apparently to do little more than purchase yet more peppers from Chorlton supermarkets. Aside from the odd hefty quote in the ever faithful *Manchester Evening News* Diary claiming time and again that Hucknall would be working with (that awful phrase) 'local musicians', it was easy to believe that the superstar had stepped back into the world of dull normality.

In May, despite Hucknall's alleged inactivity, a few scurrilous tabloid hounds remained in tow, ever ready to embellish and enhance the merest whiff of a story. As an example, one of them actually rang me on a Sunday afternoon and, adopting the usual tabloid tone not dissimilar to those pathetic school-leavers who attempt to sell double glazing at your doorstep, his disembodied voice demanded that I give him Elliot Rashman's home phone number.

I didn't have it, as it happened, but even if I had the last thing I would have done would be to hand it over to such a person. 'I'm writing a story about Kate Crabtree [keyboard player from the Dave Rowbotham period], who was once a principal member of Simply Red and was kicked out just before the band went really big. That's true, isn't it?' I told him, of course, that it wasn't true at all. That Kate Crabtree – and he would have known this if, as he claimed, he really had read this book – was a member of an extremely early Hucknall band way back in 1983 and had certainly left before any true momentum had been gained.

Naturally, this 'truth' fell upon deaf ears. The story, which appeared the very next morning, cast the peculiar vision of Kate Crabtree struggling to the local shops in Hulme, laden with shopping bags and children, while Hucknall sped past in his Porsche, dousing her with water from a roadside puddle. Unwittingly, this somewhat stupid story did seem to highlight Hucknall's uncomfortably lofty position. What was he to do? How could he win? As he didn't even patronise his own father by showering him with the rich pickings of his success, would it have been wise for him to hover about, downloading greenbacks to all who had played even a small part in his ascent? Obviously not. The tone of the article – for which, I hasten to add, Kate Crabtree should take none of the blame; her dignity remains intact – was one of ludicrously naïve indignation. And yet, if scanned briefly over a mug of breakfast tea, it conveyed just one simple message: that Mick Hucknall actually got his kicks from flaunting his success in the face of those who struggle to meet every incoming electricity bill. Utter nonsense, of course, but the story did suggest that Hucknall would not find it at all easy to bask, uncaringly, in his so-called state of 'retirement'.

But rumours that Hucknall had returned to haunt the Manchester social calendar proved, if not unfounded, then certainly overstated. Possibly due to the fact that, when he is in town, he is very visible indeed. Serious Hucknall spotters, and there are a good many of them, might have found it easier to find him in, say, Paris than Whalley Range.

Hucknall spent many nights, in the spring of '93, gallivanting around the hotter, richer, more glamorous nightspots of Paris, quite often accompanied by a showbiz accomplice, most notably his good friend Sean Penn. Attending such haunts as Le Palace, Le Central and Club De Larc, Hucknall and Penn became friendly with Parisian nightclub kings Thierry Klemenuick and Franc Rossi.

This new-found élite must have tasted sweet to Hucknall, for soon, along with Penn, Klemenuick and Rossi, he was tempted to join a consortium (also including LA-based club owners Alexis Ougril and DJ Eric Omares) which would open the BASH nightspot on Washington Avenue in the fashionable South Beach area of Miami. For Hucknall and Penn, it wasn't a huge deal.

Nevertheless, they were more than happy to be seen adding a touch of necessary celebrity glamour to the venture. Hucknall and Penn partied heartily throughout the four-day launch over Easter. Big deal or not, the rave-up was enough to see Andy Dodd and So What special projects manager David Dunne – who will be playing an important organisational role in Hucknall's non Simply Red activities during the coming years – fly to Miami to join in the celebrations.

One other incident, involving a fellow Manchester popstar, springs to mind. I refer to New Order's dry and detached frontman, Bernard Sumner, a man not noted for his personal flamboyance. Sumner found himself returning to Manchester from Italy on the same flight as Hucknall. It was rather an odd situation. Unlike Hucknall, Sumner, by choice mainly, does not bask in the recognition of the general public and the cross-section on the plane would not have been aware that they were in the presence of two popstars, rather than just one. Hucknall plumped himself down next to Sumner and the two fell into the usual rockspeak . . . or soccerspeak. As Hucknall was talking, Sumner fought hard to keep his eyes from wandering upwards, towards Hucknall's shock of hair. It was Hucknall's hair extensions, dreadlocks if you like, which captured Sumner's curiosity, especially when one of them, apparently too heavy to be held in place, became dislodged and began to move slowly down Hucknall's back before flipping off the armrest onto the floor. Unabashed by this, Hucknall continued to talk while deftly flicking the lonesome dreadlock up with his foot and, as he stood up to leave, placing it in the back pocket of his jeans. A position from which it bobbed comically for the remainder of the journey. A tiny but signifi-cant incident.

Sumner spent the rest of the journey wondering why he, unlike Hucknall, had not allowed his 'stardom' to be reflected so flamboyantly by his dress sense and style. The thought of Barney Sumner having hair extensions is clearly preposterous – he'd be laughed out of Salford – and yet Mick Hucknall wouldn't really be Mick Hucknall without such affectations.

Any notions that Hucknall's musical inactivity might cause Rashman and Dodd to 'relax the reins' a little were well and truly quashed when photographer Steve Wright rang Rashman to request permission to use a few early, yet fairly insignificant, photographs of the band. This action is in itself unusual. Photog-raphers are not noted for actually requesting permission from their subjects before sending photographs off for secondary usage in some magazine or book. Nevertheless, as Wright had been a good friend of Rashman in the early days of Simply Red and as he knew full well that the manager cherished a reputation of being a 'control freak', he thought it would be polite to ask.

'They are not bad pictures and I'm just trying to earn my living,' he stated reasonably. An initial deal was struck, whereby Wright would send shots to Rashman for approval. Although this was unusual, Wright happily agreed, comforted as he was by the thought that nobody, surely, could object to the use of such ubiquitous images. Incredibly, Rashman refused to allow any of the shots to be used and actually offered Wright a large sum of money *not* to offer them for reproduction. What was Rashman afraid of? And why? Especially as, to all intents and purposes, the Simply Red roller-coaster had ground to a rather numbing halt.

It *was* a halt, too. Nothing new, nothing polished and controlled would be coming out of that Simply Red pipeline. There was no momentum to spoil, no timing to unhinge. For the foreseeable future, the whole damn thing had ceased to be. (Those who believe that the Fritz McIntyre contribution towards the Simply Red success story is nothing short of a silent parallel to Hucknall's would, at least, be cheered to discover that the enigmatic engine stoker of the band was not using the break in activities merely to swan about nightspots. McIntyre had been freed, at long last, to work on his solo album in New York.)

With Simply Red so effectively frozen, Mick did, at least, begin to hover officially around various mixing desks, flexing his muscles as fledgling remix producer, ably assisted by Gota Yashiki. He was particularly struck by Bjork, the ex-lead singer of the Icelandic band, The Sugarcubes. Bjork's unusual vocal technique had intrigued Hucknall for some time and, as she proceeded into what looked like becoming a successful solo career, he decided to try out his expertise on Bjork's album track, *Venus As A Boy*. Generally speaking, a song is remixed without any need to call the vocalist back into the studio. Hucknall, however, believed that Bjork could improve on the original recording and requested that she return to the mike to record the song in a more emotive style. Bjork responded valiantly and, apparently, even astonished herself with the results. Her record company, equally impressed with the remix, immediately plucked *Venus As A Boy* out as the next single. Residing temporarily in Venice, Hucknall was heard frequently to refer to Bjork as 'a Billie Holliday for the nineties'.

As I write, and bear in mind that situations can alter rapidly when one is dealing with the fickle nature of an artist, I cannot think of any comparable vanishing act in the history of top level pop music. At least, no comparable 'deliberate' vanishing act. Maybe, as 1994 looms, Hucknall's muse will be nudging him into a state of galvanisation. Until then, however – and fleeting appearances behind mixing desks being used by local artists or Bjork are not sufficient to change this – we must accept the official line. The 'old bugger' really has all but retired. If, reading this, you find some of these later musings and anecdotes rather trite and inconsequential, then consider the feelings of the earnest and noticeably intelligent body of folk who belong to the Simply Red Information Service.

It is a fan club, to be sure, but it is a fan club governed by no rules of age or general taste and certainly not by fashion. It is not bland, nor – in the main – fawning. It does not exist merely to soothe the ego of Mick Hucknall, either. To tell the truth, I do not like fan clubs much. Generally, I find the joining of such an organisation to be an act of unpalatable servility. Initially, I had no reason to believe that SRIS was any different. After all, the official message which greets you, when you pay your not inconsiderable sum of money, is excruciatingly banal.

'Thank you for writing to Simply Red,' it states. 'I am sorry that Mick cannot reply personally to your letter but, as you can imagine, he does get a lot of post. However, he does care about each and every one of you and so he has set up an information service . . .'

However, the dozen or so members of this quite staggeringly disparate, not to say massive, fan club who have corresponded regularly with me since this book first appeared have seemed not at all like starstruck dullards, but people of genuine taste and perception. They have even been more than willing to debate the shortcomings of Simply Red and, in some cases, most vigorously. In Mick Hucknall, they have, they all state,

302

found something that apparently no other modern singer has been able to supply. And yet, as the summer of 1993 passed by, they all suffered from a sense that something had, if only for a year or so, vanished.

Hilary Jones was one example. Not at all a typical pop fan, Hilary is an elegant ex-teacher and mother in her mid-thirties. She had not, she told me, bothered to listen to any pop music since leaving university in Leeds back in the seventies. And yet something in Hucknall had awakened her interest.

'It seemed so sad, after that last concert,' she earnestly stated. 'It was like an end. We held a convention earlier in the year and there may be one next year but, and everyone I write to agrees with me, it just seems like the music has gone. I have made a lot of good friends through the Simply Red Information Service and they all seem to feel this loss. It's odd, isn't it?' It *is* odd . . . very odd indeed. When sophisticated people, not mere teen whimsies, feel dislodged by a singer's state of hard-earned and, surely, temporary inactivity.

Linda Ward, another SRIS agitator, added a further comment. 'This year has been strange,' she said. 'A lot of the members of SRIS have been complaining because the flow of information has dried up. He's deserved his rest, but all we have received this year are magazines written by the fans. There has been no input from So What at all. It's almost as if we are the only ones keeping the ball rolling.'

Well, I don't know. I have brought the SRIS members into the frame here, at the close of this book, simply because they seem to me to be the kind of fan club that any genuine artist would long for, and any vacuous popstar would be afraid of. They do demand a return.

As far as the 'old bugger' is concerned, one can only assume, and hope, that this period of 'nothingness' will signify an artistic reassessment. It would be foolish for him or Simply Red to emerge from this void armed with another collection of songs which echo the tempered perfection of *Stars*. It would have to be more than that. It would, most certainly, have to take a risk or two. Maybe even alienating the odd SRIS member along the way. Anything less, anything weaker, anything which lies in formula, anything which fails to provoke, or stimulate, or break some kind of new ground, just won't do. The void has created a hunger. It's up to him now.

Discography

Frantic Elevators

Voice In The Dark/Every Day I Die/Passion.
TJM 5, June 1979.

Hunchback Of Notre Dame/I See Nothing And Everything/ Don't Judge Me.
TJM, Demo only.

You Know What You Told Me/Production Prevention.
Eric's 006, November 1980.

Searchin' For The Only One/Hunchback Of Notre Dame.
Crackin' Up. Crak 1, April 1981.

Holding Back The Years/Pistols In My Brain.
No Waiting (Wait One), October 1982.

Mick Hucknall and the Frantic Elevators: The Early Years LP
TJM 101, September 1987.

Mick Hucknall and the Frantic Elevators: The Early Years CD
Receiver CD 1, 1990.

Simply Red

Money's Too Tight To Mention/Open Up The Red Box.
Elektra EKR 9, June 1985.
UK chart placing – 13.

Money's Too Tight To Mention/Open Up The Red Box/No Direction.
Elektra EKR 9T, 12 inch, June 1985.

Money's Too Tight To Mention/Open Up The Red Box.
Elektra EKR 9P, Picture disc, June 1985.

Money's Too Tight To Mention (special remix)/*Open Up The Red Box.*
Elektra EKR 9TX, 12 inch, July 1985.

Come To My Aid/Valentine.
Elektra EKR 19, August 1985.
UK chart placing – 66.

Come To My Aid (extended)/*Valentine/Gramma's Hands.*
Elektra EKR 19T, 12 inch, August 1985.

Holding Back The Years/I Won't Feel Bad.
Elektra EKR 29, November 1985.
UK chart placing – 51.

Holding Back The Years/I Won't Feel Bad/Drowning In My Own Tears.
Elektra EKR 29T, 12 inch, November 1985.

Holding Back The Years/I Won't Feel Bad.
Elektra EKR 29F, Poster sleeve 7 inch, November 1985.

Holding Back The Years/I Won't Feel Bad.
Elektra EKR 29P, Picture disc, November 1985.

Jericho/Jericho (the musical).
Elektra YZ 63, February 1986.
UK chart placing – 53.

Jericho/Jericho (the musical).
Elektra YZ 63c, red vinyl in clear PVC sleeve, February 1986.

Jericho/Jericho (the musical)/*Money's Too Tight To Mention* (live)/*Heaven* (live).
Elektra YZ 63T, 12 inch, February 1986.

Holding Back The Years/Drowning In My Own Tears.
Elektra YZ 70, May 1986.
UK chart placing – 2.

Holding Back The Years /Drowning In My Own Tears/Picture Book.
Elektra YZ 7DT, 12 inch, May 1986.

Open Up The Red Box (remix)/*Look At You Now.*
Elektra YZ 75, July 1986.
UK chart placing – 61.

Open Up The Red Box (remix)/*Look At You Now/Heaven* (the musical, live).
Elektra YZ 75T, 12 inch, July 1986.

The Right Thing/There's A Light.
Elektra YZ 103, February 1987.
UK chart placing – 11.

The Right Thing/There's A Light/Every Time We Say Goodbye.
Elektra YZ 103T, 12 inch, February 1987.

The Right Thing/There's A Light/Holding Back The Years/ Drowning In My Own Tears.
Elektra YZ 103DP, Doublepack single, February 1987.

Infidelity/Lady Godiva's Room.
Elektra YZ114, May 1987.
UK chart placing – 31.

Infidelity (stretch mix)/*Lady Godiva's Room/Love Fire* (massive red mix).
Elektra YZ 114T, 12 inch, May 1987.

Infidelity (stretch mix)/*Lady Godiva's Room*/*Love Fire* (massive red mix).
Elektra YZ 114TP, 12 inch, Picture disc, May 1987.

Maybe Someday/*Let Me Have It All* (remix).
Elektra YZ 141, July 1987.

Maybe Someday/*Let Me Have It All* (remix)/*Broken Man*.
Elektra YZ 141T, 12 inch, July 1987.

Every Time We Say Goodbye/*Love For Sale* (live).
Elektra YZ 161, November 1987.
UK chart placing – 11.

Every Time We Say Goodbye/*Love For Sale* (live)/*Every Time We Say Goodbye* (live).
Elektra YZ 161T, 12 inch, November 1987.

Every Time We Say Goodbye/*Love For Sale* (live)/*Sad Old Red*/*Broken Man*.
Elektra YZ 161CD, CD single, November 1987.

Every Time We Say Goodbye/*Love For Sale* (live)/*Every Time We Say Goodbye* (edit).
Elektra 161 TX, 12 inch Postcard pack, November 1987.

Every Time We Say Goodbye/*Love For Sale* (live)/*Sad Old Red*/*Broken Man*.
Elektra YZ 161TE, 10 inch, November 1987.

I Won't Feel Bad/*Lady Godiva's Room*.
Elektra YZ 172, February 1988.
UK chart placing – 68.

I Won't Feel Bad (Arthur Baker remix)/*Lady Godiva's Room* (Ellis/Hucknall mix)/*I Won't Feel Bad* (edit).
Elektra YZ 172 remix, 12 inch, February 1988.

I Won't Feel Bad (remix)/*Lady Godiva's Room* (remix)/*I Won't*

Feel Bad (edit)/*The Right Thing*.
Elektra YZ 172CD, CD single, February 1988.

It's Only Love/Turn It Up.
Elektra YZ 349, January 1989.
UK chart placing – 13.

It's Only Love/Turn It Up/I'm Gonna Lose You.
Elektra YZ 349T, 12 inch, January 1989.

It's Only Love/Turn It Up/The Right Thing/I'm Gonna Lose You.
Elektra YZ 349CD, CD single, January 1989.

It's Only Love (Valentine mix)/*Turn It Up/I'm Gonna Lose You*.
Elektra YZ 349TE, 10 inch numbered and limited edition, February 1989.

If You Don't Know Me By Now/Move On Out (live).
Elektra YZ 377, April 1989.
UK chart placing – 2.

If You Don't Know Me By Now/Move On Out (live)/*Shine* (live).
Elektra YZ 377T, 12 inch, April 1989.

If You Don't Know Me By Now/Move On Out (live)/*Shine* (live)/*Sugar Daddy*.
Elektra YZ 377CD, CD single, April 1989.

If You Don't Know Me By Now/Move On Out (live)/*Shine* (live)/*Sugar Daddy*.
Elektra YZ 377CDX, CD single in special package, April 1989.

If You Don't Know Me By Now/Move On Out (live)/*Great Divide*.
Elektra YZ 377TE, 10 inch in cardboard sleeve, April 1989.

A New Flame/More.
Elektra YZ404, July 1989.
UK chart placing – 17.

A New Flame/More/I Asked Her For Water (live)/*Resume* (live).
Elektra YZ 404T, 12 inch, July 1989.

A New Flame/More.
Elektra YZ 404C, Cassingle, July 1989.

A New Flame/More/I Asked Her For Water (live)/*Resume*.
Elektra YZ 404CD, CD single, July 1989.

A New Flame/More/I Asked Her For Water (live)/*Funk On Out* (live).
Elektra YZ 404TE, 10 inch, July 1989.

Something Got Me Started.
East West YZ 614, October 1991.

Stars.
East West YZ 626, December 1991.

For Your Babies.
East West YZ 642, February 1992.

For Your Babies.
East West YZ 642 CDX, February 1992.

Thrill Me.
East West YZ 671, April 1992

Your Mirror.
East West YZ 689, June 1992.

Your Mirror.
East West YZ 689CD, June 1992.

Your Mirror (live version).
UK holographic CD and box, Simp 2, July 1992.

Your Mirror.
Studio version UK holographic CD and box, Simp 1, July 1992.

Montreux EP: *Love For Sale/Drowning In My Own Tears/ Gramma's Hands/Lady Godiva's Room.*
East West YZ 16 CD, November 1992.

LPs

Picture Book.
Elektra EKT 27, October 1985.
UK chart placing – 2.

Men And Women.
Elektra WX 85, March 1987.
UK chart placing – 2.

A New Flame.
Elektra WX 242, February 1989.
UK chart placing – 1.

Stars.
East West 9031, October 1991.
UK chart placing – 1.

Index

Note: *Abbreviations used in this index are F.El for Frantic Elevators; MH for Mick Hucknall; MP for Manchester Polytechnic; SR for Simply Red.*

313

PETER GABRIEL

AN AUTHORISED BIOGRAPHY

SPENCER BRIGHT

'Well-researched and intelligent' *Today*

Born of a gentleman farmer father and a doting musical mother, he had a conventional middle-class upbringing.

At public school he was a quiet and conscientious pupil.

Then he discovered rock 'n' roll.

While still a schoolboy of seventeen, Peter Gabriel founded the band that was eventually to become the seminal group of the seventies, Genesis. When he left in 1975, speculation was intense as to what he would do next. Few would have predicted that, despite long periods of silence, he would join that elite handful of rock superstars who command both the respect of the critics and the adulation of fans worldwide.

Flamboyant on stage, shy and serious in real life, Peter Gabriel rarely gives interviews and so has remained something of an enigma. Now the man himself, his friends and colleagues have decided to give Spencer Bright their full cooperation for this book. The result is a sympathetic and provocative biography which at last reveals the man behind that legendary mask.

'Welcome and enjoyable . . . the first serious attempt to understand one of the few genuinely original talents residing uncomfortably in the wacky world of rock 'n' roll' *Venue*

'A compelling biography' *Daily Mirror*

'A compelling read' *Record Mirror*

NON-FICTION/BIOGRAPHY   0 7472 3231 8

MICHAEL JACKSON
THE MAGIC AND THE MADNESS

J. RANDY TARABORRELLI
Author of CALL HER MISS ROSS

THE INTERNATIONAL BESTSELLER
'REALLY JUICY STUFF' *ROLLING STONE*

Forget everything you ever read about Michael Jackson. The truth has never been told.

Until now.

This explosive book examines the amazing career and tumultuous private life of the legendary, enigmatic performer. Not since Garbo has a celebrity worked so diligently to protect his privacy. But Taraborrelli has cracked Jackson's carefully constructed showbiz facade – a persona that Michael has methodically manufactured to hide his private pains and personal heartaches.

Based on voluminous court documents and hundreds of interviews with Michael Jackson's closest associates and the star himself, this book unravels the startling truth behind Michael's well-known crushing isolation, his erratic behaviour, peculiar habits and highly unusual lifestyle. The result is a complex, rather sad but highly sympathetic portrait of a man whose destiny was decided for him from a very young age.

MICHAEL JACKSON: THE MAGIC AND THE MADNESS – the first fully documented, intimate portrait of the world's most famous performer.

'If you're interested in backstage backstabbing, traumatic childhoods, plastic surgery, sex scandals and media manipulation, then this terrific book is for you' *Atlantic Journal*

'Exhaustively detailed, Taraborrelli paints a tragic portrait of a family out of control' *San Francisco Chronicle*

BIOGRAPHY/POPULAR MUSIC   0 7472 3880 4

More Biography from Headline:

ROD STEWART

THE BESTSELLING BIOGRAPHY

TIM EWBANK AND STAFFORD HILDRED

The definitive biography of one of the world's most enduring sex symbols.

In this searching yet affectionate account of the man, his music and his life so far, Tim Ewbank and Stafford Hildred follow Rod's inexorable rise from the backstreets of Highgate via a short-lived soccer career and busking in Paris, through times spent with Steampacket, The Jeff Beck Group and The Faces until he finally achieved the pinnacle of international stardom that he enjoys today. And then there are, of course, the blondes...

Based on first-hand interviews with those close to Rod at every stage of his life – including ex-girlfriends – this biography highlights the many contradictions and ambiguities that make up Rod Stewart. Stripping away the hype and the hysteria, it reveals at last the man.

NON-FICTION/BIOGRAPHY   0 7472 3585 6

JUST THE ONE

THE WIVES AND TIMES OF
JEFFREY BERNARD

GRAHAM LORD

'One of the most thoroughly researched biographical enquiries I have read. It's all here, booze, women, Norman Balon, horses, "No-knickers Joyce", booze, and finally fame of a sort a writer rarely achieves in his lifetime' Patrick Marnham, *The Oldie*

Jeffrey Bernard, the legendary Soho journalist and boozer who has been popping down to the pub for 'just the one' for forty years is the most unlikely hero of our times.

What other bottle-of-vodka-and-fifty-fags-a-day hack has also been a gigolo, navvy, fairground boxer, miner, stagehand, film editor and actor? Who else has been married four times, seduced 500 lovers (including several renowned actresses) – and also written a famous column for the *Spectator*, his 'suicide note in weekly instalments'? In the astonishingly successful stage play, *Jeffrey Bernard is Unwell*, his rackety life has been portrayed by Peter O'Toole, Tom Conti, James Bolam and Dennis Waterman.

Graham Lord – who has known Bernard well for many years – has written a biography that is fun, devastatingly frank and critical, yet unexpectedly touching. Jeffrey Bernard is indeed unique – just the one.

'I wanted it to be longer. I read it from cover to cover in one sitting and laughed out loud and often' Paul Pickering, *Sunday Times*

'A gripping and unsentimental biography...an astonishing achievement' Irma Kurtz, *Sunday Express*

NON-FICTION/BIOGRAPHY   0 7472 4286 0

More bestselling non-fiction from Headline

PECKISH BUT POOR	Cas Clarke	£5.99 □
PLAYFAIR CRICKET ANNUAL	Bill Frindall (Ed)	£3.99 □
ONE LIFETIME IS NOT ENOUGH	Zsa Zsa Gabor	£5.99 □
THE MURDER YEARBOOK	Brian Lane	£5.99 □
MY FATHER LAURENCE OLIVIER	Tarquin Olivier	£6.99 □
SUPER JUICE	Beverley Piper	£4.50 □
GINGER: My Story	Ginger Rogers	£6.99 □
THE MEDITERRANEAN HEALTH DIET	Gilly Smith & Rowena Goldman	£4.99 □
THE ART OF SENSUAL LOVING	Dr Andrew Stanway	£6.99 □
THE NEW BODY TALK	Michael van Straten	£6.99 □

All Headline books are available at your local bookshop or newsagent, or can be ordered direct from the publisher. Just tick the titles you want and fill in the form below. Prices and availability subject to change without notice.

Headline Book Publishing PLC, Cash Sales Department, Bookpoint, 39 Milton Park, Abingdon, OXON, OX14 4TD, UK. If you have a credit card you may order by telephone — 0235 831700.

Please enclose a cheque or postal order made payable to Bookpoint Ltd to the value of the cover price and allow the following for postage and packing:
UK & BFPO: £1.00 for the first book, 50p for the second book and 30p for each additional book ordered up to a maximum charge of £3.00.
OVERSEAS & EIRE: £2.00 for the first book, £1.00 for the second book and 50p for each additional book.

Name ....

Address ....

....

....

If you would prefer to pay by credit card, please complete:
Please debit my Visa/Access/Diner's Card/American Express (delete as applicable) card no:

Signature ....Expiry Date ....